Jesse Feiler

Sams **Teach Yourself**

Core Data for Mac and iOS*

in **24 Hours**

SAMS   800 East 96th Street, Indianapolis, Indiana, 46240 USA

Sams Teach Yourself Core Data for Mac™ and iOS in 24 Hours

ISBN-13: 978-0-672-33577-8

ISBN-10: 0-672-33577-8

Library of Congress Cataloging-in-Publication data is on file.

Printed in the United States of America

First Printing: November 2011

Trademarks

Warning and Disclaimer

Bulk Sales

Sams Publishing offers excellent discounts on this book when ordered in quantity for bulk purchases or special sales. For more information, please contact

U.S. Corporate and Government Sales
1-800-382-3419
corpsales@pearsontechgroup.com

For sales outside of the U.S., please contact

International Sales
international@pearsoned.com

Editor-in-Chief
Greg Wiegand

Acquisitions Editor
Loretta Yates

Development Editor
Sondra Scott

Managing Editor
Sandra Schroeder

Project Editor
Mandie Frank

Copy Editor
Megan Wade

Indexer
Brad Herriman

Proofreader
Water Crest Publishing, Inc.

Technical Editor
Robert McGovern

Publishing Coordinator
Cindy Teeters

Designer
Gary Adair

Compositor
Mark Shirar

Contents at a Glance

Part V: Managing Data and Interfaces

Appendix

Table of Contents

vi

Part III: Developing the Core Data Interface

About the Author

Jesse Feiler is a developer, web designer, trainer, and author. He has been an Apple developer since 1985 and has worked with mobile devices starting with Apple's Newton and continuing with the iOS products such as the iPhone, iPod touch, and iPad. Feiler's database expertise includes mainframe databases such as DMS II (on Burroughs), DB2 (on IBM), and Oracle (on various platforms), as well as personal computer databases from dBase to the first versions of FileMaker. His database clients have included Federal Reserve Bank of New York; Young & Rubicam (advertising); and many small and nonprofit organizations, primarily in publishing, production, and management.

Feiler's books include the following:

▶ *Sams Teach Yourself Objective-C in 24 Hours* (Sams/Pearson)

▶ *Data-Driven iOS Apps for iPad and iPhone with FileMaker Pro, Bento by FileMaker, and FileMaker Go* (Sams/Pearson)

▶ *Using FileMaker Bento* (Sams/Pearson)

▶ *iWork for Dummies* (Wiley)

▶ *Sams Teach Yourself Drupal in 24 Hours* (Sams/Pearson)

▶ *Get Rich with Apps! Your Guide to Reaching More Customers and Making Money NOW* (McGraw-Hill)

▶ *Database-Driven Web Sites* (Harcourt)

▶ *How to Do Everything with Web 2.0 Mashups* (McGraw-Hill)

▶ *The Bento Book* (Sams/Pearson)

▶ *FileMaker Pro In Depth* (Sams/Pearson)

He is the author of MinutesMachine, the meeting management software for iPad—get more details at champlainarts.com.

A native of Washington, D.C., Feiler has lived in New York City and currently lives in Plattsburgh, NY. He can be reached at northcountryconsulting.com.

Acknowledgments

Thanks go most of all to the people at Apple, along with the developers and users who have helped to build the platform and imagine possibilities together to make the world better.

At Pearson, Loretta Yates, Acquisitions Editor, has taken a concept and moved it from an idea through the adventures along the way to printed books and eBooks in a variety of formats. She is always a pleasure to work with.

Mandie Frank, Project Editor, has done a terrific job of keeping things on track with a complex book full of code snippets, figures, and cross references in addition to the text. Technical Editor Robert McGovern caught numerous technical typos and added comments and perspectives that have clarified and enhanced the book.

As always, Carole Jelen at Waterside Productions has provided help and guidance in bringing this book to fruition.

We Want to Hear from You!

As the reader of this book, *you* are our most important critic and commentator. We value your opinion and want to know what we're doing right, what we could do better, what areas you'd like to see us publish in, and any other words of wisdom you're willing to pass our way.

As an Editor-in-Chief for Sams Publishing, I welcome your comments. You can email or write me directly to let me know what you did or didn't like about this book—as well as what we can do to make our books better.

Please note that I cannot help you with technical problems related to the topic of this book. We do have a User Services group, however, where I will forward specific technical questions related to the book.

When you write, please be sure to include this book's title and author as well as your name, email address, and phone number. I will carefully review your comments and share them with the author and editors who worked on the book.

Email: feedback@amspublishing.com

Mail: Greg Wiegand
          Editor-in-Chief
          Sams Publishing
          800 East 96th Street
          Indianapolis, IN 46240 USA

Reader Services

Visit our website and register this book at amspublishing.com/register for convenient access to any updates, downloads, or errata that might be available for this book.

Introduction

Organizing things is an important human activity. Whether it is a child organizing toys in some way (by size, color, favorites, and so forth) or an adult piecing together a thousand-piece jigsaw puzzle, the desire to "make order out of chaos" (as one inveterate puzzler put it) reflects a sense that somehow if we try hard enough or just have enough information, we can find or create an understandable view of the world. Or at least an understandable view of the left overs in the refrigerator or the photos in an album.

Core Data is a powerful tool that you can use with the Cocoa and Cocoa Touch frameworks on iOS and Mac OS to help you make order out of the chaos of the hundreds, thousands, and even billions of data elements that you now can store on your computer or mobile device.

Who Should Read This Book

This book is geared toward developers who need to understand Core Data and its capabilities. It's also aimed at developers who aren't certain they need the combination of Core Data and Cocoa. It places the technologies in perspective so that you can see where you and your project fit in. Part of that is simply analytical, but for everyone, the hands-on examples provide background as well as the beginnings of applications (apps) that you can create with these two technologies.

If you are new to databases or SQL, you will find a basic introduction here. If you are familiar with them, you will find a refresher as well as details on how the concepts you know already map to Core Data terminology.

Likewise, if you are new to development on Mac OS, iOS, or Cocoa and Cocoa Touch, you will find a fairly detailed introduction. If you are already familiar with them, you will see how some of the basic concepts have been expanded and rearranged to work with Core Data.

There is a theme that recurs in this book: links and connections between interface and code as well the connections between your app and the database. Much of what you find in this book helps you develop the separate components (interface, database, and code) and find simple ways to link them.

Some Points to Keep in Mind

Not everyone starts from the same place in learning about Core Data (or, indeed, any technology). Learning and developing with new technologies is rarely a linear process. It is important to remember that you are not the first person to try to learn these fairly complex interlocking technologies. This book and the code that you experiment with try to lead you toward the moment when it all clicks together. If you do not understand something the first time through, give it a rest, and come back to it another time. For some people, alternating between the graphical design of the interface, the logical design of the code processes, and the organization structure of the database can actually make things seem to move faster.

Here are some additional points to consider.

Acronyms

In many books, it is a convention to provide the full name of an acronym on its first use—for example, HyperText Markup Language (HTML). It is time to recognize that with wikipedia.org, dictionaries built into ebooks and computers, and so many other tools, it is now safe to bring a number of acronyms in from the cold and use them without elaboration. Acronyms specific to the topic of this book are, indeed, explained on their first use in any chapter.

There is one term that does merit its own little section. In this book, as in much usage today, SQL is treated as a name and not as an acronym. If you look it up on Wikipedia, you will see the evolution of the term and its pronunciation.

Development Platforms

It is not surprising that the development of Mac OS X apps takes place on the Mac itself. What may surprise some people, though, is that iOS apps that can run on iPad, iPod touch, and iPhone must be developed on the Mac. There are many reasons for this, not the least of which is that the development tool, Xcode, takes advantage of many dynamic features of Objective-C that are not available on other platforms. Also, Xcode has always served as a test bed for new ideas about development, coding, and interfaces for the Apple engineers. Registered Apple developers have access to preview versions of the developer tools. As a result, the Apple developers had access to features of Lion such as full-screen apps nine months before the general public. In fact, Xcode 4 is optimized for Lion in both speed and interface design.

Assumptions

Certain things are assumed in this book. (You might want to refer to this section as you read.) They are as follows:

- ▶ *Cocoa*, as used in this book, refers to the Cocoa framework on Mac OS and, unless otherwise specified, also to the Cocoa Touch framework on iOS.

- ▶ *iPhone* refers to iPhone and iPod touch unless otherwise noted.

Formatting

In addition to the text of this book, you will find code samples illustrating various points. When a word is used in a sentence as computer code (such as NSTableView), it appears like this. Code snippets appear set off from the surrounding text. Sometimes they appear as a few lines of code; longer excerpts are identified with listing numbers so they can be cross-referenced.

Downloading the Sample Files

Sample files can be downloaded from the author's website at northcountryconsulting. com or from the publisher's site at www.informit.com/9780672335778.

How This Book Is Organized

There are five parts to this book. You can focus on whichever one addresses an immediate problem, or you can get a good overview by reading the book straight through. Like all of the *Teach Yourself* Books, as much as possible, each chapter (or hour) is made to stand on its own so that you can jump around to learn in your own way. Cross-references throughout the book help you find related material.

Part I, "Getting Started with Core Data"

This part introduces the basic issues of the book and shows you principles and techniques that apply to all of the products discussed:

- ▶ Chapter 1, "Introducing Xcode 4"—Xcode is the tool you use to build Mac OS and iOS apps. It includes graphical editors for designing your interface and data model. The current version, Xcode 4, represents a significant step forward from previous development environments. You'll get started by learning the ins and outs of Xcode 4. After you use it, you'll never look back.

▶ Chapter 2, "Creating a Simple App"—This hour walks you through the process of creating an app from one of the built-in Xcode templates. It's very little work for a basic app that runs.

▶ Chapter 3, "Understanding the Basic Code Structure"—This hour introduces design patterns used in Objective-C as well as some of the features (such as delegates and protocols) that distinguish it from other object-oriented programming languages.

Part II, "Using Core Data"

Here you will find the basics of Core Data and its development tools in Xcode:

▶ Chapter 4, "Getting the Big Core Data Picture"—Here you'll find an overview of Core Data and a high-level introduction to its main components.

▶ Chapter 5, "Working with Data Models"—Data models have been around since the beginning of databases (and, in fact, since long before, if you want to include data models such as the classifications of plants and animals). This hour lets you learn the language of Core Data.

▶ Chapter 6, "Working with the Data Model Editor"—In this hour, you will learn how to build your data model graphically with Xcode's table and grid views.

▶ Chapter 7, "What Managed Objects Can Do"—In this hour, you'll discover the functionality of managed objects and what you can do to take advantage of it and to expand it.

▶ Chapter 8, "Controllers: Integrating the Data Model with Your Code"—The key point of this book is to show you how to link your database and data model to interface elements and your code. This hour provides the basics for Mac OS and for Cocoa.

▶ Chapter 9, "Fetching Data"—Just as the SQL SELECT statement is the heart of data retrieval for SQL databases, fetching data is the heart of data retrieval for Core Data. Here you'll learn the techniques and terminology.

▶ Chapter 10, "Working with Predicates and Sorting"—When you fetch data, you often need to specify exactly what data is to be fetched—that is the role of predicates. In addition, you will see how to build sorting into your fetch requests so that the data is already in the order you need.

Part III, "Developing the Core Data Interface"

Now that you understand the basics of Core Data, you can use it to drive the commands, controls, and interfaces of your apps:

▶ Chapter 11, "Finding Your Way Around Interface Builder: The Graphics Story"—The Interface Builder editor in Xcode 4 (a separate program until now) provides powerful tools and a compact workspace to help you develop your interface and app functionality.

▶ Chapter 12, "Finding Your Way Around Interface Builder: The Code Story"—This hour shows you the graphical tools to link the code to the interface.

▶ Chapter 13, "Control-Dragging Your Way to Code"—A special aspect of linking your interface to your code is using the tools in Xcode 4 to actually write the interface code for you.

▶ Chapter 14, "Working with Storyboards"—One of the major advances in Xcode 4, storyboards let you not only create and manage the views and controllers that make up your interface but also let you manage the sequences in which they are presented (segues). You will find that storyboards can replace a good deal of code that you would otherwise have to write for each view you display.

Part IV, "Building the Core Data Code"

Yet another aspect of the connections between Core Data, your code, and your interface consists of the data source protocol and table views. This hour explains them:

▶ Chapter 15, "Saving Data with a Navigation Interface"—Originally designed for iPhone, navigation interfaces are an efficient use of screen space for organized data. This hour shows you how to use them.

▶ Chapter 16, "Using Split Views on iPad"—Split views on iPad provide a larger-screen approach to data presentation than navigation interfaces. As you see in this hour, you can combine navigation interfaces with a split view on iPad. Data sources provide your Core Data data to the table view. This hour shows how that happens and moves on to how you can work with tables and their rows and sections. You'll also see how to format cells in various ways.

▶ Chapter 17, "Structuring Apps for Core Data, Documents, and Shoeboxes"—This hour goes into detail about how and where your data can actually be stored.

▶ Chapter 18, "Validating Data"—When you use Xcode and Core Data to specify what data is valid, you do not have to perform the validation yourself. This hour shows you how to set up the rules

Part V, "Managing Data and Interfaces"

▶ Chapter 19, "Using UITableView on iOS"—Table views let you manage and present data easily. The UITableView structure on iOS is designed for seamless integration with Core Data.

▶ Chapter 20, "Using NSTableView on Mac OS"—NSTableView on Mac OS is revised in Lion. The older versions of table views still work, but as you see in this hour, some of the new features of UITableView have been backported to Mac OS.

▶ Chapter 21, "Rearranging Table Rows on iOS"—The ability to rearrange table rows by dragging them on the screen is one of the best features of iOS. It is remarkably simple once you know the table view basics.

▶ Chapter 22, "Managing Validation"—This hour shows you how to build on the validation rules from Hour 18 to actually implement them and let users know when there are problems.

▶ Chapter 23, "Interacting with Users"—On both iOS and Mac OS, it is important to let users know when they are able to modify data and when it is only being displayed.

▶ Chapter 24, "Migrating Data Models"—You can have Core Data automatically migrate your data model to a new version. This hour shows you how to do that, as well as how to use model metadata and alternative types of data stores.

Appendixes

▶ Appendix A, "What's Old in Core Data"—There are some legacy features in the sample code you'll find on developer.apple.com and in apps you might be working with. This appendix helps you understand what you're looking at and how to modernize it.

HOUR 1

Introducing Xcode 4

What You'll Learn in This Hour:

- ▶ Understanding the new development paradigms
- ▶ Exploring the Xcode workspace window
- ▶ Defining projects and workspaces
- ▶ Debugging with breakpoints
- ▶ Caring for your source code with repositories and versions

The Origins of Xcode 4

Xcode 4 has its roots in Project Builder and Interface Builder, the two development tools created for NeXTSTEP. The NeXTSTEP operating system ran on the NeXT computer, which was manufactured by NeXT, the company Steve Jobs founded when he left Apple in 1985. The hardware side of the business was not successful, and NeXTSTEP morphed into OPENSTEP, which ran on Sun's Solaris operating system, and later on Windows. After Apple purchased NeXT in 1996, the software became Rhapsody and, later, Mac OS X. A branch of the software became the iPhone operating system which, after the introduction of iPad, became iOS.

Project Builder and Interface Builder remained the developer tools through all this time. Project Builder was the tool you used to write code, and Interface Builder was the graphically oriented tool you used to draw the interface. Project Builder was renamed Xcode in 2003; it contained significant changes to its user interface at that time.

At Apple's 2010 Worldwide Developer Conference, Xcode 4 was given its debut. It was released as the official version in spring 2011. One of its most significant features was the integration of Project Builder and Interface Builder in a single tool.

This book is based on Xcode 4. If you are using an earlier version, it is time for you to update to the latest software because by the time this book is published, Xcode 4 will be more than a year old (depending on whether you start counting from the demonstrations or from the official release). Now that you know the history and origins of Xcode 4, there is no reason to distinguish it from its predecessors: From this point on, it is simply referred to as *Xcode*.

Getting to Know Xcode

Everything you do in the development of Mac and iOS apps is done in the context of Xcode. First demonstrated at Apple's Worldwide Developers Conference in June 2010, it was released in several preview versions until the final release in the spring of 2011. Xcode 4 is not just a revision to the interface of Xcode 3; it is a rethinking of the way in which developers work on their apps.

This hour helps you understand this new way of working and why it is so relevant to apps written for Mac and iOS in today's world. Not only will you find out how to use Xcode 4, but you will see why it is structured the way it is and how you can best take advantage of its new features.

As you use Xcode 4, try to use the new features and new ways of working so that you understand what the people at Apple think a productive development process can look like today. And bear in mind one important point about Apple's developer tools: for many years, these tools have been testing and proving grounds for new ideas about interface design. What you see in Xcode 4 includes some novel approaches to interface design that you may consider using for your own apps both on Mac and iOS.

> ▶ One of the most important features of Xcode is its simulator: software that lets you test iOS apps on your Mac. You'll find out more about the simulator in Part II of this book, "Using Core Data."

Goodbye "Hello, World"

For many people, their first program was something along the lines of the well-known Hello World program shown in Listing 1.1. It is from the classic *The C Programming Language* by Brian Kernighan and Dennis Ritchie (1978).

LISTING 1.1   Hello, World

```
main( ) {
  printf("hello, world");
}
```

Many people still think of this as a model of what programming is all about: You start with a blank piece of paper or a blank screen, you type in your code, you run it, you make revisions, and you continue on to the next program on its own blank piece of paper or blank screen.

Today's programming is based on several commonly used paradigms. Two of the most important have to do with how programs function—declarative and imperative paradigms. A third, object-oriented programming, has to do with the structure of programs.

Working with Imperative and Declarative Programing Paradigms

Today's apps are much more complex than just printing or displaying a line of text. How do you get from Hello, World to an app such as iTunes? Even an app that appears to be text-based such as Pages in the iWork suite is a far cry from Hello, World. And when you consider that Mac OS X and iOS are basically just very large apps, it is hard to see how they evolved from Hello, World.

When Hello, World first was written, the programming world was already moving away from this linear do this/do that paradigm (called *imperative* or *procedural* programming) to a new paradigm called *declarative* programming, in which the mechanics of *how* something is done are less important than *what* is done.

Procedural programming is used in the code you write; most of that is Objective-C when you are writing for Mac OS X and iOS. For most people, writing procedural code "feels" like programming. (In addition to its procedural programming concepts, Objective-C uses object-oriented programming, hence it's name.)

Languages that are declarative (that is, focusing on what is done) are particularly common on the Web. Most people consider Cascading Style Sheets (CSS), regular expressions, and the basics of SQL (SELECT statements, for example) to be examples of declarative languages. Markup languages in general—including HTML itself—are declarative rather than procedural because they describe what the end result should look like. For many people, designing databases and web pages doesn't "feel" like programming (and many people do not think that it is).

The distinction between these two programming paradigms is not a matter of good versus bad or old versus new: It is simply a contrast between two ways of developing software. As you approach Xcode, Mac OS X, and iOS, you do not have to make a choice because both paradigms are supported in Xcode. Most of the time, a specific editing function is implemented only in procedural or declarative styles because one or the other is the natural way of editing that particular set of instructions.

NOTE

In at least one case—the creation of interface views—you can choose between procedural and declarative styles. In those cases, this book will point out some of the differences that affect your finished app.

If you are starting building apps for Mac OS X or iOS that use Core Data, you will use descriptive editors for the Core Data side of things just as you do with many SQL-based development environments, and you will use procedural editors for the text-based code that you write to manipulate the interface and the database.

Working with Object-Oriented Programming

Object-oriented programming is now so pervasive that for many people, it is the only kind of programming they do. Instead of the simple and relatively unstructured code shown in Listing 1.1, *objects* are created that encapsulate data and functionality. These objects interact with one another to get the work of the program done.

When people first started using object-oriented programming techniques, some critics pointed out that it took much more code and programming time to use object-oriented techniques and languages than to use traditional techniques and languages. The idea of writing a program with the three lines shown in Listing 1.1 is unthinkable in the object-oriented programming world.

However, the arguments made by proponents of object-oriented programming and borne out by decades of experience are that

▶ Object-oriented programming is easier to maintain and modify over time in part because of its inherent structures.

▶ It might take many more lines to write a very simple program using object-oriented programming techniques, but as the complexity of the program increases, the incremental effort to build each new feature can be significantly less than with traditional techniques.

When you put these points together, you can see that there is a significant difference between simple and complex programs no matter whether you are using object-oriented programming or traditional programming. The benefits of object-oriented programming really only appear in complex programs, whereas the limitations of traditional programming methods do not appear in short programs.

In practical terms, this means that to learn how to use the tools of Mac OS X and iOS along with Xcode, you have to work with hefty examples. And if you try to use a simplified example, you might wind up thinking that these tools are overly complex. That is true in one sense: Using these tools to write something very simple is overkill. But not using tools like this to write complex software is frequently self-defeating.

As you begin to work with Xcode, Core Data, Mac OS X, and iOS, you will find yourself at the helm of a sophisticated and powerful development environment. In this book, you will see how to start small and build up to very complex apps. In the initial hours, because the examples are small, you may be tempted to worry about the complexity, but just remember that the complexity will pay off as the examples become more complex.

▶ With that overview, you might be interested in the Tutorial "Using Xcode to Write 'Hello, World'" in Hour 1 of *Apple's Xcode Quick Start Guide*. It is 20 pages long and demonstrates precisely these points.

TIP

If you have not done so already, register as a developer with Apple at developer. apple.com. A variety of developer programs are available, but the most common are the Mac OS X developer program ($99/year), the iOS developer program ($99/year), and the Safari developer program (free). All these programs are built on your registration as a developer with Apple, which is free.

Without even registering, you have access to libraries of documentation. All Apple documentation referred to in this book is available through developer.apple.com. Any documentation that is not available through developer.apple.com will be identified.

You can visit http://developer.apple.com/programs/which-program/ to compare the various developer programs and to choose the one that makes sense for you.

Hello, App Development for Mac OS X and iOS

To get started, register and sign up for a developer program so you can download Xcode from developer.apple.com. If you are not certain that you want to register as a developer, you can purchase Xcode alone from the Mac App store. It is currently free. By default, Xcode is installed in the root view of your boot disk, as you can see in Figure 1.1. Although it is an application, it is installed in a special Applications folder inside the Developer folder.

Launch Xcode to open the window shown in Figure 1.2. (While you are at it, you might want to set the option to keep it in the Dock. Some people like to launch

Xcode directly; others launch it by opening the Xcode project document they are currently working on.)

FIGURE 1.1
Xcode is auto-
matically
installed in your
Developer
folder.

FIGURE 1.2
Launch Xcode.

TIP

If you have run Xcode before, preferences might have changed and you may see a different welcome screen—or none at all.

As you can see in Figure 1.2, from this point you can create a new project, get help, and generally get started with Xcode.

▶ At this point, you can get started using Xcode by creating a simple app as described in Hour 2, "Creating a Simple App," p. 49.

This hour continues with an exploration of the Xcode window and how to use it.

Getting Started with Xcode

Whether you are creating a new Xcode project or reopening an old one, you see the Xcode workspace window shown in Figure 1.3. Note that depending on your project and your Xcode preferences, the details of the window (not to mention the code) will very likely be different.

Navigation
Selector bar   Toolbar   Jump bar   Inspector Selector bar

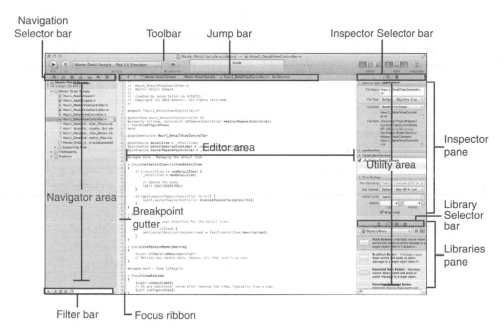

FIGURE 1.3
You work inside the Xcode workspace window.

Editor area

Inspector pane

Utility area

Navigator area

Breakpoint gutter

Library Selector bar

Libraries pane

Filter bar   Focus ribbon

Using the Workspace Window

As noted previously, Apple developer tools often provide a test bed for new interface features (and, under the hood, performance advances such a advanced threading). In its first demonstration of Mac OS X 10.7 (Lion), Apple showed how full-screen apps could take over the screen in much the same way that all apps do on mobile iOS devices. As Apple has moved forward, Xcode has provided an example of how a full-screen app can work. It was compelling and relatively simple to demonstrate full-screen implementations of existing apps such as Preview, iCal, iPhoto, and Mail, which Apple did as long ago as fall of 2010.

But how would full-screen apps work with data that is not visual the way that photos, calendars, and the documents shown in Preview are? The answer was under developers' eyes right at the first preview: They just had to download a beta version of Xcode 4.

The window is a combination of panes and panes-within-panes that can be shown or hidden as well as resized. At first glance, Figure 1.3 can be daunting. But when you look at it a second time, you will see that it is actually fairly simple. It uses and reuses three components. Each component exhibits the same behavior wherever it appears. In addition, you can show or hide almost all the components, rearrange them, and resize them.

These are the main components of the workspace window:

▶ **Areas**—There are three areas shown in Figure 1.3. At the left is the navigator area, at the right is the utility area, and hidden at the bottom is the debug area. Each of these can be shown or hidden by using the three View buttons at the upper right of the workspace window. The editor area, in the center of the workspace window, is always visible.

▶ **Bars**—At the top of the navigator, editor, and debug areas, you will find a bar you can use to select different views for the area. The bar above the editor area is the jump bar, but the others are the navigator selector bar and the debug bar.

▶ **Panes**—The utility area is divided into two panes, each of which can be resized. The combined height of the utility area remains constant within the window size, so if you enlarge the height of the library pane, you automatically reduce the height of the inspector pane. Selector bars appear at the top of the panes in the utility area.

There are three lesser components in the workspace window:

▶ **Filter bar**—At the bottom of the navigator area, this lets you filter the lists in the navigator to include or exclude certain types of items, such as class symbols, files with unsaved changes, and so forth.

▶ **Breakpoint gutter**—This appears in the editor area and lets you insert and delete breakpoints for debugging.

▶ **Focus ribbon**—This lets you expand or collapse sections of code in the editor.

TIP

The best way to explore the workspace window is to open or create a project and then explore the menu bar. This hour can only provide a high-level summary of the workspace window.

There you have it: The workspace window is a compact and powerful environment to let you manage your development process. The same interface elements are used over and over, which means you do not have to learn a multitude of interfaces and functions. This is the result of the consolidation of Project Builder and Interface Builder along with a great deal of hard work and imagination.

Xcode is designed to be customizable with all kinds of preferences; these, together with the basic interface components, allow you to work the way you want to work on the projects you want to work on (An iPhone app? A Mac OS app? And if you work for Apple, Mac OS X itself?). For these reasons, there is no sequential way to start working with Xcode. The sections that follow highlight some of the main components: Feel free to skip around.

NOTE

This overview of Xcode walks through the workspace window. There is an Xcode menu bar, as you would expect in a Mac app, but menus today are not nearly so important as they were many years ago. If this book had been written 10 years ago, it is quite likely that the overview would have walked you through each menu and each command in that menu. Now, however, we are in a world of direct manipulation where buttons, commands, and hot items are located throughout the interface—they are placed where you want to use them. This means that that lengthy mouse trip up to the menubar is often not necessary because the interface element that does what you want to have done is right on the window itself. (Hmmm, just like on an iOS device.) The menu commands are more often than ever available with keyboard equivalents. For many people, the menubar and its commands serve largely as a place to go to find the keyboard equivalent for a command. For these reasons, you will find the menu commands scattered through this hour; they are dealt with in the interface elements they affect.

Using the Navigator

The starting point for this exploration is the navigator pane at the left of the workspace window. You show or hide it with the leftmost View button, as pointed out in Figure 1.3. At the top of the navigator is a selector bar. The seven items in it control which navigator is displayed. You can use commands in the Navigators submenu of the View menu or keyboard equivalents instead of the selector bar if you want.

TIP

If the navigator is not visible, the menu command will automatically open it.

If you want to hide the navigator, use the leftmost View button or the View > Navigators > Hide Navigator command (⌘–0).

The next sections explain the navigators, their keyboard equivalents, and what they do.

Project ⌘–1

Figure 1.4 shows the project navigator. When you have first created a new project, it will very likely look like this. At the top of the navigator is a single item with a disclosure triangle to its left.

Click the disclosure triangle, and the single project item opens revealing its files and groups, as you see in Figure 1.5.

NOTE

Groups are shown with folder icons, but they are not file system folders. The groups into which you organize your project's files are a construct within Xcode. The files can be anywhere you want.

Figure 1.5 also demonstrates another feature of Xcode: the parts of the workspace window know about one another. When you click the project icon at the top of the navigator, the editor area of the workspace window shows information about the project, as you can see in Figures 1.4 and 1.5.

FIGURE 1.4
The project is shown in a collapsed form in the navigator right after you have created it.

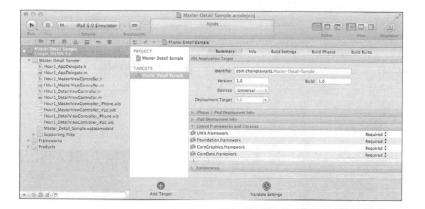

FIGURE 1.5
You can expand groups in the project navigator.

Click one of the files in the project, and it appears in the editor area shown in Figure 1.6.

FIGURE 1.6
Click a file to edit it.

Clicking a file opens it in the editor area no matter what kind of file it is. Figure 1.7 shows an interface file (a *nib* file) in the editor area. Note that new projects for iOS have the option to use storyboards instead of nib files; for older projects and on Mac OS, nibs remain the standards.

▶ Learn more about storyboards in Hour 14, "Working with Storyboards."

Figure 1.8 shows a Core Data data model file in the editor area.

In Figure 1.9, you see that if you have added an image file to your project, clicking it opens the image in the editor area.

FIGURE 1.7
Edit a nib file in
Xcode.

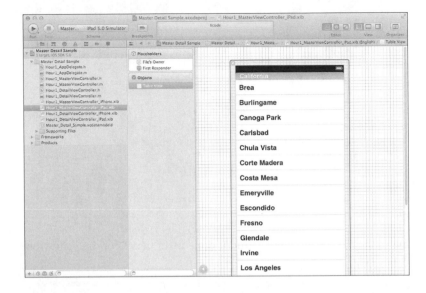

FIGURE 1.8
Edit your data
model in Xcode.

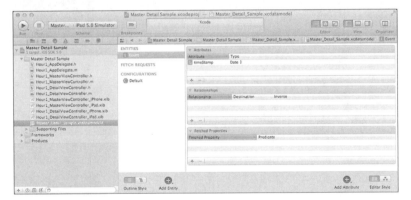

FIGURE 1.9
Open resource
files.

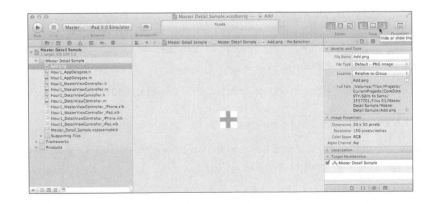

In other words, no matter what kind of file it is, select it in the project navigator and edit it in the editor (for the file types that Xcode supports).

You have seen how to use the navigator to explore your project and its files, but how do you manage the files themselves? When you create a project, as you will see in Hour 2, the files are automatically created for you. In your own projects, you might need to add files to it. Control-click in the project navigator to bring up the shortcut menu shown in Figure 1.10. For many people, right-clicking the mouse will have the same effect. You can add the new file anywhere you want and move it to the right position in the navigator just by dragging it. If you control- or right-click in a group, the file will be added to that group and you might not have to move it.

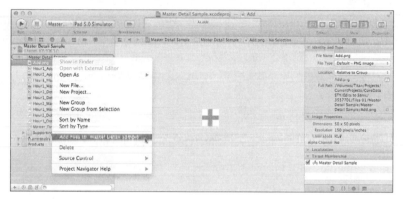

FIGURE 1.10
Use the shortcut menu to add files to the project.

Once you have selected a file to add, the sheet shown in Figure 1.11 opens.

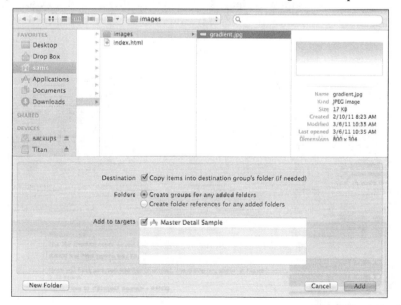

FIGURE 1.11
Specify a file to add.

The most important part of this dialog box other than the filename is the Destination checkbox. This determines whether the project will use the file that may be somewhere else on your disk or network or whether it will copy it into your project. Normally, you do want to copy the file into the project so that you can then move the entire project folder to another computer if necessary.

TIP

Sometimes, a filename will appear in red. This indicates that it is part of the project but that it is missing. For example, before you have built your project, the file named <MyProjectName>.app appears in red. After you have successfully built your project, the name appears in black.

The filter bar at the bottom of the project navigator lets you filter by filename (or part thereof). The + in the bottom-left lets you add a new file with a template (it is not the same as the add file to project command shown in the shortcut menu in Figure 1.10). Three symbols to the right of the + limit your navigation. From left, here are their effects:

▶ Show only recently edited files

▶ Show only files with source-control status such as modified

▶ Show only files with unsaved changes

Symbol ⌘–2

The symbol navigator, shown in Figure 1.12, shows you the symbols in your project: the classes (indicated with C), methods (M), and properties (P). Interface Builder actions (A) and outlets (O) manage the interactions between your code and your interface.

FIGURE 1.12
Use the symbol navigator.

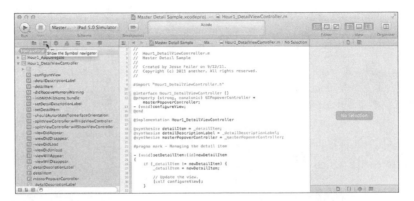

Properties are identified by P unless they are Interface Builder outlets—a special kind of property. The synthesize directive that is the companion to a property directive is flagged with a V (for variable).

▶ You will find out more about the property and synthesize directives in Hour 3, "Understanding the Basic Code Structure," p. 63.

At the bottom of the symbol navigator, you can filter the display. Use the search box to type text to search for in symbol names. To the left of the filter bar, symbols let you choose what to display and hide. From left, the following effects are available:

▶ Show only class symbols—that is, no globals

▶ Show only symbols defined in the project

▶ Show only containers such as classes and categories, do not show members

Search ⌘-3

The search navigator packs a lot of searching into a small space. You can use it by simply typing a search term into the box; Xcode will search for it through the project. The list of results (if any) is shown in the search navigator. You will see the relevant filename, a symbol such as the ones shown previously in Figure 1.12, and the beginning of the line of code. The search term is highlighted in yellow in each line. Sometimes this means that you do not see the beginning of the line, but never fear—a click on the line will display it in the editor area, or you can hover the pointer over it to see a tooltip with the full text.

You can switch between searching and replacing text at the upper-left, as shown in Figure 1.13. In addition, at the bottom of the search navigator, the filter bar lets you search within the results. In Figure 1.13, for example, the find was executed on "detail." (You can see this because "detail" is highlighted in all of the search results.) The filter bar is used to filter on "item." If you look at the search results, you will see that "detail" is always found, but each of those results also contains "item," which is not highlighted because it was not part of the original search. You can duplicate these results for yourself. Conduct a search without a filter, and then add a filter. You'll see that the number of results is reduced.

Just to the right of the magnifying glass in the search field, a disclosure triangle lets you show or hide the Find Options shortcut, as shown in Figure 1.14. It also lets you repeat recent searches.

FIGURE 1.13
Specify a
search.

FIGURE 1.14
Show or hide
Find Options
shortcuts.

The search navigator searches throughout the project. The Edit menu has traditional
single-file Find commands, as shown in Figure 1.15.

FIGURE 1.15
The Edit menu
provides a mul-
titude of search
and replace
options.

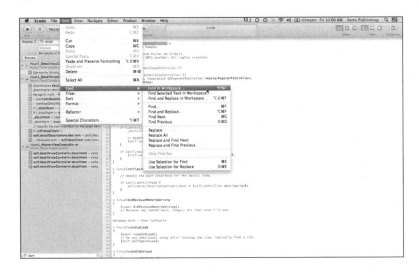

Issue ⌘–4

The issue navigator lets you view the issues with your project. In the old days, these used to be called *compile errors*, but with Xcode, you will have many fewer compile errors. Do not get your hopes up, though. That is because Xcode has a powerful parser that checks your code as you type. It is as lively as a spell-checker, but it looks for syntax errors as well as ordinary misspellings. This means that compile errors now show up much earlier—just as you are typing them in many cases. The issue navigator lets you see them. You can display them by file (the traditional way of showing compile errors), but you can also display them by type so that like errors are grouped together. Sometimes that can make fixing the errors faster, particularly if you are consistently mistyping a variable name.

Figure 1.16 shows the issue navigator. In addition, note that, in the breakpoint gutter at the left of the editor area, symbols show up as soon as you have made the offending keystroke. (An extra *s* has just been added to synthesize—synthessize.)

FIGURE 1.16
The issue navigator helps you correct errors as you type.

Debug ⌘–5

Debug shows you the calling sequence for each of your app's threads (in the simplest case, there is only one). For example, Figure 1.17 shows the app stopped in DetailViewController viewWillAppear. That was called from UISplitViewController viewWillAppear, and so on back to the bottom of the calling sequence—main, which starts the program running.

FIGURE 1.17
Use the debug
navigator to
track a calling
sequence.

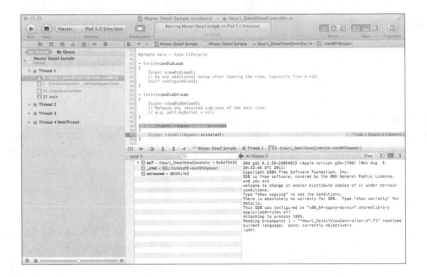

Breakpoint ⌘–6

Breakpoints let you stop program execution at specific lines of code. You place a
breakpoint in the breakpoint gutter to the left of the editor area and, when the program is about to execute that line of code, it stops. You can then inspect the variables in the debug area. In Figure 1.17, a breakpoint was set in the editor area at
[super viewWillAppear:animated]. The program stopped just before executing
that line of code. The calling sequence is visible in the debug navigator. In the editor
area, you see the breakpoint, and, to its right, a small green arrow that points to the
line of code about to be executed. If you have several breakpoints, you need to know
which one has just stopped the app.

Beneath the editor area, the debug area shows you information about the breakpoint. On the left is a view of the variables at this moment. On the right are console
messages. Buttons at the upper-right of the debug area let you choose which—or
both—views to display. In the view of variables, you can expand and collapse containers as you examine exactly what data is where.

TIP

Breakpoints can be useful even if they do not trip. When you cannot figure out why
a line of code does not work properly, set a breakpoint on it to examine the data. If
the breakpoint is not tripped, work backwards to see where the app goes off the
rails. Command-click on a breakpoint to edit it. For example, you can stop only
after the nth pass through the breakpoint and only if a certain data condition is
true. You can add actions to the breakpoint such as a sound, a log message, a
shell command, or even that trustworthy and powerful tool, an AppleScript script.

To remove a breakpoint, drag it out of the breakpoint gutter. You can also use the breakpoint navigator to list the breakpoints. Clicking one will take you to the line of code. You can drag breakpoints out of the breakpoint navigator to remove them if you prefer not to drag them out of the breakpoint gutter.

TIP

Note that there is a global breakpoint control in the toolbar. Use it to turn all breakpoints on or off. This is helpful in debugging when you are done with the breakpoints but might want to turn the breakpoint back on the next time a bug appears.

Log ⌘–7

Finally, the log navigator keeps track of what you've been doing with this app. Figure 1.18 shows the log navigator. The events are in reverse chronological order (latest first). As always in the navigator, a filter bar lets you filter the entries so you can easily find builds or other specific types of entries; you can also use the control at the bottom-left to see the most recent log entries. Clicking a log entry shows you the console results for that compile, build, or other action.

FIGURE 1.18
The log navigator keeps track of your work.

Using Editors

The center of the workspace window is reserved for editing your project and its files. As you have seen, different editors are automatically opened for the different types of files in your project.

▶ This section focuses on text editors; other editors are discussed in Hour 6, "Working with the Data Model Editor," p. 117, and Hour 11, "Finding Your Way Around Interface Builder: The Graphics Story," p. 189.

Using Editing Modes

Three editing modes are available in Xcode:

▶ **Standard**—This displays a single file in the edit area.

▶ **Assistant**—This displays two or more related files in the edit area.

▶ **Version**—If you are using source control, you can compare a file with its previous version or versions.

▶ Refer to the "Working with Assistant" on p. 29 of this hour for details about the Assistant mode.

You select the editing mode with the trio of buttons marked Editor at the right of the top of the Xcode window, as shown in Figure 1.19. You can also use View, Editor to choose among them.

FIGURE 1.19
Select the assistant you want to use.

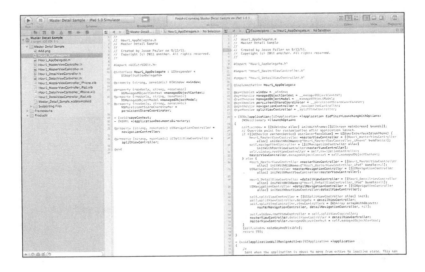

Using the Jump Bar

The *jump bar* appears at the top of the editor area no matter what mode you are in. As you can see in Figure 1.20, the jump bar above the editor area shows the path to the file you are working on relative to the project and lets you quickly navigate to a file, method, property, or class in the file. If you have several files open (as is often the case in Assistant and Version editor panes), each has its own jump bar.

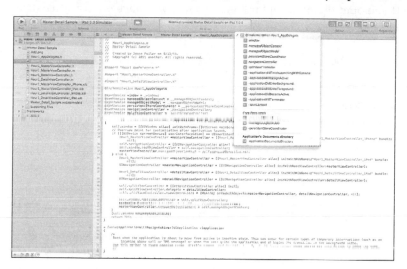

FIGURE 1.20
Jump bar in action.

You can use it to quickly navigate to a file or to a method, property, or class in the open file.

Thus, at the left, you see the icon for the project (Master Detail Sample); within that, you see a group (Master Detail Sample—shown with a Finder folder icon), and within that, the filename is shown (Hour1_AppDelegate.m). The next level down is a list of the methods, properties, and classes in that file.

> **TIP**
>
> It is important to note that this is the logical structure of the project, files, and groups. If you move the project to another folder, drive, or computer, this structure will remain the same.

Organizing Your File's Pop-Up Menu List

In addition to the names of the methods, properties, and classes, titles appear in the pop-up list. You put titles into the file using a pragma directive:

```
#pragma mark - headingName
```

There actually are three variations on this directive:

▶ The example shown provides a bold-faced heading with a dividing line above it, as shown in Figure 1.20.

▶ If you omit the hyphen, the dividing line is not shown and you only have the name.

▶ If you omit the name but use the hyphen, you have an unnamed dividing line.

You can use the bold-faced heading with a dividing line for major sections of your code; then use dividing lines without headings to further divide each major section.

Using headers forces you to keep your file organized because related methods, properties, and classes are physically co-located in the file.

TIP
Be aware that the code that is commented out will not appear in the pop-up menu list.

Using Xcode's Organization Tools

Xcode keeps track of the relationships among your files. At the left of the jump bar, the related items menu lets you quickly jump to related files. You can see the related items menu in Figure 1.21.

Related items menu

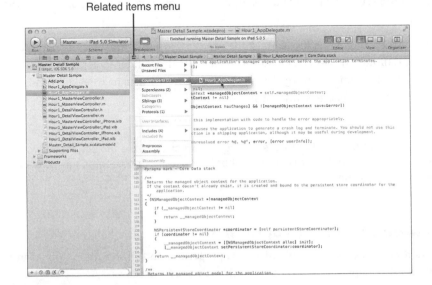

FIGURE 1.21
Use the related items menu.

At the top of the menu, submenus show you unsaved files and recent files. Submenus show you these types of related files when you are looking at source code. Other types of files, such as nib files and Core Data model editor files, have different submenus:

▶ **Counterparts**—This means the .h files for .m files, and vice versa.

▶ **Superclasses**—There is always a superclass (except for NSObject). This list is organized in order so that the last item at the bottom is always NSObject.

▶ **Subclasses**—If any.

▶ **Siblings**—These are classes that share the same immediate superclass.

▶ **Categories**—This is an Objective-C construct that allows you to add methods to an existing class.

▶ **Protocols**—This Objective-C features lets you declare a set of methods that can be implemented by several classes in their own ways and with their own data structures. Protocols provide functionality similar to multiple inheritance in some other object-oriented languages.

  ▶ Both categories and protocols are discussed in Hour 3, "Understanding the Basic Code Structure," p. 63.

▶ **Includes**—These are the files that are included in the file you are looking at.

▶ **Included By**—From an included file, you can return easily to this file; you can also see the other files in your project that may include this file.

With these various navigational tools available and updated by Xcode, you might want to use the adjacent forward and back arrows. They function just as forward and back arrows do in a browser. This means that you can use the related items menu to explore the rest of your project and get back to where you started from with just a few mouse clicks.

Working with Assistant

Assistant lets you see several files in the same pane of the window, and it can take advantage of the fact that Xcode keeps track of the relationships among files that you have already seen in the related items menu. As soon as you think about displaying several files in the same pane, the question arises as to how to display them. Xcode gives you a variety of choices, as shown in Figure 1.22.

FIGURE 1.22
Control the layout of assistant panes.

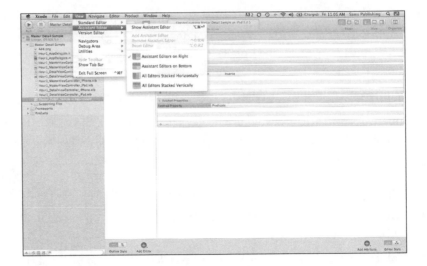

Experiment with the various layouts. Most people switch back and forth among them, depending on the size of their display and the files that they are working with. Sometimes, you are dealing with short lines of code that look good side-by-side, but in other cases, you have large chunks of code that need the width of your computer display.

Once you are using an assistant, you might be able to open additional panes in the assistant. Figure 1.23 shows two panes displayed, one above the other. When you have several panes in the assistant window, each has its own jump bar.

Also, note that small widget at the right of a jump bar let you close that pane or add another pane.

FIGURE 1.23
You can open additional assistant panes.

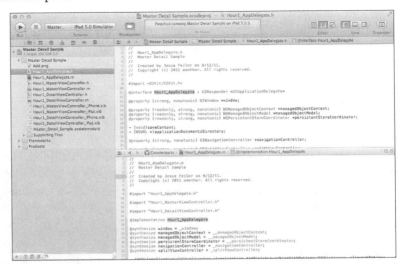

Getting Help in an Editor Window

You can option-click on a word in an editor window to bring up help and documentation, as shown in Figure 1.24.

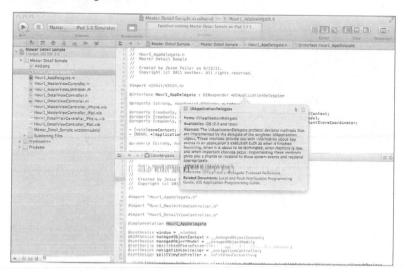

FIGURE 1.24
Use option-click to get more information about code syntax.

Where possible, there will be two links to the documentation—the filename is a link, as is the file icon with .h in the upper-right of the window. The book in the upper-right opens the reference in the Organizer window, which is described later in this hour.

▶ Find out more about help and documentation in the "Using the Organizer Window" section on p. 45 of this hour.

Using Utilities—Inspectors

At the right of the workspace window is the utility area. This consists of two panes stacked one above the other. You can drag the divider between them to change their sizes, but they always fill the utility pane.

At the top of utilities are the inspectors. They change as you select objects in the editor window. The content of the pane depends on what is selected in the editor, as well as on which of the buttons at the top of the inspector is selected. However, as you will see, a consistent framework applies to all selected objects.

In Figure 1.25, you see the file inspector as it appears when a file is selected in the project navigator; if a line of text within a file is selected in the text editor, the display may look the same.

FIGURE 1.25
Use the file
inspector.

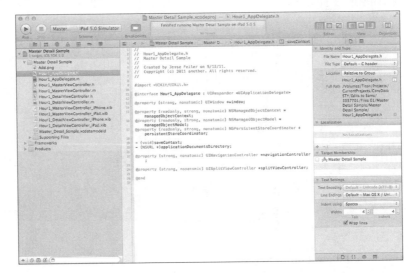

At the left of the top of the inspector, the small icon lets you view the information about the file you have selected. Information about the filename and file type is available. Each section of the file inspector has its own heading; you can expand or collapse each one.

These settings are self-explanatory, but one of them needs careful attention if you want to avoid problems. The location of each file can be set to one of six settings:

▶ Absolute Path

▶ Relative to Group

▶ Relative to Project

▶ Relative to Build Products

▶ Relative to Developer Directory

▶ Relative to SDK

Relative to project means that if you move the project to another computer, folder, or disk, all the files within the project move together and the internal file structure stays intact. An absolute path is great if the path is to a location on a shared server that a number of people will be using. In that case, the project files stay in one place, but the developers can move from computer to computer.

Relative to Group can be a good structure for a multiperson project where components are being developed by different people at different times. Each person can structure a group without worrying about how they will be arranged together. The remaining choices are useful in specific cases that typically are involved with large projects or special conditions.

TIP

Of course, by using a source code repository, you can handle the issues of sharing and version control easily.

To the immediate right of the file inspector button is a Quick Help button. If an element in the editor is selected and help is available, it will be displayed as shown in Figure 1.26.

FIGURE 1.26
Quick Help is available wherever possible in the inspector pane.

In Figure 1.27, an Interface Builder document is open. The file inspector is still the left-most button at the top of the window, and its data is much the same. Immediately to its right, a help inspector will reflect information about the selected item in the editor. However, new inspectors are available to let you inspect items in the interface.

FIGURE 1.27
Inspectors
change depend-
ing on what is
selected in the
editor.

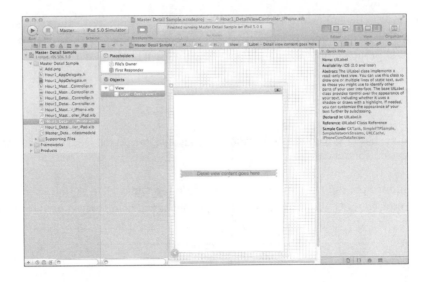

FIGURE 1.27
Inspectors
change depend-
ing on what is
selected in the
editor.

For example, in Figure 1.28, you see the Identity inspector in action. It identifies a selected object in the interface.

FIGURE 1.28
Use the Identity
inspector.

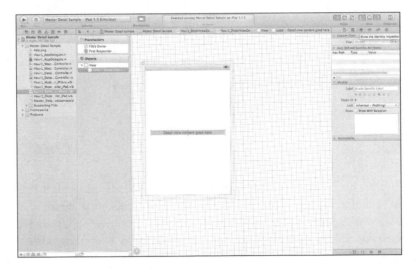

▶ Refer to Hour 11, p. 189, to find out more about how you can use these inspectors to set everything from an object's location to its behavior as people type in it.

Using Utilities—Libraries

The bottom pane of the utility area is for libraries. These are collection of items that you can add to your apps just by dragging them to the appropriate place in an editor.

▶ More information on libraries is included in Hour 11.

The selector bar at the top of the library pane lets you choose from four libraries:

- **File templates**—[ctrl][option][command]1
- **Code snippets**—[ctrl][option][command]2
- **Objects**—[ctrl][option][command]3
- **Media**—[ctrl][option][command]

You can also use the View, Utilities submenu to select the library you are interested in. If the Utilities submenu is hidden, use the View menu or the rightmost of the three View buttons at the upper-right of the workspace window to show it.

> **TIP**
>
> Alternatively, if the utility area is hidden, choosing View, Utilities, File Template Library or any of the other commands in the View, Utilities menu will show utilities and select the appropriate library with one command (or one keyboard shortcut).

Figure 1.29 shows the general components of the library pane. At the top of the library pane, a pop-up menu lets you navigate to sections within that library. To its right, buttons let you display the contents of that library as icons or in a list. The icon view can make finding images or objects such as graphic elements very fast; for other items such as code snippets, the list view is better.

At the bottom of the library pane, a search field lets you filter the library shown above it.

When you select an item in the library, a description appears floating over the editor area, as shown in Figure 1.30. This description is generally somewhat lengthier than the summary in the library list.

File Templates Library

These file templates give you a headstart for whatever type of code you want to write. The pop-up menu at the top of the library pane lets you choose between iOS and Mac OS X file templates.

FIGURE 1.29
Use the library pane to take advantage of existing code, objects, and media.

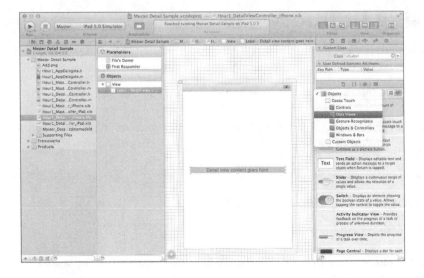

FIGURE 1.30
Select an item in the library to see its description.

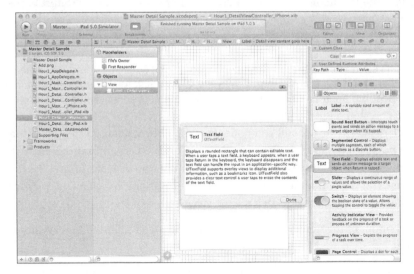

You select the appropriate file template from the file template library and drag it into the project navigator, as shown in Figure 1.31.

TIP
Remember, that for this to work, you need to have both the project navigator and the file template library visible.

FIGURE 1.31
Use a file
template.

You can also use file templates by choosing File, New, New File, as shown in Figure 1.32. The templates in this interface are shown grouped by their SDK and area of functionality. However, as you can see in Figure 1.32, by comparing the descriptions of NSManagedObject subclass in the library and in the sheet, they are the same. The menu command gives you the organization by SDK and area, while the library provides you with the ability to search with the filter at the bottom of the pane. The choice is yours.

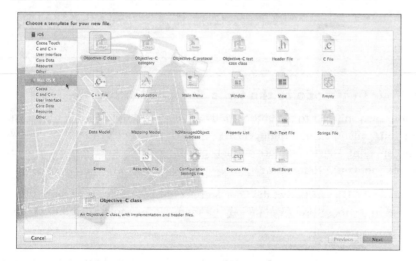

FIGURE 1.32
Use either the
library or the
menu to access
a template.

Code Snippet Library

Code snippets can only be dragged into text editing files. They provide common examples and templates. The pop-up menu lets you choose from iOS, Mac OS X, and your own snippets (which you can add).

If you select a code snippet, its code appears as shown in Figure 1.33. Sometimes, if you have just forgotten a small piece of syntax, this refresher is enough and you do not have to worry about actually dragging the snippet into your file. Other times, the snippet gets you started with your own programming.

FIGURE 1.33
Select a snippet to see its contents.

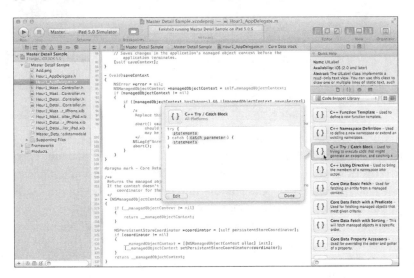

Try It Yourself

Add Your Own Code to the Code Snippet Library

Add your own snippets to the library to save time or to enforce standards on yourself or your colleagues in a multiperson project. (A particularly useful snippet would be the copyright notice you place at the beginning of each file if you want to protect you work [not you].) Here's how:

1. Show the User section of the Code Snippet library. If necessary, show utilities and choose User from the pop-up menu at the top of the library pane.

2. Select the code you want to make into a snippet.

3. Drag the code into the Users pane of the code snippet library. It will appear in the list, as shown in Figure 1.34.

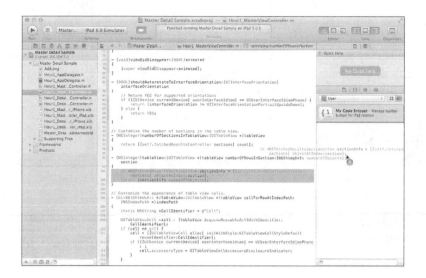

FIGURE 1.34
Drag the code into the library.

4. Provide a title and summary. Also, check that the code is complete (check the first and last characters in case of sloppy mousing).

5. Provide the other information (optional). The more information you provide, the more useful your snippet will be. In particular, specifying the language as shown in Figure 1.35 will remove it from the code snippet library for files that cannot use it. And, of course, a title other than My Code Snippet will increase the usability of the code.

FIGURE 1.35
Identify the snippet language.

6. Click Done, and your snippet is added to the library.

▲

To change the snippet's name, summary, or other data, select it and then click the Edit button, as shown previously in Figure 1.33. Click Done to save the changes.

Object Library

The Object library contains objects you use in building interfaces. This includes visible interface elements, such as views and buttons, as well as objects that work behind the scenes, such as view controllers.

▶ See Hour 11, p. 189, and Hour 12, "Finding Your Way Around Interface Builder: The Code Story," p. 209, for more details on developing your app's interface.

Media Library

The Media library brings together media files (icons, sounds, and images) from your workspace or from the system. Particularly when you have large projects, this helps you keep things organized. It also means that in creating your file groups, you can organize them functionally rather than putting all media files in one group and all code files in another.

Using the Text Editor

The text editor in Xcode is similar to many text editors that you have probably used already. Two areas deserve your attention even if you are used to using text editors:

▶ **Editing preferences**—Xcode provides extensive preferences for displaying and auto-completing code. Even if you have used other text editors, take a quick look at these preferences so that you can find out what's new in Xcode and, if you are used to another text editor, how to customize colors and behaviors to what you are used to.

▶ **Fix-it and Live Issues**—The LLVM compiler in Xcode 4 is not just for formal compiles. Its engine runs in the background checking syntax as you type so that errant keystrokes are caught in many cases as soon as you make them. Not only is the LLVM engine looking for misspellings, but it is aware of common syntax errors that can take a long time to track down, even though they are absurdly simply (once you know what the error is). One

such error is demonstrated in this line of code that almost every developer
has typed more than once:

```
if ( x = 3 ) {...
```

That is a replacement statement, not a logical comparison. Fix-It would most
likely suggest the following:

```
If ( x == 3 ) {...
```

Setting Editing Preferences

As in most Mac apps, preferences are set from the application menu (that is, the
Xcode menu in this case). Tabs at the top let you set different collections of preferences, and, as in the case of text editing, further tabs let you set more details such as
the editing and indentation preferences.

Figure 1.36 shows the editing preferences. Most are familiar to users of other code
text editors, but two may be new to you. The code folding ribbon appears to the
right of the gutter and the left of the main text editing area. It lets you collapse
blocks of code so you can focus on other areas. If the code folding ribbon is shown,
you have a further option—to focus on code as you hover the pointer over it.

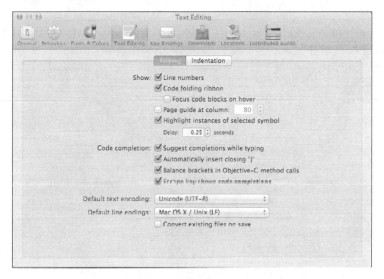

FIGURE 1.36
Set editing
preferences.

Figure 1.37 shows this behavior in action.

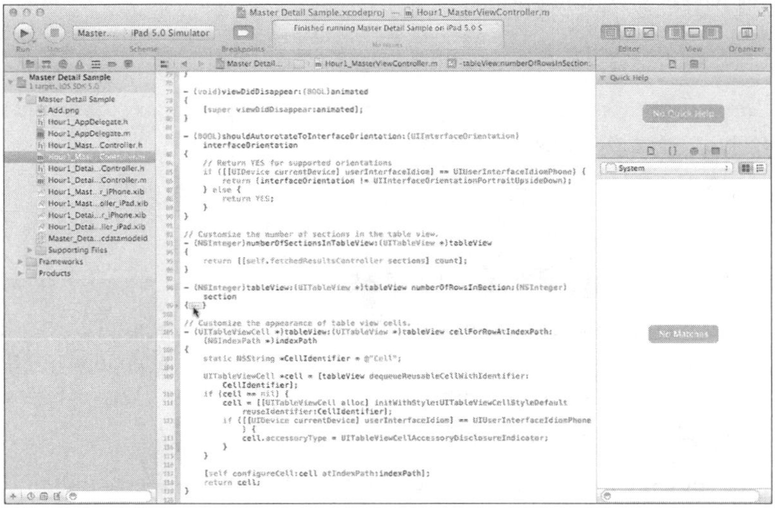

FIGURE 1.37
Highlight blocks
of code by
hovering
over them.

Many people have this option on at all times. As you move the mouse over code, you will quickly spot unmatched brackets or quotation marks because the highlighted block of code will be illogical.

Syntax-aware indenting can be set, as shown in Figure 1.38. Just as with the highlighting of code in the code ribbon, this can provide an early warning of unbalanced punctuation.

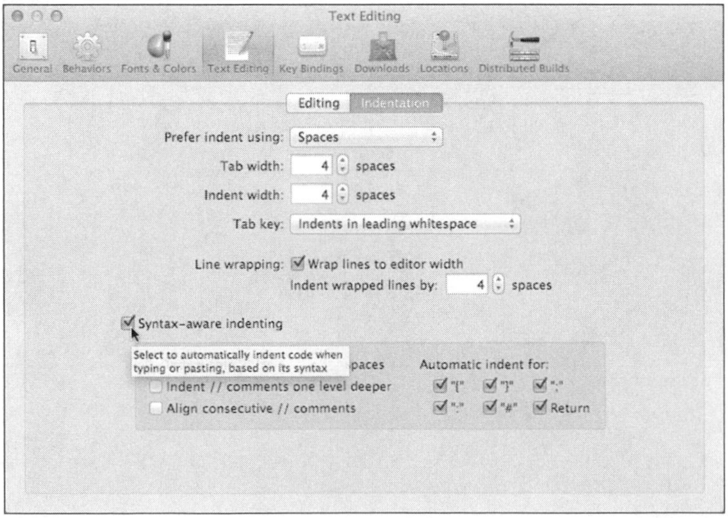

FIGURE 1.38
Syntax-aware
indentation
makes your
code neater
and catches
some keystroke
errors as well.

The final preference you should look at is Fonts & Colors, as shown in Figure 1.39.

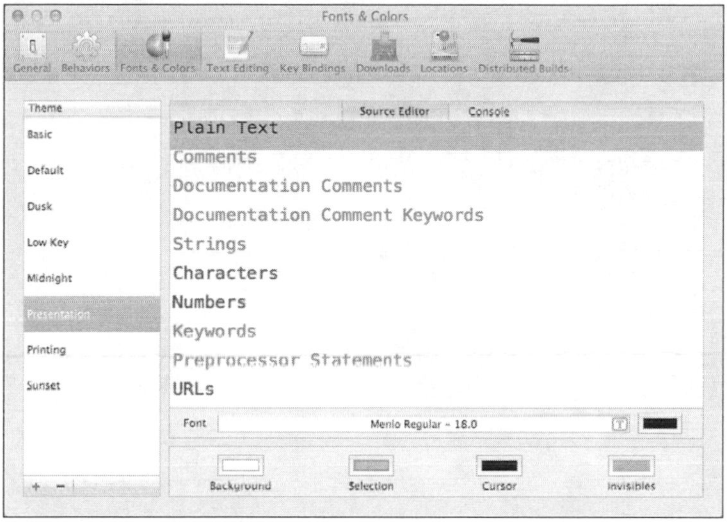

FIGURE 1.39
Set Fonts &
Colors.

A variety of predefined styles are available, and you can switch back and forth among them as you wish. The color wells at the bottom of the window bring up a color picker for you to use to replace any of the colors in the theme for the syntax element that you have highlighted in the main body of the window. The font for the highlighted syntax element is identified in the font field; click the T at the right of the field to bring up the font panel and change the size, style, or font.

Among the provided themes is one called Presentation. For some people, this is one of the most frequently used themes. Whereas the other themes ship with fonts that are 11 points, the Presentation theme ships with an 18-point font. Not only is Xcode used to build Mac OS X and iOS as well as Apple apps, it is also often used to prepare slides for conferences such as the Worldwide Developer Conference—and that is where the presentation theme comes in handy. Even if you are not presenting at WWDC, the Presentation theme can be useful for code reviews and documentation in your own organization.

Using Fix-It and Code Completion

Xcode is constantly indexing your project and its files in the background. As it does so, it can provide code completion (type-ahead) tips for you. Figure 1.40 shows this feature in action. As you type each character in a symbol name, a list of the possible completions appears. You can select one of them or continue typing to narrow down your search. In many cases (such as your own variables), there is no list; there is just a grayed-out completion displayed. Pressing Return accepts the completion.

FIGURE 1.40
Use code
completion.

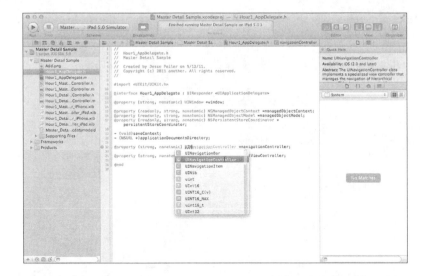

You will note that in a case in which there are alternatives, Xcode indicates what type of object each one is. Figure 1.40 shows several classes and typedefs.

Finally, the LLVM engine tries to catch syntax errors as soon as you type them. It will flag them with warnings or errors in the gutter; clicking the symbol will bring up the error itself and, if possible, a Fix-It, as shown in Figure 1.41.

FIGURE 1.41
Use Fix-It.

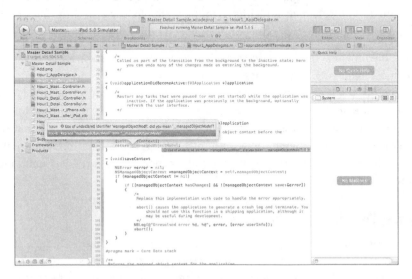

You can press Return to accept the Fix-It.

NOTE

With both code completion and Fix-It, do pay attention to what you are accepting. Certain types of errors can generate incorrect corrections or completions. The main benefit may come simply from stopping you to let you know there is an error. If you automatically accept any suggested correction, you are likely to make the same type of mistake that can result in using the wrong word in English.

Using the Organizer Window

The companion to the Xcode workspace window is the Organizer window, shown in Figure 1.42.

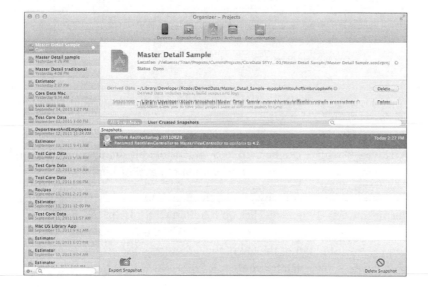

FIGURE 1.42
The Organizer window keeps track of files in repositories and archives, projects, devices, and documentation.

The five tabs at the top let you switch from one view to another:

▶ **Devices**—Primarily for iOS, this is a list of devices you have provisioned through Apple's developer program. This process is described on developer. apple.com. It is the process whereby you present your developer credentials to Apple and receive a digitally signed signature that lets your app run on specific devices that are listed here.

▶ **Repositories**—Xcode supports industry-standards Git and Subversion as source code repositories for version control. Both are widely used open-source projects. Xcode puts a graphical user interface onto them. The functionality of both is the same in Xcode as it is in other environments.

▶ **Projects**—This tab lets you organize snapshots of your project created while working on your project. You can create them manually from File, Create Snapshot, but it is easier to have Xcode create them automatically at critical moments. As you can see in Figure 1.43, you can use File, Project Settings and the Snapshots tab in your workspace window to turn on these automatic snapshots and set the locations for their storage. (You can also set these locations in the Locations tab of Xcode preferences.) Snapshots require Git to be installed. (That is an option in the Xcode 4 install.)

FIGURE 1.43
Use snapshot
at critical
moments in
restructuring
your project.

▶ **Archives**—Archives can be used to create installable archives of your app for deployment. There is more information at developer.apple.com.

▶ **Documentation**—For many people, the most commonly used tab is for documentation. When you click on a link in Quick Help, the detailed documentation opens in the documentation tab of the Organizer window. You can use the jump bar at the top of the Organizer to select the appropriate area in which to search for your topic.

Summary

Xcode 4 is not just a cosmetic change to previous versions; it is a new development environment complete with a new compiler (LLVM) that includes an engine that runs in the background to catch basic errors as you (occasionally) make them. This hour helps you get ready to write code using the latest and greatest technologies for software development.

The workspace window gives you all of a project's data and controls in a single multi-paned window. You can control which panes are shown, and, to a certain extent, you can even rearrange their positions as they are shown. For most people, this is not a matter of setting up a preferred workspace and sticking with it: Depending on what you are doing, you often show and hide parts of the workspace window so you can focus on the task at hand.

Xcode 4 includes interfaces to source code management tools such as Git and Subversion (Git is preferred). As a result, you can manage your code—even on a multiperson project—and keep track of revisions. In addition, Xcode provides a snapshot feature that can capture your entire project at specific moments, such as when you ask and when you are about to perform project-wide automated changes.

Q&A

Q. *What is the best way to get started with Xcode?*

A. Use it. Open it and create a test project based on one of the built-in templates. Explore and experiment, and then throw it away. If you start working with it on a real project, your beginning mistakes will be around to haunt you for a long time.

Q. *What is the best way to handle the periodic updates to operating systems and SDKs?*

A. Registered developers are notified in advance of these updates; you can download the pre-release versions of both OSs and SDKs as well as new releases of Xcode. This enables you to test your apps with the new environmental software and prepare to use new features. Typically, you are warned not to use this software for production use. Apps developed with the new OS and SDK cannot be submitted to either App Store until a few weeks before the release of the software to the public. This process allows developers to get up to speed with the new technologies. The period of a few weeks before the public release of the new software allows the App Store to be stocked when the software is in final versions.

Workshop

Quiz

1. *How do you get a copy of Xcode?*

2. *If you are used to another development environment, can you use it to develop software for Mac OS X and iOS?*

Quiz Answers

1. Register at developer.apple.com. Various registration categories are designed for different types of developers. The paid levels of developer registration include technical support assistance (two incidents for the basic programs). There are also free registrations that provide no support but do allow you to download Xcode. You can also buy Xcode through the Mac App Store. It is currently free.

2. Only with great difficulty, and you will not be able to submit your apps to the App Store.

Activities

As you start to work with Xcode, take advantage of its productivity features such as code snippets. In particular, add your own snippets as you think of them. It generally is best not to sit down and make a list of snippets that you think you will need—that is often a waste of time. Instead, keep alert and, whenever you find yourself typing something that might be useful as a snippet, add it right then and there. These snippets are stored in your environment—not just in a single project.

Many people shy away from the debugging tools, but you will find that they can save you a large amount of time and effort. Some of them are for advanced developers but practice using breakpoints. This is a simple technology, and it is very easy to just click in the gutter of the editor to set a breakpoint. The debug area will let you examine local variables; it also will help you track the path of execution so you can see why a certain section of code is or is not being executed.

HOUR 2

Creating a Simple App

What You'll Learn in This Hour:

- ▶ Choosing a template
- ▶ Creating the app
- ▶ Deciding where to make changes

Starting to Build an App

Whether you are starting out to build an iOS app or a Mac App, there is one thing you will not do: start from scratch. With Xcode, the welcome screen shown in Figure 2.1 gives you choices, such as reopening recent projects that you have been working on, learning about Xcode, connecting to a source code repository such as Git, or going to developer.apple.com to get the motherload of documentation and help. You are not starting from scratch.

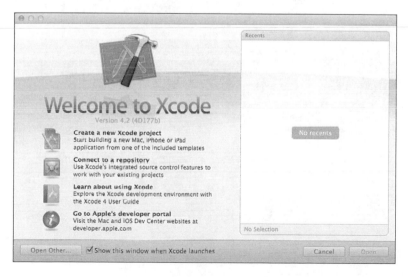

FIGURE 2.1
Xcode helps you start with your project.

NOTE

At the bottom of this window, a checkbox lets you opt to bypass it in the future. If you do so, you can always get back to it with View, Welcome to Xcode, which opens the window again; you can adjust the checkbox if you want to change the default behavior.

But when you are getting ready to work on your own app, Xcode gives you a variety of templates with the appropriate files and even snippets of code already written.

Working with Code Samples

Apple's website, developer.apple.com, provides resources for developers including extensive documentation, tutorials, and sample code. You can get to it from the welcome screen if you want.

TIP

To locate sample code, log in to the iOS Dev Center or the Mac Dev Center. However, before you can search for sample code, you must have registered as a developer.

Click Sample Code at the left of the window and then search for the topic or technology you are interested in, as shown in Figure 2.2. You can search on keywords and can also sort each of the columns just by clicking the header. If you click the header of a column that is already sorted, the direction of the sort is reversed.

FIGURE 2.2
Search for sample code.

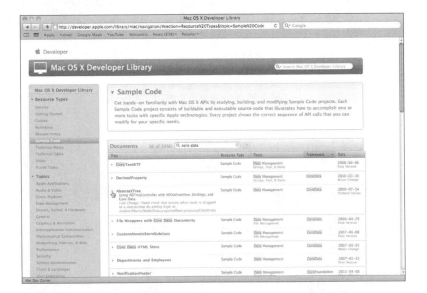

You can get to developer resources with using Xcode's organizer or with a web browser. When you access the resources using Safari on iPad, a richer experience awaits you than you will find on either Xcode's organizer or even Safari on Mac OS.

You can use the disclosure triangle to the left of the name of each sample code project to see a summary, as is shown in Figure 2.2, for the AbstractTree sample. Click any code sample's name to go to its documentation on the Web, as shown in Figure 2.3. Each of the samples has the same basic information, such as the following:

- ▶ General information

- ▶ Complete code listings

- ▶ Archive of the project files you can download with a button at the upper-left of the window

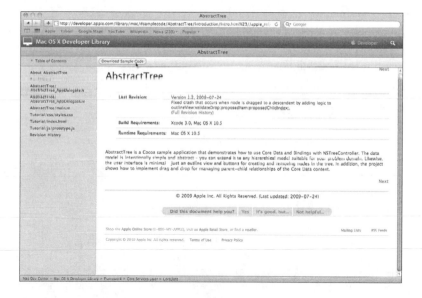

FIGURE 2.3
Download samples to explore them.

Code Samples Developed with Older Versions of Xcode

You can normally open a code sample directly in Xcode, build it, and run it. In a few cases, the code samples were developed using older versions of Xcode, and you might have difficulty opening them. In general, code samples that are a number of years old and have not been revised might be problematic in this way. Furthermore, a few of the code samples remain online but have been deprecated for one reason or another.

If you cannot open a code sample or see that it is deprecated, you can search for other code samples that might help you. If you are just interested in finding out how to code a certain feature of the sample app, remember that you can browse all the code on developer.apple.com, even if you cannot open an old version of the downloadable code. Often it is enough to just read the relevant line or two of code.

TIP

Although the layouts and formatting are the same, the code samples in the Mac Dev center are different from those in the iOS Dev Center.

Working with Xcode Templates

When you choose to start from a template as shown previously in Figure 2.1 or by using File, New, New Project, you are presented with choices for the platform and for specific projects within it.

As you choose a platform at the left and a category of projects, the window changes to show your choices. It is worth experimenting with this interface to get an idea of what is available. Even if you only read the descriptions of the projects and do not actually build or run them, you will have a guided tour of the goodies waiting for you.

Building the Project

Having selected a template on which to build your project, you next provide information about the project so that Xcode can prepare it for use.

Identifying Your Files and Projects

Xcode automatically identifies your files and projects using your company name. This is one of those "just works" features that are hallmarks of Apple software, but because this automatic naming has "just worked" in several different ways over time, here is a summary of how it works today—and is likely to work this way for the foreseeable future. (Translation: If you are confused, be leery of doing an Internet search on the topic because you might turn up discussions and articles from years ago that are no longer relevant.)

The identifier for your project is used to identify the bundle for the project—the heart of the executable code. It is constructed using your company or organization name in reverse-domain format. Reverse-domain formats take the globally unique domain names such as champlainarts.com and reverse them to names such as com.champlainarts. The names are still unique, but they cannot be mistaken for actual URLs, thus preventing confusion. (This notation was first widely used in Java.) When you create a new project for the first time in Xcode, the company identifier field is blank. Just type in your company identifier in reverse-URL style, and Xcode will concatenate it with the product name you have selected (replacing spaces with hyphens). Thus, you have a globally unique name for your project.

Here is the part that has changed over time. To change your company identifier, just type a new one into the field. Xcode will remember it for the next project. To change it again, just retype it. You do not have to get your hands dirty with property lists or command-line instructions.

The file identification information is also used to automatically insert a copyright line and other identifying information at the top of each file, such as the following:

```
//
//  MyClass.h
//  My New Project
//
//  Created by Jesse Feiler on 6/14/11.
//  Copyright 2011 Champlain Arts. All rights reserved.
//
```

This information is collected from the name of the file you create, the name of your project, and your username or account name (they are used synonymously). If you have a Me card in Address Book (that is, a card that you have identified as being your own with Card, Make this My Card), the company—if any—that you have used on that card is used in the copyright notice.

This practice works seamlessly for most projects where the identifier is set at the beginning of the project and for most files when they are created by people working for the company. In the case of a project where several developers working for different companies work on the project and where their work is copyrighted individually and not as part of the overall project, you will need to manually change the copyright notice in each file. You might need to consult an attorney for the correct wording of these relatively unusual cases.

Try It Yourself

Creating an iOS Project ▼

iOS project templates are often a bit more fleshed out than Mac projects. In part, this is because iOS projects started from scratch along with iOS. They are built with a more powerful operating system and SDK than the very first Mac projects which, at this time, are often a decade old. Even so, these projects are not out-of-date if they have been updated to incorporate new technologies. Do the following:

1. Select a project from the iOS choices shown in Figure 2.4.

2. Click Next.

FIGURE 2.4
Select a template to work with for an iOS app.

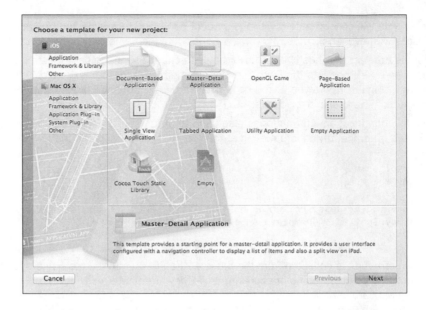

3. Provide options and a name for the project, as shown in Figure 2.5. For iOS, your options are whether to use Core Data (and, if you are reading this book, that is probably your choice) and whether to include the unit test code (which is beyond the scope of this book, so you probably want to leave that box unchecked). Beginning with Xcode 4.2, you have the ability to create document-based apps as described later in the Mac OS section.

FIGURE 2.5
Name your project and choose options.

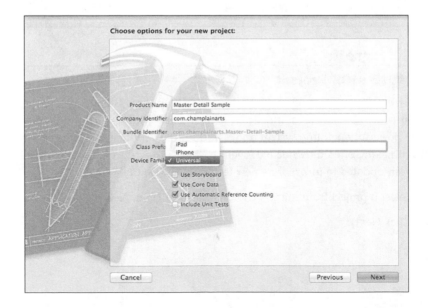

4. Choose a folder in which to place the project, as shown in Figure 2.6. You can also choose to create a new Git repository for the project. Many people leave this checkbox unchecked for quickie projects that are designed to test a particular aspect of code or design. Check this checkbox for projects that will be kept and developed over time—particularly if they will be worked on by a number of developers at the same time.

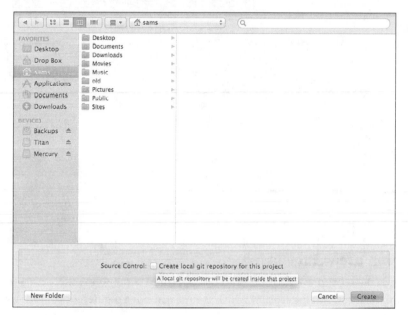

FIGURE 2.6
Select a folder and possibly a Git repository.

5. Click Create to create the project. The project is created with all its files; the project summary shown in Figure 2.7 opens, and you are ready to begin.

6. Build and run the project. The simulator should launch and the basic app should run. If it does not, track down the issues; they will not disappear by magic.

FIGURE 2.7
The iOS project
is created.

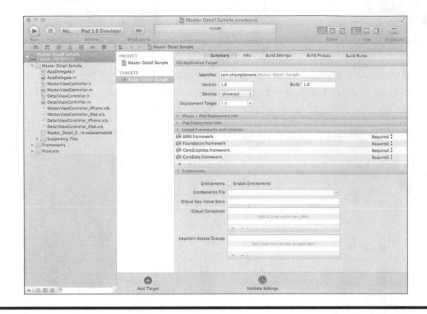

Try It Yourself

Creating a Mac Project

Although the basic process for creating a Mac project is the same, there are some minor differences, not the least of which is that you have a different collection of templates to start from:

1. Select a template from the Mac choices, shown in Figure 2.8 (usually it will be a Cocoa application).

FIGURE 2.8
Select a tem-
plate to work
with for a Mac
OS X app.

2. Click Next.

3. Provide options and a name for the project, as shown in Figure 2.9. Compared to iOS apps, you have several additional options you can set. You can choose a category for the App Store here (you can always change it later).

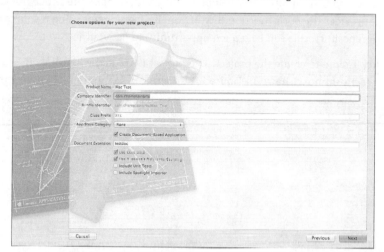

FIGURE 2.9
Name your project and choose options.

Perhaps most important is that you can choose to create a project based on a document. If you do so, you need to identify the class for the document that you will be creating, and you will need to provide an extension for that document. In general, apps that use Core Data rely on Core Data itself for data storage rather than separate documents, so you often just ignore the option to create a document-based application.

You also can choose to take advantage of Spotlight Importer.

4. Choose a folder in which to place the project, as shown in Figure 2.10.

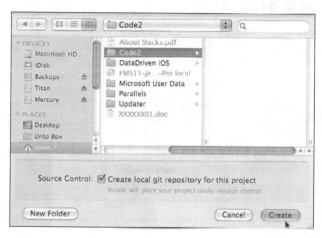

FIGURE 2.10
Select a folder and possibly a Git repository.

Just as with iOS apps, you can also choose to create a new Git repository for the project. Many people leave this checkbox unchecked for quickie projects that are designed to test a particular aspect of code or design. Check this box for projects that will be kept and developed over time—particularly if they will be worked on by a number of developers at the same time. (The Xcode interface to Git provides the basic functionality. If you are leery about using a source control repository, this can be a good opportunity to get your feet wet.)

5. Click Create to create the project. The project is created with all its files; the project summary shown in Figure 2.11 opens, and you are ready to begin.

FIGURE 2.11
The Mac project is created.

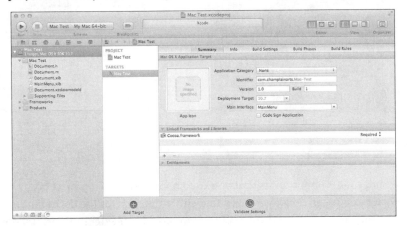

6. Build and run the project by clicking Run at the left of the toolbar. In most cases, all you will see is an empty window, but that is all you should be seeing. You should not be seeing errors in the build process.

Exploring the App

Explore the app in the simulator (iOS) or with its menus (Mac). See what has already been created for you.

TIP

On the iOS simulator, remember to experiment with the hardware menu so you can see how the app responds to device rotation.

Also explore the structure of the project and the files that have been created. In evaluating what you have created, you might want to explore the data model. Although this topic is discussed in more detail in Part II, "Using Core Data," a quick glance at the data model can help you to understand what the code sample or template is prepared to do. Look for a file in the project navigator with an extension of xcdatamodeld: That is the data model. Click it to open the data model editor, as shown in Figure 2.12.

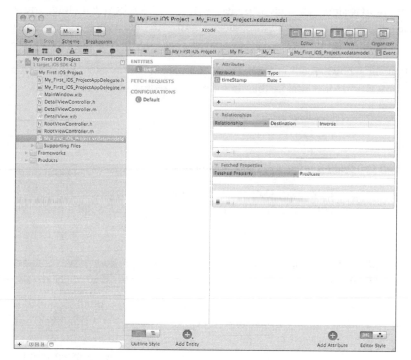

FIGURE 2.12
Explore the
data model.

The *entities* are the object of the data model—employees and departments in a corporate data model, products in a merchandising model, and so forth. The *attributes* are fields, columns, properties, or variables (the terms are often used interchangeably at this point). Thus, for the employee entity, you might have attributes such as name, address, salary, and so forth.

Relationships are the heart of the relational database model. They relate employees to departments in the corporate model. In the code samples and templates, these objects are named fairly clearly so that you can understand what is beneath the data model hood. As you explore code samples and templates, look at the data models to see what has been implemented.

NOTE

In your explorations, you might find it most profitable to look for common organizational structures rather than exact data matches. For example, the structure of employees in departments is often quite the same as the structure of students in classes and even of inventory items in a warehouse. Modifying a data model for employees and departments might be better for your purposes than working with a data model that focuses on employees and training courses.

Summary

It is very hard to start from a blank project with Xcode. You have templates and sample code to get you started, so you almost always start with at least half a dozen files and with a significant amount of code—both placeholder code and actual code that works.

This hour has shown you how to find code samples and templates and how to build them for iOS and Mac. Explore the (literally) hundreds of code samples on developer.apple.com for more ideas.

Q&A

Q. *Can you build a project for both iOS and Mac?*

A. Not directly. Using Core Data, you can build two projects that share the same database structure and the same data. On iOS, you can build a project for both iPhone and iPad.

Q. *The structure of groups of files in some of the sample code projects and the templates is different. Should I pick one structure and use it for all my projects?*

A. If you are working from sample code or a template, it is often a good idea to keep the structure until you are familiar with the project. Remember that with Xcode, the structure of files on disk is separate from the structure of groups within Xcode. You can modify the group structure at any time without breaking the project.

Workshop

Quiz

1. *When do you use a code repository like Git?*

2. *Do you use document-based apps with Core Data?*

Quiz Answers

1. Use Git or Subversion to manage your code if it is a multiperson project or one that will extend over time. It is usually not necessary to worry about a code repository if you are building a throw-away project just to test a piece of code or a concept.

2. For many people, a database structure such as Core Data is separate from the document model of apps. Starting with iOS 5 and Lion, the use of Core Data inside document-based apps is becoming very much mainstream in Mac OS and iOS development.

Activities

Periodically visit developer.apple.com, show the list of sample code, and sort on the last-update date so you can see what is new and updated. You will note that between releases of Xcode and new versions of the operating system, the developers at Apple are hard at work continually updating the code samples.

HOUR 3

Understanding the Basic Code Structure

What You'll Learn in This Hour:

▶ Exploring the world of Objective-C

▶ Getting inside Objective-C objects

▶ Managing inheritance

▶ Using delegates and protocols

▶ Using model/view/controller

Working with the Code

Mac OS and iOS apps are written using the Objective-C language. Right there, some people might panic and throw up their hands, but do not worry. As pointed out previously, you write very little code from scratch. Much of the code that you run is already written for you using Objective-C; that code is in the Cocoa and Cocoa Touch frameworks that support everything from animation to native platform appearance and the Core Data and various table view classes that are the topic of this book. (Cocoa Touch is the version that runs on iOS; unless otherwise noted, references to Cocoa include Cocoa Touch in this book, just as references to iPhone include iPod touch.)

When you're working inside the Cocoa framework and the other components of iOS and Mac OS, most of your work consists of calling existing methods and occasionally overriding them for your own purposes. Xcode 4 provides a new development environment that is heavily graphical in nature. You will find yourself drawing relationships in your data model and, in the interface, drawing connections between objects on the interface and the code that supports them.

NOTE

Actually, Cocoa is an ever-evolving set of frameworks. You can find an overview at http://developer.apple.com/technologies/mac/cocoa.html.

Blank pages are rarely part of your development environment.

NOTE

This hour provides an overview of Objective-C. It provides some comparisons to other object-oriented languages such as C++, but its focus is on Objective-C and, particularly, in the ways in which it differs from object-oriented languages you might already know. You can find many introductions to object-oriented programming on the Web and in bookstores, so if you are unfamiliar with that basic concept, you might want to get up to speed on the basics.

Objective-C 2.0

First announced at the 2006 Worldwide Developers Conference and released in Mac OS X v.10.5 (Leopard) in October 2007, Objective-C 2.0 is now the standard implementation. It is fully supported in Xcode 4. The primary changes from the original version of Objective-C include the addition of automatic garbage collection, improvements to runtime performance, and some syntax enhancements. Those syntax enhancements are fully reflected in this book (after all, this book is written more than five years after the announcement of Objective-C 2.0). Some legacy software still uses old syntax, and there is generally no problem with that.

Objective-C 2.0 is often referred to as *modern,* while the previous version is referred to as *legacy.* The modern version is not to be confused with Objective-C *modern syntax*, a project in the late 1990s that changed the presentation of its syntax and which was ultimately discontinued.

As a general rule, legacy Objective-C code runs without changes in the Objective-C environment (there are some exceptions). Much of the sample code for Mac OS X on developer.apple.com is from the legacy period and, with few exceptions, it compiles and runs well. During the transition period, developers often continued to use legacy syntax. This meant that for shared code (and for sample code), developers did not have to worry about whether the code would be compiled or run in the modern or legacy system—it would generally work.

Today, there is no reason to write legacy code because the tools are all updated to Objective-C 2.0. It is safe to write code that will not compile or run in the legacy environment because people are not (or should not be) still using it.

▶ This is particularly relevant to *declared properties,* which are discussed later in this hour in the "Using Declared Properties" section, p. 68.

What You Do Not Have to Worry About

You do not have to worry about designing an entire program in most cases. You are writing code that will be a part built on a template, the behavior of which is known by users, so what you have to do is to fit in. You need to write the code that is specific to your app, but you do not have to worry about implementing an event loop.

In fact, if you decide to develop the app's infrastructure yourself, you might find that users are disappointed at its unfamiliarity and—more important to many people—your app might not find a place in the App Store.

Instead of writing code from scratch, much of what you will do is to investigate the code that you have in the Xcode templates or in Apple's sample code. You need to explore what is written and how it has been designed so that you can understand how and where your functionality will fit in. It is a very different process than writing it from scratch.

Introducing Objective-C

Objective-C is built on C; in fact, if you write ordinary C code, you can compile it with an Objective-C compiler (that includes Xcode). The main extension to C that Objective-C provides is its implementation of objects and object-oriented programming.

Today, object-oriented programming rates a big yawn from many people; that is the kind of programming that most people are used to. When Simula 67, the first precursor of Objective-C and all modern object-oriented languages, was developed, this was a new notion, and many people were not certain it was worth the extra effort (not to mention the time it took to learn what then was a new and not fully formed technology). It is against this background that the extensions to C needed to implement Objective-C were created. One of the goals was to prove that very little was needed to be added to C to implement object-oriented programming.

Basically, what was added to C was a messaging and object structure based on Smalltalk. Over the years, additional features such as protocols and delegates as well as categories and blocks were added to the language. Some other features were added. Some of them are not as important to developers writing for iOS or Mac OS X, while others of them simply never caught on with developers at large. Thus, this section provides an overview of the major components that are in use today in the context of iOS and Mac OS X.

At the same time as additional features were being added, the use of the language was refined particularly in the environments of NeXT, Apple, Mac OS X, and iOS.

These refinements include conventions such as naming conventions and even code formatting conventions. They are not part of the language itself, but they represent best practices that are followed by the vast majority of Objective-C developers.

Looking at Object-Oriented Programming in the Context of Objective-C

The heart of the implementation of object-oriented programming consists of the objects themselves and the roles that they can play. With Objective-C, there is another point to notice about the implementation of the language; because it is a *dynamic* language, some of the work that would be done in the compile and build process for a language such as C++ is done at runtime. This means that the runtime environment, which, for all intents and purposes is the operating system, is a much bigger player than it is in other languages.

Differentiating Classes, Instances, and Objects

The first point to remember is that objects, classes, and instances are related but different concepts. These concepts exist in most object-oriented languages:

▶ **Class**—A *class* is what you write in your code. It typically consists of a header file (ending in .h) with an *interface,* as well as an implementation file (ending in .m) that provides the code to support the interface.

▶ **Instance**—At runtime, a class can be *instantiated.* That converts it from instructions in your program to an object that has a location in memory and that can function.

▶ **Object**—*Object* is a term that is commonly used in contexts where most people understand what is meant. The word can be used to refer to instances or classes, but most of the time, it refers to instances.

Understanding What Is Not an Object

Some basic types are declared in Foundation/Foundation.h. Each of these is implemented as a struct (NSDecimal), a typedef (NSUinteger), or an enum (NSComparisonResult). Sometimes these hide the actual implementation, such as this definition of NSInteger, which resolves to a long on a 64-bit application and to an int otherwise:

```
#if __LP64__ || TARGET_OS_EMBEDDED || TARGET_OS_IPHONE ||
   TARGET_OS_WIN32 || NS_BUILD_32_LIKE_64
typedef long NSInteger;
#else
typedef int NSInteger;
#endif
```

Using these types makes your code more maintainable and portable than using native C types.

NOTE

The NS prefix refers to NeXTSTEP.

With the exception of basic types such as these, almost everything you deal with is an object. You will find some non-object entities in the Core Foundation framework and in specialized frameworks that often deal with low-level operations such as Core Animation.

Understanding the Three Purposes of Objects

Building on Smalltalk's structure, objects in Objective-C have three purposes and functions:

▶ **State**—Objects can contain *state,* which in practical terms means that they can contain data and references to other objects. In implementation and use, state usually consists of member variables, instance data, or whatever terminology you use.

▶ **Receive messages**—Objective-C objects can receive messages sent from other objects.

▶ **Send messages**—Objective-C can send messages to other objects.

▶ Communication between objects is via these messages, which are highly structured. This is covered in more detail in the "Messaging in Objective-C" section later in this hour, p. 73.

Data is *encapsulated* within objects in Objective-C. That means it is accessible only through messages. Objects cannot access another object's data (state) directly as can happen in other object-oriented languages. This is a general goal of all good object-oriented programming, but it is enforced in Objective-C in ways that are often best practices in other languages.

Declared properties, which are discussed in the next section, shows you how this is done in Objective C. This section also explains why, at first glance, it can appear that you can access internal data from another object and why, at second glance, you will see that it is only the appearance of direct access.

Using Declared Properties

One of the most significant new features of Objective-C 2.0 was the introduction of *declared properties*. The concept is quite simple and eliminates a great deal of tedious typing for developers. The feature is best demonstrated by showing before-and-after examples.

Declaring a Property

Listing 3.1 shows a typical interface using legacy syntax. This is the .h file, and it contains the interface in a section starting with the compiler directive `@interface`. `@` always introduces compiler directives; note the `@end` at the end of the file. Interface code can appear in other places, but the .h file for a class is the primary place.

NOTE

Notice that because the code in Listing 3.1 was generated by Xcode, the comments are automatically inserted.

LISTING 3.1 Legacy Class Declaration

```
//
//  My_First_ProjectAppDelegate.h
//  My First Project
//
//  Created by Sams on 6/14/11.
//  Copyright 2011 __MyCompanyName__. All rights reserved.
//

#import <Cocoa/Cocoa.h>

@interface My_First_ProjectAppDelegate : NSObject <NSApplicationDelegate> {
@private
  NSWindow *window;
}

  - (IBAction)saveAction:sender;
@end
```

The class shown here, My_First_ProjectAppDelegate, has an interface with one variable. After that, a single method, (IBAction)saveAction:sender, is declared. By convention, variable names that begin with underscores are private and should not be used directly. Also, note that all the variables are references—the * indicates that at runtime, a reference to the underlying object's structure is to be used and resolved as needed. The @private directive means that these variables are private to this class; by contrast, @protected would allow descendants of this class to use them. @public, which is rarely used (and which is considered poor syntax), allows any object to access these variables directly. This syntax is described later in this hour.

As you can see, there is no method declared that will allow another object to access the data inside this object. Listing 3.2 adds *accessor* methods to access the data. These are referred to generally as *accessors* and specifically as *getters* or *setters*. By using this coding best practice, the variables are encapsulated and can be accessed only through these methods.

LISTING 3.2   Legacy Class Declaration with Accessors

```
//
//  My_First_ProjectAppDelegate.h
//  My First Project
//
//  Created by Sams on 6/14/11.
//  Copyright 2011 __MyCompanyName__. All rights reserved.
//

#import <Cocoa/Cocoa.h>

@interface My_First_ProjectAppDelegate : NSObject <NSApplicationDelegate> {
@private
  NSWindow *window;
}

- (NSWindow*) getWindow;
- (NSWindow*) setWindow: (NSWindow*)newwindow;

- (IBAction)saveAction:sender;
@end
```

Listing 3.3 demonstrates the use of declared properties in Objective C 2.0.

LISTING 3.3   Modern Class Declaration

```
//
//  My_First_ProjectAppDelegate.h
//  My First Project
//
//  Created by Sams on 6/14/11.
//  Copyright 2011 __MyCompanyName__. All rights reserved.
//
```

```
#import <Cocoa/Cocoa.h>

@interface My_First_ProjectAppDelegate : NSObject <NSApplicationDelegate> {
}

@property NSWindow* window;

- (IBAction)saveAction:sender;
@end
```

The individual declarations of the variables are gone; they are replaced by *declared properties* that are implemented with compiler directives. As compiler directives, these are merely instructions to the compiler. They are not part of the program's syntax.

Synthesizing a Property

A declared property directive works together with a companion synthesize directive that appears in the implementation file. The companion synthesize directive to the property declaration is shown in Listing 3.4.

LISTING 3.4   Synthesize Directives to Match Listing 3.3

```
@synthesize window;
```

When the program is compiled, these two directives generate code. If, as in Listing 3.3, the variables are not declared, the declarations are created. They will look just like the code that has been typed into Listings 3.1 and 3.2. In addition, getters and setters will be automatically generated. They will look exactly like those typed at the bottom of Listing 3.2.

And, perhaps most important, the declared properties allow for the use of *dot syntax* that automatically invokes the relevant accessors. It also provides the appearance of direct access to the encapsulated data of the object. Given the code in Listings 3.3 and 3.4, you could write the following code to reference the data within an object of type My_First_ProjectAppDelegate that has been instantiated with the name jf_ My_First_ProjectAppDelegate:

```
jf_ My_First_ProjectAppDelegate.managedObjectContext
```

The appropriate accessor (getter or setter) will be invoked as needed. Note that within the implementation code of an object, you can always use self to refer to the object itself. Thus, you can write

```
self.managedObjectContext = <another managedObjectContext>;
```

Or

```
<myManagedObjectContext > = self.managedObjectContext;
```

You save a great deal of typing and make your code much more readable by using declared properties.

You can still declare the variables if you want to. At compile time, the same-named variables you have declared will be accessed by the property. However, a common use of properties is to reinforce the hiding of internal variables. The property declaration can provide a name that is used by programmers while the underlying variable is not accessed. This is common in the framework code you deal with.

For example, here is a declaration of a private variable:

```
NSWindow *__window;
```

Here is a companion property declaration:

```
@property nonatomic, retain, readonly NSWindow* window;
```

The synthesize directive would normally create the window variable because there is none. However, you can use the following synthesize directive to have the property's accessors, which are created during compilation by the synthesize directive, point to __window if you have declared it, as shown in Listing 3.5.

LISTING 3.5   Using a Private Variable in a Property

```
@synthesize window = __window;
```

You can access the private variable by using its name if you are allowed to do so, which in practice generally means for code in the class itself. Thus, you can write:

```
__window = <something>;
```

Using dot syntax, you go through the property and, as a result, the following code can have the same effect:

```
self.window = <something>;
```

NOTE

There is one case in which the direct access with dot syntax does have a difference. If you have set a variable to an object that has been allocated in memory, the appropriate way to set it to another value is to dispose of the first object and then set it again. Disposing of an object that is no longer needed prevents *memory leaks*—the bane of developers. Because the accessors can perform any operations you want, they can dispose of no-longer-needed objects as part of their setting process.

In practice, synthesize directives usually are a bit more complex. You can provide *attributes* by placing them in parentheses after the property directive. A common set of attributes in a synthesize directive is the following:

```
property (nonatomic, strong, readonly)
  NSPersistentStoreCoordinator *persistentStoreCoordinator;
```

Attributes reflect the reality of today's environment and the features of modern Objective-C. It is no longer enough to know that a variable is of a specific type. Many other attributes come into play, and the property directive allows you to set them. Its syntax also allows for the expansion of attributes in the future as the language evolves. Thus, property directives together with the appropriate attributes combine to create rich, useful objects that are easy to use and maintain over the lifespan of the app.

Table 3.1 shows the current set of attributes and the available values. The default values (having a synthesize directive create the accessors, assign, and atomic) are most commonly used. Notice also that the opposite of the atomic attribute is to omit it—in other words, there is no separate "nonatomic" attribute. (Over time, these attributes have changed to add new features. Consult the release notes for new versions of Xcode for these changes.)

TABLE 3.1   Attributes for Declared Properties

Attribute	Values	Notes
Accessor	getter = <name of your getter>	Accessors are synthesized for you unless you provide your own.
	setter = <name of your setter>	You can go further by specifying your own custom accessors. You will have to write them, but it might be worthwhile in special cases.
Writability	readwrite	
	readonly	
Setter	assign (default)	
Semantics	retain	Retains the object after assignment and releases the previous value.
	copy	Copies the object and releases the previous value.
Atomicity	nonatomic	Default is atomic so that getters and setters are thread-safe.

Using Dynamic Properties

Instead of a synthesize directive, you can use a dynamic directive for any property. The format is as follows:

```
@dynamic myValue;
```

The dynamic directive indicates that your code is going to be providing the appropriate values for the property at runtime. This entails writing some rather complex code, but there is an alternative. Core Data implements the functionality promised by the dynamic directive, so you do not have to worry—just keep reading.

Messaging in Objective-C

Objective-C is a *messaging* environment, not a *calling* environment. Although the end result is very much the same as in a calling environment, you send a message to an object in Objective-C. That message consists of an object name and a method of that object that can respond to the message. Here is an example:

```
[myGraphicsObject draw];
```

In a language such as C++, you would call a method of the object, as in:

```
myGraphicsObject.draw();
```

> **NOTE**
>
> There is a lot of information in Apple's documentation as well as across the Web detailing the technical differences and how the two styles evolved. The most important point to remember is that a primary purpose of Objective-C was to show that object-oriented programming could be implemented very simply with a small set of Smalltalk-based variations on top of C. More than three decades later, whether Objective-C is simpler than C++ is a topic of much debate (although many reasonable people have moved on to other matters).

The arguments sent to a function (or method) in C are placed in parentheses, and their sequence is determined by the code. In Objective-C, the arguments are named. Thus, a C-style function looks like this:

```
resizeRect (float height, float width){
  return height * width;
}
```

If that function were part of an object in C++, you would invoke it with the following:

```
myRect.resizeRect (myHeight, myWidth);
```

An Objective-C-style function looks like this:

```
-(void) resizeRect: (float*) height newWidth:(float*)width {
}
```

You invoke it with the following:

```
[myRect resizeRect: myHeight newWidth: myWidth];
```

The most important difference you notice is that the parameters in Objective-C are labeled, whereas the parameters in C or C++ are strictly positional. Do not be misled: The labels do not imply that the order of the parameters can vary. The following Objective-C function is not identical to the previous one because the labels (that is, the order of the parameters) are different:

```
-(void) resizeRect: (float*)width newHeight:(float*)height {
```

> **WARNING**
>
> Technically, the labels before the colons are optional. Omitting them is a very bad practice. It is best to assume that they are required in all cases.

Despite the fact that there are many similarities, you will find it easier to learn Objective-C if you avoid translating back and forth to and from other programming languages you know. The principle is just the same as it is for learning a natural language—start thinking in the new language right away.

Naming Conventions

The definitive reference about naming items in your code is in "Coding Guidelines for Cocoa" located at http://developer.apple.com/library/ios/#documentation/ Cocoa/Conceptual/CodingGuidelines/CodingGuidelines.html. These are detailed guidelines to help you make your code consistent with best practices and standards.

There is one guideline that is sometimes an issue. As noted previously in this hour, you can begin an instance variable name with an underscore to indicate that it is private. In some documentation, developers are advised that only Apple is to use this naming convention. That is all well and good, but some of the Xcode templates and example code do use underscores at the beginning of names for private variables. As you expand and modify your projects built on these templates and examples, you may choose to make your code consistent so that the naming convention is the same for the variables named by Apple in the template and those named by you that are syntactically parallel. Just be aware of the issue, and make your choice.

The other naming conventions are normally adopted by most developers. When there are deviations, it often is the case that a developer is not aware of the conventions.

Using Protocols and Delegates

Many people consider protocols and delegates to be advanced topics in Objective-C. However, as you will see, they are critical in the table views that are often used to manipulate Core Data objects as well as in Core Data itself. They are also used throughout the iOS and Mac OS frameworks. This section explains that there are several pieces to the puzzle, but they fit together the same way in every case. Once you've worked through a few of them, they will become very natural. In particular, you will see that a lot of the details need no attention from you when you use a protocol or delegate. This section shows you how they work, but soon you will appreciate the fact that they are another part of the operating system that just works without too much of your attention.

Looking Up the Background of Protocols and Delegates

Object-oriented programming offered (and continues to offer) very powerful ways to build and maintain code. One issue arose quite early—multiple inheritance. For simple classroom examples, it is easy to propose a base class of Toy, with subclasses of Ball, Jump rope, and Puzzle. It is also easy to propose a base class of Sports Equipment with subclasses of Ball, Jump rope, Puzzle, Net, and Score board.

Both of these object hierarchies refer to real-life objects, and both make sense to most people. However, as soon as you start programming with those objects, you might find that you want an object such as a ball to have some variables and behaviors that descend from Toy and some that descend from Sports Equipment. In other words, can a ball have two superclasses (or ancestors)?

Many proposals have been made and implemented for solving the multiple inheritance problem. Objective-C started out addressing that issue and has evolved a structure that handles multiple inheritance. However, it also covers a number of other long-time object-oriented programming issues.

NOTE

This overview of history is not only simplified, but also benefits from 20/20 hindsight so that it is now possible to construct plausible and rational sequences of events. At the time that they occurred, though, the overall picture was not yet visible to the participants.

The Objective-C approach that has evolved allows you to share functionality between two objects without using inheritance. To be sure, inheritance is used throughout Objective-C, but the very deep inheritance hierarchies that often evolve in languages such as C++ are far less common in Objective-C. Instead, you can take a defined chunk of functionality and share it directly.

A major distinction between extending a class by subclassing it and extending a class by adding a protocol to it is that a subclass can add or modify methods and can also add new instance variables. Protocols, like categories that are described briefly at the end of this section, only add methods.

Using an Example of a Protocol

An example of this is found in the iOS sample code for Multiple Detail Views (http:/ /developer.apple.com/library/ios/#samplecode/MultipleDetailViews/). This code addresses an issue that arises with some iPad apps. iOS supports a split view in which the main view fills the screen when the device is vertically oriented; when the device is horizontally oriented, the right and larger part of the screen shows the detail view, but, at the left, a list of items controls what is shown in the larger view.

In the vertical orientation, a control bar at the top of the window contains a button that will let you open a popover with the list of items that can be shown at the left.

The problem arises because the control bar at the top of the window can be a navigation bar or a toolbar. These are two different types of controls. The button to bring up the popover needs to be shown (in portrait mode) and hidden (in landscape mode). The code to implement this differs whether the button is added to a toolbar or to a navigation bar.

The key to this consists of four steps:

▶ **Declaring a protocol**—A protocol is declared. It is a set of methods presented as they would be in an interface.

▶ **Adopting the protocol**—Any class in this sample app that wants to be able to use this protocol must *adopt* it in its header. Adopting a protocol means that the class declared in the header must implement methods from the protocol. (Note that ones marked optional do not have to be implemented. This is another Objective-C 2.0 improvement.)

▶ **Implementing the protocol**—Any class that adopts the protocol must implement all required methods and might implement other methods. The implementations might use variables and other methods of the particular class that adopts the protocol.

▶ **Using the protocol.**

The code is described in the following sections.

The first step is to define the protocol in RootViewController.h, as shown in Listing 3.6.

LISTING 3.6   Defining the Protocol

```
@protocol SubstitutableDetailViewController
- (void)showRootPopoverButtonItem:(UIBarButtonItem *)barButtonItem;
- (void)invalidateRootPopoverButtonItem:(UIBarButtonItem *)barButtonItem;
@end
```

Beginning with Objective-C 2.0, you can indicate which methods are required or optional. The default is required, so the code in Listing 3.6 actually is the same as the code shown in Listing 3.7.

LISTING 3.7   Marking Protocol Methods Required or Optional

```
@protocol SubstitutableDetailViewController
@required
- (void)showRootPopoverButtonItem:(UIBarButtonItem *)barButtonItem;
- (void)invalidateRootPopoverButtonItem:(UIBarButtonItem *)barButtonItem;
@end
```

After you have declared a protocol, you need to adopt it. Listing 3.8 shows the code from the sample app for a view with a toolbar. Although the protocol is declared in RootViewController.h, it is adopted in FirstDetailViewController.h (and in the second one, too).

LISTING 3.8   Protocol Adoption with a Toolbar

```
@interface FirstDetailViewController : UIViewController <
SubstitutableDetailViewController> {

UIToolbar *toolbar;
}
```

Listing 3.9 shows the protocol adopted by another view that uses a navigation bar.

LISTING 3.9   Protocol Adoption with a Navigation Bar

```
@interface SecondDetailViewController : UIViewController <
SubstitutableDetailViewController> {

UINavigationBar *navigationBar;
}
```

Each of the classes that has adopted the protocol must implement its methods. Listing 3.10 shows the implementation of the protocol with a toolbar in FirstDetailViewController.m.

LISTING 3.10   Implementation of the Protocol with a Toolbar

```
#pragma mark -
#pragma mark Managing the popover

- (void)showRootPopoverButtonItem:(UIBarButtonItem *)barButtonItem {


// Add the popover button to the toolbar.

NSMutableArray *itemsArray = [toolbar.items mutableCopy];
  [itemsArray insertObject:barButtonItem atIndex:0];
  [toolbar setItems:itemsArray animated:NO];
  [itemsArray release];
}

- (void)invalidateRootPopoverButtonItem:(UIBarButtonItem *)barButtonItem {


// Remove the popover button from the toolbar.

NSMutableArray *itemsArray = [toolbar.items mutableCopy];
  [itemsArray removeObject:barButtonItem];
  [toolbar setItems:itemsArray animated:NO];
  [itemsArray release];
}
```

In Listing 3.11, you see how you can implement the protocol with a navigation bar. (This code is from SecondDetailViewController.m.)

NOTE

In Listing 3.11, you will also see how certain types of operations, such as adjusting buttons on a navigation bar, can be easier than the corresponding operations on a toolbar.

LISTING 3.11   Implementation of the Protocol with a Navigation Bar

```
#pragma mark -
#pragma mark Managing the popover

- (void)showRootPopoverButtonItem:(UIBarButtonItem *)barButtonItem {

// Add the popover button to the left navigation item.
  [navigationBar.topItem setLeftBarButtonItem:barButtonItem animated:NO];
}

- (void)invalidateRootPopoverButtonItem:(UIBarButtonItem *)barButtonItem {

// Remove the popover button.
  [navigationBar.topItem setLeftBarButtonItem:nil animated:NO];
}
```

The next step is to adopt another protocol. This protocol, UISplitViewController Delegate, is part of the Cocoa framework, so you do not have to write it. All you have to do is adopt it as the RootViewController class in the example does. The interface is shown in Listing 3.12 together with the adoption of the protocol in RootViewController.h. To repeat, what that adoption statement (in the < and >) means is that all required methods of the protocol will be implemented by this class.

> **TIP**
>
> In addition, remember that without an optional directive, all methods are required.

LISTING 3.12 Adopting the **UISplitViewControllerDelegate** Protocol

```
@interface RootViewController : UITableViewController
  <UISplitViewControllerDelegate> {
UISplitViewController *splitViewController;

UIPopoverController *popoverController;
UIBarButtonItem *rootPopoverButtonItem;
}
```

Having promised to implement the required and (possibly) optional methods of the UISplitViewControllerDelegate protocol, RootViewController.m must do so. The sample app implements two of the methods as shown in Listing 3.13. In doing so, it has fulfilled the promise made when it adopted the UISplitViewController-Delegate protocol.

There are two critical lines, one in each method of Listing 3.13. Those lines are the same in both methods and are underlined. It is easiest to start reading them from the middle. The heart of each line is the assignment of a local variable, *detailViewController, using the split view controller's array of view controllers and selecting item one.

This local variable is declared as being of type UIViewController and adopting the SubstitutableDetailViewController protocol shown previously in Listing 3.6. Because it adopts the protocol, it is safe to assume that it implements all the required methods. Because nothing is marked optional, both methods are required, so it is certain that they will be there (if they are not, that assignment statement will fail).

LISTING 3.13   Implementing the protocol in `RootViewController.m`

```
- (void)splitViewController:(UISplitViewController*)svc
  willHideViewController:(UIViewController *)aViewController
  withBarButtonItem:(UIBarButtonItem*)barButtonItem
  forPopoverController:(UIPopoverController*)pc {

// Keep references to the popover controller and the popover button, and tell the
// detail view controller to show the button.
  barButtonItem.title = @"Root View Controller";

self.popoverController = pc;

self.rootPopoverButtonItem = barButtonItem;

UIViewController <SubstitutableDetailViewController> *detailViewController =
  [splitViewController.viewControllers objectAtIndex:1];
  [detailViewController showRootPopoverButtonItem:rootPopoverButtonItem];
}

- (void)splitViewController:(UISplitViewController*)svc
  willShowViewController:(UIViewController *)aViewController
  invalidatingBarButtonItem:(UIBarButtonItem *)barButtonItem {

// Nil out references to the popover controller and the popover button, and tell
// the detail view controller to hide the button.

UIViewController <SubstitutableDetailViewController> *detailViewController =
     [splitViewController.viewControllers objectAtIndex:1];
     [detailViewController invalidateRootPopoverButtonItem:rootPopover
        ButtonItem];

self.popoverController = nil;

self.rootPopoverButtonItem = nil;
}
```

You might have to trace through the code again, but it is worth it to get the hang of it. The point is that this locally declared class inherits from a standard class in the framework (`UIViewController`). However, by creating and adopting its own protocol, two separate classes with two different ways of implementing control bars can both promise to do the same thing, albeit in different ways because they have different types of control bars to work with.

NOTE

There is a related concept in Objective-C, called categories. A *category* consists of methods (no instance variables, just like protocols) that are added to a specific class. This allows people to modify a class without having access to the code that is used for it to perform its work. At runtime, there is no difference between the basic class and the methods that have been added with a category.

Using Delegates

Protocols are often paired with *delegates*, another key Objective-C concept. As noted previously in this hour, instead of calling procedures, messages are sent to objects in Objective-C. That makes the use of delegates possible. A class can declare a delegate for itself. That delegate processes messages sent to the object itself. Frequently, functionality is wrapped up in a protocol as you have seen here, and some of those protocols are designed to be used by delegates.

> **NOTE**
>
> One of the most common uses of a delegate is a delegate for the application class. Messages send to the application are passed along to the application delegate. This enables you to add functionality to an application without subclassing it: you just add your new functionality to the delegate.

For example, you saw in Listing 3.12 that the RootViewController class adopts the UISplitViewControllerDelegate protocol. This means that a RootViewController can be named as the delegate of an object that requires that protocol to be implemented.

> ▶ This is a high-level view of delegates and protocols. You will find more examples and much more detail in Part IV, "Using Data Sources and Table Views." If it is a little fuzzy now, do not worry.

Using the Model/View/Controller Concepts

One of the critical pieces of iOS and Mac OS is the model/view/controller (MVC) design pattern. Along with object-oriented programming, this is another concept that evolved in the heady days of the 1970s and 1980s when the technology world was addressing the rapidly changing environment in which personal computers were becoming more prevalent and vast numbers of people started using their own computers (and programming them).

Model/view/controller got a frosty reception from some people at the start because it seemed like an over-complicated academic exercise. In retrospect, it seems that perception might have arisen in some cases because the benefits of MVC only become apparent when you apply the pattern and concepts to large systems. Writing "Hello World" using MVC concepts is indeed over-complicated. However, writing Mac OS or iOS in Basic, COBOL, or even C would be something close to futile.

Fortunately, we have complex problems and powerful computers today and MVC has come into its own. The concepts are quite simple:

- **Model**—This is the data you are working with. With Core Data, you will always have a data model.

- **View**—This is the presentation of the model and the interface for users to manipulate it.

- **Controller**—This code is the glue between model and view. It knows details of both, so if either changes, the controller normally needs to be changed, too. However, a change to the view typically does not require a change to the model, and vice versa. The addition of new data to the model will require a change to the view, but that is only because the underlying reality affects both.

One of the mistakes people made early on was to draw a conceptual diagram with a large bubble for the model and another large bubble for the view. The controller was relegated to a small link. In practice, that is far from the case. The controller is often the largest set of code modules. For people used to traditional programming, working on a controller feels most like traditional programming. Both the model and the view can be highly structured, but it is in the controller that all the idiosyncrasies emerge and collide.

Importing and Using Declarations in Files

A compiler instruction that you have seen in many of the code snippets in this hour is `import`. It is broadly similar to the C `include` statement but bypasses some of the issues that arise with multiple uses of the `include` statement. In Objective-C, `import` checks to see if the file has already been imported and does not repeat the import if it is unnecessary. Files within your project are identified by their filenames enclosed in quotes; files that are part of the frameworks are enclosed in < and >.

Typically, an interface (.h) file imports other interface files. An implementation file (.m) imports it own interface file, and it might import other interface files (usually not implementation files).

In an interface file, it is common to declare protocols and classes that will be defined later in the build process. Thus, instead of using

```
#import "myclass.h"
```

you might be better off simply declaring

```
@class myclass
```

The templates and samples demonstrate this style in many cases.

Summary

This hour provides an introduction to Objective-C and its concepts, as well as a general comparison to other object-oriented languages you might know. The biggest differences from other object-oriented languages are its messaging syntax (rather than function calling syntax), the ability to extend code in ways other than subclassing (protocols, delegates, and categories), and its somewhat more rigorous enforcement of basic object-oriented design principles when compared to languages such as C++ (this last point remains a topic of much discussion and dissension).

You have seen some examples of Objective-C code at work, and you will see more—and write more—throughout this book. For some people, the syntax and nomenclature is daunting with all its square brackets. Have no fear; if you start to use it, you will soon become accustomed to it. Furthermore, that syntax helps you access some of the powerful features of Objective-C that have no direct parallels in other programming languages.

Q&A

Q. Where is the best place to start learning about model/view/controller?

A. Start with controllers and, in particular, start with some of the view controllers such as the ones described in Part IV. The basics of both the view and model components of MVC are quite simple—one is your data and the other is your interface. The controller is pretty much where all the programming you are used to takes place.

Q. Are there naming conventions for methods and instances?

A. Naming conventions for instance variables are usually dependent on the project or developer. Inside the frameworks, you will find a number of standard types of methods. These are typically implemented in subclasses of the major framework classes. They have names such as viewWillAppear and viewDidAppear so that you can insert your code at the right place. The documentation on developer.apple.com helps you to understand which parts of the creation of objects such as views (and the corresponding destruction) are done in which step.

Workshop

Quiz

1. *What is one of the biggest differences between subclassing and extending a class with a protocol or category?*

2. *What are the benefits of using declared properties?*

Quiz Answers

1. You can add instance variables to a subclass. Protocols and categories allow you to only add methods.

2. You can save yourself some typing, your code will be more readable, you can use dot syntax to use the accessors, and the attributes you can assign to the properties can help you take advantage of runtime features.

Activities

If you have not already done so, create a new Xcode project from one of the templates. Go through the code and pick out the Objective-C constructs that have been discussed in this hour. Be certain to run the code! Only hands-on experience with the code will help you understand what the code is doing.

Explore one or more of the sample code projects on developer.apple.com (these are often more complex than the Xcode projects). You might want to search for specific features, such as protocols or delegates, that you want to explore.

Getting the Big Core Data Picture

What You'll Learn In This Hour:

- ▶ Understanding the core data objectives
- ▶ Exploring the core data stack
- ▶ Working with fetch requests

Starting Out with Core Data

The section provides a brief introduction to Core Data. The remaining hours in this part of the book provide you with more details. The next part of the book shows you how to merge Core Data with the frameworks and code you saw in the first part of the book.

This overview is descriptive. There are several tips for places you might want to come back to if you want to—for example, change the name of your database—but the point of the hour is a high-level view. Starting with the next hour, you will get into creating your own Core Data code.

Tracing the Origins of Core Data

Core Data had its origins in Enterprise Objects Framework (EOF), which was developed at NeXT as part of WebObjects in the early 1990s. When Apple purchased NeXT in 1996, EOF came along for the ride. It morphed into the Core Data framework and was released as a part of Mac OS X 10.4 (Tiger) and, later, as a part of iOS.

The initial objective was to deliver a solution to an important challenge in the programming world of that time: something to combine the techniques of object-oriented programming with the functionality of a relational database.

NOTE

Object-oriented databases—sometimes referred to as *object databases*—were created in the 1980s. Today they are generally considered as a niche in the much larger database market.

Core Data today is a powerful tool for building database functionality into your apps for Mac and iOS. In and of itself, it is not a database. It is designed to store data using a *persistent store*. On iOS and Mac, that can be an SQLite database (SQLite is part of both operating systems); on Mac, it can also be an XML file.

As a developer, your interaction with the actual data management tool (SQLite in most cases) is through the Core Data model editor in Xcode. You use it to create and develop a Core Data model file (with extension .xcdatamodeld). The Core Data model editor is shown in Figure 4.1. At the left of the editor is a pane for top-level components. The larger section at the right contains details for a selected component.

FIGURE 4.1
Xcode contains a Core Data model editor.

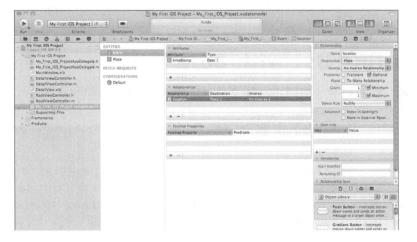

There are two modes for the editor. Figure 4.1 shows the table mode; Figure 4.2 shows the graph mode. You switch from one to the other with the switch at the lower-right of the editor titled Editor Style.

▶ The Core Data model editor is covered in more detail in Hour 6, "Working with the Data Model Editor," on p. 117.

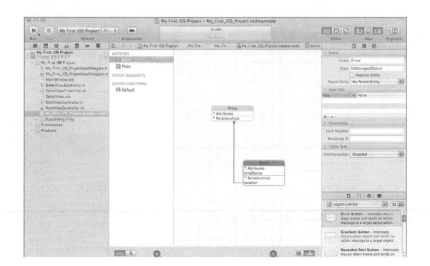

FIGURE 4.2
Switch to graph
mode.

NOTE

There are many options you can use when you create a project from a template. In Figures 4.1 and 4.2, the option for universal code (that is, separate code for iPad and iPhone) is used along with the option to not use storyboards. Storyboards are the topic of Hour 14, "Working with Storyboards." They are only available on iOS, so the older technology—nib files—is used to start.

Talking Core Data

In the world of relational databases, data is stored in *tables*. Each table has a number of *rows* or *records* (the terms are basically interchangeable). Inside a row, data is stored in *columns* or *fields* (again, basically interchangeable terms). Core Data hides this from you so that when you access the data, it appears as objects. This means a little bit of renaming from the rows, columns, records, and fields of database-speak.

In Figure 4.3, the data model shown previously in Figures 4.1 and 4.2 has been enhanced with some additional elements. *Entities* are in many ways similar to tables. An entity can have any number of *attributes*, which are roughly the same as columns or fields.

As you see in Figure 4.4, attributes can have a *type* just as an instance variable can. In addition, relationships can have attributes, they can be optional or not, and then can have a specified number of related objects. This will be described as you continue in this hour.

Figure 4.4 shows the supported data types in Core Data. They are common database data types.

FIGURE 4.3
Enhancing the basic model.

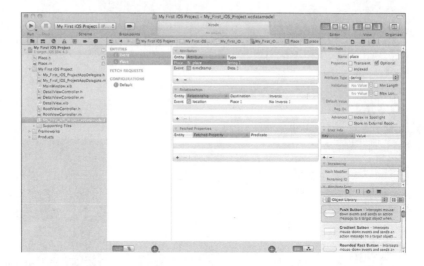

FIGURE 4.4
Choose a Core Data data type for a selected attribute.

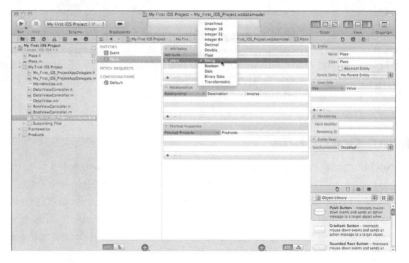

As you will see in Hour 6, Xcode can translate your data model into actual code. This is the bridge from the world of relational databases to the world of object-oriented programming that was at the heart of the initial project. Listing 4.1 shows the automatically generated code for the Place entity shown in the previous figures in this hour. Listing 4.2 shows the automatically generated implementation file.

LISTING 4.1   Place.h

```
//
//  Place.h
//  My First iOS Project
//
```

```
//   Created by Jesse Feiler on 9/13/11.
//   Copyright (c) 2011 another. All rights reserved.
//

#import <Foundation/Foundation.h>
#import <CoreData/CoreData.h>

@interface Place : NSManagedObject

@property (nonatomic, retain) NSString * address;
@property (nonatomic, retain) NSSet *event;
@end

@interface Place (CoreDataGeneratedAccessors)

- (void)addEventObject:(NSManagedObject *)value;
- (void)removeEventObject:(NSManagedObject *)value;
- (void)addEvent:(NSSet *)values;
  (void)removeEvent:(NSSet *)values;

@end
```

LISTING 4.2   Place.m

```
//
//   Place.m
//   My First iOS Project
//
//   Created by Jesse Feiler on 9/13/11.
//   Copyright (c) 2011 another. All rights reserved.
//

#import "Place.h"


@implementation Place

@dynamic address;
@dynamic event;

@end
```

As you can see, the Place entity in the data model is now a Place class in the code.
The attribute of the Place entity in the data model is now a declared property.

NOTE

If there were more attributes, they would all be treated the same way.

And finally, the address attribute of the Place entity in the data model is an
NSString in the code, whereas in the data model, it was a string.

Two points about Listing 4.2 are worth noting:

▶ Although the `Place` entity in the data model has been transformed into a `Place` class in the code, it could have been used as an `NSManagedObject` in the code. `Place` (or any other class derived from Core Data) is a descendent of `NSManagedObject`.

▶ Note that what would have been a `@synthesize` directive for most declared properties is a `@dynamic` directive when working with a Core Data property.

If you are used to using graphical database management tools, you can look around for a button or command that lets you browse the data in the database. There is no such button or command. This is an editor for the data model, and, in fact, the database might not exist at this time. Generally, the database exists only when you are using the Core Data model editor to make modifications to an existing model. The data model will interact with the database at runtime, which is the topic of the next section of this hour.

Many experienced database users and designers appreciate the fact that databases make it easy to store, retrieve, and modify structured data, as well as making it possible for several people to use the database at the same time without falling over one another. SQLite is designed for single-user use. It definitely can be used in a multiuser environment, but it is primarily used today for a single user. For example, it often manages data within a user's browser. Apple's use of SQLite is geared to a single user.

Remember that this is just a preview of the detailed discussion of the Core Data model editor in Hour 6.

Examining Core Data at Runtime: The Core Data Stack

The Core Data model should be familiar to anyone who has used a database. It is basically the *schema* of the database—the description of rows and columns or records and fields.

At runtime, the data model is combined with two other objects: a *managed object context* and a *persistent object store*.

NOTE

The persistent object store is often an SQLite database, but it can be other types of storage entities.

Using Managed Object Contexts— NSManagedObjectContext

At runtime, each managed object is made part of a managed object context. You can have a number of managed object contexts in your app at any time. A single entity from the data model can be instantiated into several managed objects, but each instance of a managed object must be in a separate managed object context. When you want to save changes, it is the managed object context that you save. That act saves the data in the persistent store. The use of multiple managed object contexts helps facilitate undo and redo, among other features.

> NOTE
>
> A managed object is the object created from an entity in the data model and, possibly, from data stored in the persistent store.

Using Persistent Stores—NSPersistentStore

A persistent object store in most cases is a file that can be a database. This is where the mapping between a database entry and a runtime object happens. Just as you can have multiple managed object contexts, you can have multiple persistent stores. In the case of persistent stores, an NSPersistentStoreCoordinator does the management; there is no corresponding object to manage managed object contexts.

In your code, you work with managed objects, a persistent store coordinator, and a managed object context. That is the simplest and most common scenario. If you need multiple managed object contexts, you can create them to handle undo commands, for example. It will be the managed object context that actually commits a change to a persistent store.

In the common and most basic scenario, the persistent store coordinator "coordinates" a single store. However, this structure provides little added complexity in exchange for a powerful and extendable environment

Building the Core Data Stack at Runtime

If you use any of the Xcode templates with Core Data enabled, or if you use sample code that includes Core Data, you will find that your core data stack is set up for you with little effort on your part. This section shows you how the stack is created and the places where you might need to adjust the code.

This section uses the Master-Detail Application–based template in iOS that is built in to Xcode. You can always create it for yourself by starting a new project in Xcode.

If you do not have the iOS templates and SDK installed, try using the Cocoa Application template under Mac OS. Just remember in both cases to click the checkbox to use Core Data on the screen where you name the project. Because this code is built in to Xcode and you can easily re-create it with File, New, New Project, some of the code is compressed here.

> Even though the focus of this section is on the Core Data code, some interface elements such as the lines including IBOutlet are explained in Part III, "Developing the Core Data Interface."

Listing 4.3 shows how the app delegate declares the key core data elements. What matters here are the declared properties for the managed object context, the managed object model, and the persistent store coordinator.

LISTING 4.3   AppDelegate.h for a Core Data Project

```
//
//  AppDelegate.h
//  My First iOS Project
//
//  Created by Jesse Feiler on 9/13/11.
//  Copyright (c) 2011 another. All rights reserved.
//

#import <UIKit/UIKit.h>

@interface AppDelegate : UIResponder <UIApplicationDelegate>

@property (strong, nonatomic) UIWindow *window;

@property (readonly, strong, nonatomic) NSManagedObjectContext
  *managedObjectContext;
@property (readonly, strong, nonatomic) NSManagedObjectModel
  *managedObjectModel;
@property (readonly, strong, nonatomic) NSPersistentStoreCoordinator
  *persistentStoreCoordinator;

- (void)saveContext;
- (NSURL *)applicationDocumentsDirectory;

@property (strong, nonatomic) UINavigationController *navigationController;

@property (strong, nonatomic) UISplitViewController *splitViewController;

@end
```

The implementation file, shown in Listing 4.4, supports the declared properties. Names beginning with one or two underscores are reserved for Apple; these getters get instance variables declared inside the framework code by Apple.

LISTING 4.4   **Synthesize the Core Data Stack Properties**

```
@implementation AppDelegate

@synthesize window = _window;
@synthesize managedObjectContext = __managedObjectContext;
@synthesize managedObjectModel = __managedObjectModel;
@synthesize persistentStoreCoordinator = __persistentStoreCoordinator;
@synthesize navigationController = _navigationController;
@synthesize splitViewController = _splitViewController;

@end
```

The elements of the Core Data stack are all provided on an as-needed basis. If they have not yet been created, their accessors create them. For example, Listing 4.5 shows the getter accessor for the managed object context. Note that several comments have been added to the template code.

LISTING 4.5   The Getter for `managedObjectContext` in `AppDelegate.h`

```
- (NSManagedObjectContext *)managedObjectContext
{

if (__managedObjectContext !- nil)
  {

    return __managedObjectContext;
  }

  // Set a local variable to the persistent store coordinator
  NSPersistentStoreCoordinator *coordinator = [self persistentStoreCoordinator];

if (coordinator != nil)
  {
    // Create the managed object context with the persistent store coordinator
    __managedObjectContext = [[NSManagedObjectContext alloc] init];
    __managedObjectContext setPersistentStoreCoordinator:coordinator];
  }

return __managedObjectContext;
}
```

If the internal instance variable is not nil, it is simply returned, and that is the end of things. In other cases (that is, it is nil), it is created. The setter is the default setter created with the synthesize directive, so do not bother to search for it in the code. The getter is overridden because it performs extra steps to create the managed object context if it does not exist, and, therefore, the default setter is not sufficient.

A managed object context requires a persistent store, so the accessor for the persistent store is used to set a local variable. If you track down that accessor, you will see that it uses the same type of structure, as shown in Listing 4.6.

Just as in Listing 4.5, if the persistent store coordinator exists, it is returned. If it does not exist, it is created. To do so, the managed object model must exist, and the process continues with the accessor for the managed object model.

A comment has been added to highlight the name of your database; it is constructed by the template from your project's name. If you change the name of your project, you might want to change this filename.

TIP

Keep in mind that when your project's name is used for your database name, the underscores are replaced with spaces. If you can avoid spaces in your project's name, you do not have to worry about these details.

LISTING 4.6   Access (and Possibly Create) the Persistent Store Coordinator

```
- (NSPersistentStoreCoordinator *)persistentStoreCoordinator
{

if (__persistentStoreCoordinator != nil)
  {

    return __persistentStoreCoordinator;
  }


NSURL *storeURL = [[self applicationDocumentsDirectory]

  URLByAppendingPathComponent:
  // HERE IS THE NAME OF YOUR DATABASE FILE

@"My_First_iOS_Project.sqlite"];


NSError *error = nil;

__persistentStoreCoordinator
  [[NSPersistentStoreCoordinator alloc]
  // PICK UP THE MANAGED OBJECT MODEL FOR THE PERSISTENT STORE COORDINATOR

  initWithManagedObjectModel:[self managedObjectModel]];


if (![__persistentStoreCoordinator
```

```
addPersistentStoreWithType:NSSQLiteStoreType

configuration:nil URL:storeURL options:nil

error:&error])
{

NSLog(@"Unresolved error %@, %@", error,
        [error userInfo]);

abort();
}


return __persistentStoreCoordinator;
}
```

The same pattern is repeated for the managed object model, as shown in Listing 4.7. If it exists, it is returned; if not, it is created.

CAUTION

Note that the model itself is placed in the application bundle during the build process. You do not have to worry about naming or renaming it. However, if you do so, the corresponding line in this method in the app delegate needs to be changed.

LISTING 4.7   Accessing the Managed Object Model

```
- (NSManagedObjectModel *)managedObjectModel
{

if (__managedObjectModel != nil)
  {

    return __managedObjectModel;
  }
NSURL *modelURL = [[NSBundle mainBundle]

  URLForResource:@"My_First_iOS_Project " withExtension:@"momd"];

__managedObjectModel = [[NSManagedObjectModel alloc]
  initWithContentsOfURL:modelURL];

return __managedObjectModel;
}
```

In this way, the three components of your Core Data stack are created at runtime. They are built from the name of your SQLite file and from your object model. Both are set automatically in the template when you create your project. If you change the name or location of the SQLite file, you need to make a change here, and if you change the name of the data model resource (rarely necessary), you need to make the corresponding change here.

You might be thinking that you may need to change the name of the model if you are making changes to the app and want to keep two different models around as you are working on them. Have no fear: The Core Data model editor allows you to create multiple versions of a model, so you do not have to worry. By default, the latest version is used, but you can override that without coming into the code to change the resource name.

▶ See Hour 24, "Migrating Data Models," on p. 423 for more detailed information about maintaining multiple versions of your data models.

Working with Fetched Results

When you want to access your data, you do so with a *fetch request*. If you are used to working with SQL, you may think that this is the point at which you start typing SELECT, but you are in the world of Core Data and objects, so that type of procedural programming has no place.

NOTE
To be completely accurate, procedural programming does have a place, but it is deep inside Core Data where you do not have to worry about it.

In the simplest and most common cases, you create a fetch request and a *fetch request controller*. It will interact with the Core Data stack to get the data for you. The select statement will be generated deep inside the Core Data stack and will be executed by the stack. For that reason, do not go searching around in the template or sample code for select statements.

And before you go searching around for the code that moves the fetched data into the interface, do not worry about that either. If you are using a UITableView (which is what you typically use to display the data), a protocol to provide data source functionality will actually interact with the fetch request.

In MasterViewController, this process is played out. That class adopts the NSFetched
ResultsControllerDelegate protocol. That protocol lets a NSFetchedResults
Controller notify its delegate that fetch results have changed. The setup for this
process is not extensive (and, again, it is provided in the template). Because
MasterViewController adopts the protocol, it implements the necessary methods.
They are identified with a pragma mark named Fetched results controller. In most
cases, you will not need to reimplement or change these methods, so they are not
repeated here.

What you do need to do is to set up the fetched results controller. The same pattern
used for the Core Data stack is repeated here. If the object does not exist, it is created. Listing 4.8 shows the code.

LISTING 4.8   Accessing the Fetched Results Controller (in
MasterViewController)

```
- (NSFetchedResultsController *)fetchedResultsController
{
  if (__fetchedResultsController != nil) {
    return __fetchedResultsController;
  }

  // Set up the fetched results controller.
  // Create the fetch request for the entity.
  NSFetchRequest *fetchRequest = [[NSFetchRequest alloc] init];
  // Edit the entity name as appropriate.
  NSEntityDescription *entity = [NSEntityDescription entityForName:@"Event"
    inManagedObjectContext:self.managedObjectContext];
  [fetchRequest setEntity:entity];

  // Set the batch size to a suitable number.
  [fetchRequest setFetchBatchSize:20];

  // Edit the sort key as appropriate.
  NSSortDescriptor *sortDescriptor = [[NSSortDescriptor alloc] initWithKey:
  @"timeStamp"
    ascending:NO];
  NSArray *sortDescriptors = [NSArray arrayWithObjects:sortDescriptor, nil];

  [fetchRequest setSortDescriptors:sortDescriptors];

  // Edit the section name key path and cache name if appropriate.
  // nil for section name key path means "no sections".
  NSFetchedResultsController *aFetchedResultsController =
    [[NSFetchedResultsController alloc]
    initWithFetchRequest:fetchRequest
    managedObjectContext:self.managedObjectContext sectionNameKeyPath:nil
    cacheName:@"Master"];
  aFetchedResultsController.delegate = self;
  self.fetchedResultsController = aFetchedResultsController;
```

```
NSError *error = nil;
if (![self.fetchedResultsController performFetch:&error]) {
   /*
   Replace this implementation with code to handle the error appropriately.

   abort() causes the application to generate a crash log and terminate. You
     should not use this function in a shipping application, although it may be
     useful during development.
   */
   NSLog(@"Unresolved error %@, %@", error, [error userInfo]);
   abort();
}

   return __fetchedResultsController;
}
```

Toward the bottom of the code listing, note the line in which this object
(MasterViewController) becomes the delegate for the newly created fetched results
controller. That is the link that makes this object be the delegate and that requires it
to implement the NSFetchedResultsControllerDelegate protocol.

The only line of code you might change is the name of the entity to retrieve. Note
that this is the most basic retrieval: It gets all these items and sorts them. Keep in
mind that you do need some kind of sort descriptor. Except for the name of the
entity to retrieve and the sort descriptor key, you can use this code in most cases
with no changes.

▶ See Hour 9, "Fetching Data" on p. 153 for more information on implementing fetch requests and controllers.

Sometimes it is difficult for people to adjust to this new paradigm. You do much
more setup than you would do in a traditional SQL program, but it pays off when
you do not have to write any code to unload the select statement and none at all to
populate the interface with the results.

Summary

This hour has provided an overview of the Core Data framework. You will move on in the following hours to implementing your own database. In those hours, you will notice that in order to use Core Data, you will need the code shown in this hour but rarely have to write or even rewrite it. Most of your work is built on this code and on the extensions to it that you will write. But the infrastructure is usually untouched.

Q&A

Q. *What are the main purposes of Core Data in addition to the actual storing of data?*

A. One of the most important is the combination of object-oriented programming and relational databases.

Q. *Is SQLite a part of Core Data?*

A. Core Data can use SQLite as a data store on Mac and iOS; on Mac, it can also use XML. SQLite is a library that is included with Mac OS and iOS. It is frequently used for the data store, but it is not required.

Workshop

Quiz

1. *What are the components of the runtime Core Data stack?*

2. *What are managed objects?*

Quiz Answers

1. Managed object context, managed object model, and persistent store coordinator.

2. These are objects defined in the data model and created as needed at runtime from the persistent data store.

Activities

This book uses SQLite for many of its examples. If you have not already done so, get a SQLite browser that you can use to examine what happens behind the scenes. Search for SQLite browser Mac, and you will find a number of examples. Download and install one to be ready to explore.

HOUR 5

Working with Data Models

What You'll Learn in This Hour:

▶ Defining entities: the what of data
▶ Describing attributes: the characteristics of data
▶ Connecting entities with relationships
▶ Locating your data

Making the Abstract Concrete

In many ways, the role of Core Data is to turn the abstractions of a data model into concrete reality that ultimately can be stored on disk (and, of course, to manage the reverse transformation). This hour gets to the heart of the matter. You start by learning the data model and end by seeing how to write the concrete database to disk. Along the way, there are many adventures and options, which are covered in the hours that follow.

NOTE

You might be chomping at the bit to get your hands into code, but the data model requires the simplest of tools: pencil and paper, a whiteboard, or a sketch on an iPad. Once that is done, have no fear. You will be launching Xcode to try things for yourself at the end of this hour. In the next hour, you will be building another data model to get more detailed experience with the process.

Naming the Data Model

If you have worked with databases before, you have been introduced to *schemas*, *data models*, and perhaps *entity-relationship diagrams*. All are different approaches to the abstraction of objects and activities. All these abstract concepts share one important characteristic: You can design an entire data model down to the smallest unit of data without entering any data into it.

TIP

The differences between data models, schemas, and entity-relationship diagrams are beyond the scope of this book. However, searching for them on the web with a single search query will provide a multitude of references and comparisons. Suffice it to say that, in the world of Core Data, the term is *data model*.

Designing the Data Model

Designing the data model without putting data into it is a skill that some people seem to come by naturally; for others, it is more difficult. Whichever camp you find yourself in, rest assured that others have been there before. Even the most experienced data modelers often do work with paper or whiteboards during the design phase. With these tools, you can put data into your hand-drawn data model and see how it fits. Every refinement you make to a data model before it has been implemented can save you time and money.

The issue is the same as it is for physical objects. If you are building your dream house, there will be a big difference in the final cost if you realize that you need three bedrooms instead of two when the house is still in architectural drawings. If you only discover the need for that third bedroom when your parents show up for a holiday dinner, the cost might be much greater.

Testing with Real Data

This brings up another point that experienced database designers have learned (often the hard way). Use your data model and the app as it is developed with real data. You might wind up with several suites of test data to use during your development process. One might have only two items in the database, another might be a very complex and rare set of data, and so forth. Avoid creating test data from scratch.

Only by turning to real data will you fall over the data conditions that you (or your client) know never occur. Because you think they never occur, you might wind up developing an app that cannot handle them, and when they do occur, problems arise. A common example is a retail store that has a strict policy of no refunds on custom orders. This makes sense because, if someone orders something that is customized (perhaps embossed with his initials), the shopkeeper might not be able to sell it to someone else. If someone placed such a customized order, you might ask that he sign a form indicating that there are no refunds once work starts.

A few weeks later, if a sobbing and grieving person walks into the store and explains that he is the surviving spouse of the now-deceased customer, would you make an exception to the no refunds policy? It is this type of thing that is assumed to never happen, but when it does, this can cause problems. Good database designers are skeptical of every absolute statement from a client.

With that, it is time to move on to designing the data model. This is the entire data design for your app and its data. Parts of the data model might be designed only on paper to be implemented in a phase two or three, but it is a good practice not only to focus on the exceptions to the always or never rules, but also to prepare for future enhancements. It is relatively easy to draw additions to the data model on paper or a whiteboard, and it is worth taking some time to figure out how you would accommodate changes that might occur in the future.

Working with Entities

The heart of the data model is one or more *entities*. These are often physical objects that are part of the process (customers, invoices, items for sale, and the like), but they might also be intangible objects that are part of a different type of process (medical diagnosis and school curriculum, for example). In many real-life situations, the objects are a combination of tangible and intangible objects (patients, diagnoses, prescriptions, and appointments for example). In this hour, you will think through the process of developing a data model for a shopping cart.

> **NOTE**
>
> A shopping cart app is chosen because it is a common type of app, one that is familiar and simple to describe and one that demonstrates data modeling very well. The basic model applies to a shopping cart and its purchases, but it also applies to a class and its students, a warehouse and its goods, as well as a party and its guests. Yet another variation on this model is a vendor or service provider who keeps track of customers and the jobs for each customer. In each of these cases, there are items (purchases, students, goods, guests, or jobs) that are contained by or grouped into collections (a shopping cart, a class, a warehouse, a party, or a customer).
>
> This last variation (jobs and customers) was used in a simpler form as the Estimator example in the author's book *Data-Driven iOS Apps for iPad and iPhone with FileMaker Pro, Bento by FileMaker, and FileMaker Go* published by Que. In that book, you learn how to implement it in each of these FileMaker products; in the next hour of this book, you will learn how to implement it in iOS and Mac apps.

Every entity in your data model needs to have a name. You should choose meaningful names, but you must abide by the rules:

▶ Start with a capital letter.

▶ After the capital letter, use upper- and lowercase letters and underscores only. Your entity for the web shopping app might be `ShoppingCart` or `Shopping_cart`.

If you are used to databases, you will probably note that entities are very similar to *tables*. In fact, they do function in that way, but there are some minor distinctions that do not matter in most cases. When it is populated with data, a table will have a number of rows of data—one row per patient, perhaps—and there will be several values for that row or patient.

The first step in setting up your data model is settling on what your entities will be. This is often pretty obvious, but many data models require working through to the end and coming back to rethink the entities. One of the common changes you make to entities is to reflect their state or condition. Imagine a web storefront where people can choose items for their shopping carts. When they are ready to check out, they pay for the items in their shopping carts.

Everything seems simple until you learn that many web shoppers never complete the sale. They add one or more items to their shopping cart and then move on to another site or another activity. Estimates of the number of abandoned web shopping carts are high—as much as 70%. This is not simply a web phenomenon because people frequently walk out of stores without buying things. Sometimes a sale is not completed because it just takes too long (a problem on the Web, too), but other reasons might apply. Many other processes do not complete: Students drop out of courses, and sometimes party guests never leave. In any event, as the designer of an app to handle retail sales, you might have thought that you would have a nice data structure of goods for sale and a shopping cart to contain them.

But as you get deeper into the situation, it is apparent that the shopping cart has some characteristics you will need to track. Not only will you need some way of keeping track of the items in the cart, but you will also need to keep track of whether it has checked out. You also might want to keep track of who started to fill the shopping cart so that if that customer returns, the shopping cart is ready to continue shopping.

In other words, you need to describe the state of the shopping cart itself—not its content, but the entire cart and the cart process.

Adding Attributes to Entities

Every entity has one or more *attributes* that apply to the data in a specific element of the entity (that is, to a particular shopping cart). Attributes are simple data types that are defined in Core Data. Your choices for attributes in Core Data are the following:

- ▶ Undefined
- ▶ Integer 16
- ▶ Integer 32
- ▶ Integer 64
- ▶ Decimal
- ▶ Double
- ▶ Float
- ▶ String
- ▶ Boolean
- ▶ Date
- ▶ Binary Data
- ▶ Transformable

Most of these are standard data types across many platforms. Their implementation in Core Data is no different. However, the last four (Boolean, Date, Binary Data, and Transformable) require special attention.

- ▶ Three of these are described in this hour; transformable data is described in Hour 7, "What Managed Objects Can Do," p. 133.

For example, to manage the abandoned shopping cart problem, you might add these attributes to your shopping cart entity:

- ▶ dateStarted (Date)
- ▶ dateFinished (Date)
- ▶ shopperName (String)

Two points are worth noting here:

- ▶ By convention, attribute names start with a lowercase letter. They cannot contain anything other than letters and numbers as well as underscores.

Thus, to create a meaningful name for the date a shopping cart was started, your choices basically are `dateStarted` and `date_Started`.

▶ There is no field to indicate that a shopping cart has been abandoned...or is there? One principle of good database design is *normalizing* your data. There is no need for an indicator that a cart has been abandoned because, by definition, a cart with a value of nil for `dateFinished` has not been checked out. Whether it is abandoned or not is hard to tell, although there are a number of strategies you can use depending on whether you want to err on the side of retaining possibly abandoned shopping carts for possible future sales or on the side of clearing them out.

Using Dates

In most cases, dates work as you would expect them to, but you should know how they are handled internally in case you need to work with them in more than a superficial manner. Dates are stored as Cocoa objects—`NSDate`. The representation internally is a `NSTimeInterval`, which is a double containing a reference date—the number of seconds since midnight on January 1, 2001. For dates before that time, you can supply a negative number.

`NSDate` objects can present their date and time using the `description` method common to most objects in Cocoa. `NSDate` has another method, `descriptionWithLocale`, which takes an `NSLocale` object. What all of this means to you is that if you are storing dates, you should know that what is being stored is seconds and that the `Date` attribute type can be displayed as dates or as times or as both. In addition, if time zones matter to you, they need to be stored separately. All dates are assumed to be Coordinated Universal Time (UTC). If time zones do not matter to you, this does not matter.

Using Binary Data

You can store binary data as Binary Large Objects (BLOBs) or as Character Large Objects (CLOBs). These are concepts, and they are relative—"large" is in the eye of the beholder and in the context.

NOTE

If you are using an SQLite database with Core Data (the most common configuration), the database is not shared. In the discussion that follows, *sharing* refers to the general concept of database sharing whether it is implemented with a shared database or with apps sharing and communicating with multiple instances on multiple devices.

The three basic ways to store binary data are as follows:

▶ You can store relatively small amounts of binary data directly in a record. This is almost always safe for something like a small image in an unshared database. As the amount of data gets larger or the number of simultaneous users of the database gets larger, this method can pose performance problems. The advantage of this method is that it is as easy to store binary data as an integer.

▶ You can store a URL to the location of the data either on disk, on the Internet, or in your app's bundle resources. This method puts no performance burden on the database; any burden is directly on the app when a user wants to read or write the data. Apple recommends this strategy for large data files.

▶ An intermediate method is to store the data in a normalized table—that is, a table (entity) with an attribute for the binary data and with a relationship back to the main data table. This keeps the large binary data object in the database and therefore in a shared environment; it can pose performance problems, but it does keep everything together.

As always when addressing performance issues, there is no substitute for prototyping, modeling, and live testing.

NOTE
There is an additional storage option for relatively small amounts of data that need to follow an individual user. Key-value coding can be used with iCloud to store data for access across all of the user's devices. This keeps it out of a data store such as Core Data, but may be appropriate in some circumstances.

Using Boolean Data

The issues with Boolean data are a matter of Cocoa rather than Core Data, but you should be aware of them in your code. The BOOL data type is a signed char. The constants in Objective-C are YES and NO rather than true and false. The numberWithBool class method of NSNumber converts a BOOL to a number, as in the following:

```
myNumber = [NSNumber numberWithBool: myBool];
```

Linking Entities with Relationships

What about the items in your shopping cart? Obviously, you have to keep track of them. Many people start by creating attributes for them—item1, item2, and so forth. Because you will need prices and quantities, you can add additional attributes such as item1quantity and item2quantity, as well as item1price and item2price. Although this is the first thought that many people have, it is wrong. The correct way to do this is to create a new entity that will have one row for each item in the cart.

That entity can be named *Item*, and its attributes would be as follows:

- ▶ itemName (String)

- ▶ itemPrice (Decimal)

- ▶ itemQuantity (Integer 16)

The Item and Cart tables will be joined by a relationship. This will enable you to query any item to find out what cart it is in; you will also be able to list all the items for a given cart.

- ▶ In Hour 6, "Working with the Data Model Editor," p. 117, you will see how to implement relationships.

TIP

Whenever you are designing a database for any environment (Core Data, FileMaker, Bento, Oracle, or Microsoft SQL Server), if you catch yourself tempted to created fields with names like item1, item2, and item3, chances are you are making the mistake described here. The technical term for it is creating an "unnormalized data model," but the easiest term to remember is "wrong."

Keeping Track of Your Data in Files and Documents

As noted previously, you can look at Core Data as a tool that bridges the worlds of object-oriented programming and relational databases, in effect "speaking" both tongues. As part of this bridging, Core Data can support a number of databases to manage its stored data—its *persistent stores*.

Understanding Core Data Persistent Store Types

On iOS and Mac OS, Core Data supports SQLite and binary data stores; on Mac OS, it also supports XML. XML is not strictly speaking a database, but it can be used to describe structured data so that XML documents can be used as data stores with Core Data.

NOTE

Core Data has its roots in Enterprise Objects Framework, which was a part of WebObjects. In that incarnation, EOF supported databases including OpenBase, MySQL, Microsoft SQL Server, Oracle, and Sybase among others. (This information is from WebObjects Compatibility Guide of October 4, 2008—http://support.apple.com/kb/TA26741?viewlocale=en_US.) Whether such support is provided again in the future will depend on the priorities of Apple and its users.

With the currently supported data store formats, your data that is managed by Core Data is going to be stored—somewhere—in a file (or, in the case of binary data, perhaps in memory). Depending on your project, you might have to choose which type of data store to use or your choice might have been made for you. If you do have a choice, there are two considerations, both of them have to do with performance:

▶ **Speed**—XML is slower than the other storage techniques. In part, this is because XML documents are relatively verbose with their markup codes. Look at a typical data element in an XML document, and you will see that the ratio of non-data elements to data itself can be large. The actual data in the following code is underlined:

```
<first_name>George</first_name>
```

▶ **What is read or written**—SQLite allows you to work with a part of the database at a time, whereas the other formats do not permit this. Note, however, that it is very easy to slow down SQLite by requiring substantial writes of updates to ensure data integrity. For this reason, the actual timing of performance in any database configuration always has to be done with real data on the anticipated production environment. Theoretical discussions are notoriously unreliable in predicting database performance on every platform from an iPhone to a supercomputer.

Locating the Database

For most purposes, the database that you use with Core Data will be either binary or SQLite, with the XML option for Mac OS. Binary databases are useful for relatively small amounts of data, but when people approach Core Data for most projects, they approach it with SQLite in mind. One of the issues you have to consider is where this database will be located. For relatively small or transient databases, you can use a persistent store in memory that is not even written out. More often, you will want to write out the data so that it can be read back in at another time.

The two basic approaches to this are as follows:

▶ **Semi-Hidden files**—You implement this strategy by storing your data in a file with a known name that is placed in a known location such as /~/LIbrary/Application Support/. Neither the name nor the location is changeable by the user, and the user generally is discouraged from accessing the file.

▶ **Documents**—Most operating systems that are built on the desktop model metaphor let users manage their own data using files and folders. Instead of automatically reading from and writing to a specific file within Application Support, users are prompted to provide a name and location for the data that they want to save in a document. They can store their documents all over the place. Depending on your point of view, this is one of the glories or disasters of the desktop metaphor.

Semi-Hidden Files on Mac OS X

You implement this strategy by storing your data in a file with a known name located in a known location that is not designed for the user to get to it directly (that is what your app is for). The files are not technically hidden, which would be the case if their names started with a dot; however, they are not placed right in front of the user on the desktop or the Documents folder.

On the Mac, the appropriate location is usually in the user's home directory at the path /~/Library/Application Support/<your app name>. (Note that <your app name> can be a variation on the app's actual name; if you want to call your app Nifty App and store it in /~/Library/Application Support/NiftyApp with no space, that is fine. However, Apple recommends that the Application Support subdirectory should use the same name as the bundle identifier, which is shown in the Identifier field of the project summary in Xcode. Change it by changing the target name at the left of the project editor.) Because that folder in Application Support is for your app's files, you can manage the naming conventions within it. This structure lets your app have a single database for all its data, which is something users often want. For example, Bento stores its database inside /~/Library/Application Support/Bento.

Sometimes, you want files to be shared by various applications. Mail is a good example of this because its files are stored in /~/Library/Mail rather than inside Application Support. This makes them available to the various apps that might need to access them.

Either of these strategies stores your files inside a user's home directory. At the root level of the boot disk is a comparable file structure that applies to all users on that disk. At the root level, you will find iWork Tour in /Library/Application Support/iWork. This means that it can be found by any user on that computer who is running iWork; it is put there during the installation, and it should be available to everyone.

If you explore /Library for the root level, you will find files that are shared by all users and by more than one application. For instance, after a typical Mac OS install, all the desktop pictures are in /Library/Desktop Pictures. When you use System Preferences to select your desktop picture, you can choose pictures from this folder or from your own iPhoto images.

In all these cases, users are not involved with this files. They can move or rename them, but they are discouraged from doing so.

NOTE

These are Apple's guidelines for the placement of app files. There are some special circumstances in which developers might have used other file locations.

Try It Yourself

Create a Semi-Hidden Database File on Mac OS X

Here are the steps involved in creating a semi-hidden database file:

1. Launch Xcode and create a new project with File, New, New Project. You can also click New Xcode Project on the startup screen.

2. At the left, select Mac OS X and Application, and then select Cocoa Application at the right, as shown in Figure 5.1.

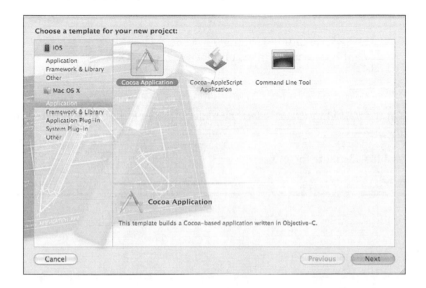

FIGURE 5.1
Create a Cocoa application.

3. Click Next.

4. As shown in Figure 5.2, provide a name for the app. Also provide an identifier for the company. This typically is the reverse of your domain name. You might add extra items at the end to create something like com.champlainarts.test.

FIGURE 5.2
Name the new app.

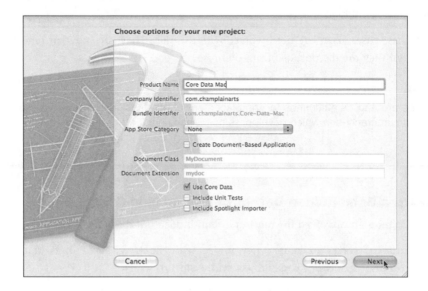

5. Select Core Data and do not click anything else (particularly do not select Create Document-Based Application).

▶See Hour 24, "Migrating Data Models." p. 423, for how to use document-based applications on Mac OS X and iOS.

6. Click Next.

7. On the following screen, select the folder location for the new app and click Create.

8. Xcode will create the project.

With the settings shown in Figure 5.2, Xcode will create a project that stores the database in the /~/Library/<your app name folder>. It will name it with the name of the project you typed in in Figure 5.1. If you have spaces in the name, Xcode will replace them with underscores. This code is placed in the app delegate file. Figure 5.3 shows the app delegate file selected in the project navigator at the left of the Xcode window. The relevant code is highlighted.

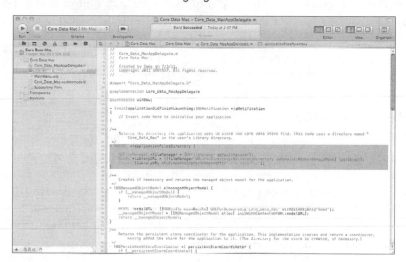

FIGURE 5.3
The code for the default filename and location is created by Xcode.

Change the Filename or Location

If you want to change the filename or location, you can do so by modifying the code for applicationFilesDirectory in the app delegate file. Listing 5.1 shows the code; the sections you might change are underlined.

LISTING 5.1 applicationFilesDirectory (Mac OS)

```
- (NSURL *)applicationFilesDirectory {

  NSFileManager *fileManager = [NSFileManager defaultManager];
  NSURL *libraryURL = [[fileManager URLsForDirectory:NSLibraryDirectory
    inDomains:NSUserDomainMask] lastObject];
  return [libraryURL URLByAppendingPathComponent:@"Core_Data_Mac"];
}
```

NSLibraryDirectory specifies /Library/. If you want to use /Library/Application Support/, change NSLibraryDirectory to NSApplicationSupportDirectory. NSUserDomainMask specifies the user's home directory. If you want to use the directory at the root of the disk, change NSUserDomainMask to NSLocalDomainMask. To find other options you can use, go to the Xcode Organizer and search on any of these constants.

In the last line of this method, the name of the app is automatically filled in for the name of the folder within the chosen library and domain. You can change that default folder name if you want.

The final step is to name the file itself (rather than the directory that is being used). That line of code is already created for you in the Xcode template. It is at the bottom of persistentStoreCoordinator. As you can see, it builds on the code elsewhere in the app delegate file that was shown in Listing 5.1. Here is the code that is generated by Xcode:

```
NSURL *url = [applicationFilesDirectory
  URLByAppendingPathComponent:@"Core_Data_Mac.storedata"];
```

Hidden Files on iOS

One of the important features of iOS and Cocoa Touch is that the folder structure is much the same as it is on Mac OS, but those folders in the library that users are asked to keep out of are not generally visible. Thus, to hide your database file, you need do nothing special except place it in the correct location. The code in Listing 5.2 parallels the Mac OS code shown previously in Listing 5.1. The main difference is that it is generating the application documents folder URL rather than the application files director. (This code applies to any document-based iOS app.)

LISTING 5.2   applicationDocumentsDirectory (iOS)

```
- (NSURL *)applicationDocumentsDirectory
{
  return [[[NSFileManager defaultManager] URLsForDirectory:NSDocumentDirectory
    inDomains:NSUserDomainMask] lastObject];
}
```

The final step is to add the filename to the directory path. As with Mac OS, this is done in persistentStoreCoordinator. Here is the code:

```
NSURL *storeURL = [[self applicationDocumentsDirectory]
  URLByAppendingPathComponent:@"Core_Data_iOS.sqlite"];
```

NOTE

Note that the two methods in Mac OS and iOS have some different structures, but these lines that you might need to change are the same in both versions.

Visible Files on iOS

If you want to make the application documents directory visible to iTunes for your iOS app, you simply change the app settings. Select the project at the top of the project navigator, and then select Info in the editor pane, as shown in Figure 5.4. Select any of the items in Custom iOS Target Properties. Hover the mouse at the right over the + and choose Application Supports iTune Sharing, as shown in Figure 5.4. This will add a new row below the selected row. Now, when users use iTunes to customize an app, they will see the contents of the directory and can add or remove files.

FIGURE 5.4
Set the app to support iTunes File Sharing.

NOTE

The formalization of sandboxes for apps allows iCloud to participate in sharing files and data automatically. If you are interested in these features, check out the iCloud documentation on developer.apple.com.

Summary

This hour has introduced you to the basics of data models in Core Data. You have seen how entities, attributes, and relationships work together.

Q&A

Q. *What is the purpose of the data model?*

A. The data model is the structural design of the database.

Q. *Do all the entities in a data model need to be related somehow?*

A. No. In many models, there is one root entity that is related in various ways to all the other entities, but that is not necessary.

Workshop

Quiz

1. *What is the difference between a relationship and an attribute?*

2. *Where is the actual database stored?*

Quiz Answers

1. A relationship is a link from one entity to another; an attribute is a data value for an entity.

2. You control where it is stored. It can be visible to the user or hide it.

Activities

As you work with data in your own life, try to figure out what the underlying data model might look like—what the entities are, what their attributes might be, and how they are related to one another. You can work through this exercise with accounting data, project management data, and even a web page with changing data (such as a news site).

HOUR 6

Working with the Core Data Model Editor

What You'll Learn in This Hour:

- ▶ Getting to know the Core Data model editor
- ▶ Creating entities
- ▶ Adding attributes
- ▶ Relating tables to one another
- ▶ Writing code with the Core Data model editor
- ▶ Creating fetch requests

Moving the Data Model from Paper to Xcode and the Core Data Model Editor

In the previous hour (Hour 5, "Working with Data Models"), you learned how to think about your data model and its structure—its entities, attributes, and relationships. In this hour, you will move the data model into Xcode and its Core Data model editor. Xcode will store the model and include it in your app's bundle when you build it.

> **NOTE**
>
> Hour 5 provides the logical and structural rationale for your data model. Many people prefer to jump right into Xcode and "real" development, although whiteboard and pencil-and-paper sketches are no less real. If you prefer to jump into Xcode (that is, you have skipped Hour 5), do not worry. Just remember that Hour 5 contains background about data models. As you work with the Xcode Core Data model

editor, if something is unclear or confusing, just flip back to Hour 5 and read it or just the relevant section to fill in the gaps. App development is definitely a linear process, but the line is never straight.

The basic prococess is simple:

1. Create a new Xcode project.

2. Select the option to use Core Data.

3. Continue into the Core Data model editor to create your data model.

Whether you are a Core Data novice or an experienced developer, it is much, much easier to let Xcode and its templates add the basic Core Data code to your project at the start. Retrofitting Core Data into an existing project is not an easy task, particularly if you are not experienced. The developer documentation from Apple does go through this process, but it is complicated and involves a number of detailed steps that must be done accurately. If you have any say in the matter, start from a new project so that all this is done for you automatically.

If you have an existing app to which you want to add Core Data, you can still take advantage of the Xcode Core Data templates. The process might be counterintuitive, but it works in many cases. Use Xcode to create a Core Data–based app. Next, take your existing app and move it into the Core Data–based app. In many cases, you can build and run your app right away. The Core Data code simply won't be used; if some of it is used at startup time, it will ignored. Your next step is to gradually migrate your existing code to use Core Data. If your existing code does not store data at all, this means simply using Core Data as you implement storage.

▶ This hour builds on Hour 2, "Creating a Simple App," p. 49, where you see step-by-step how to build an iOS and Mac app. The templates used here are Master-Detail Application on iOS and Cocoa Application on Mac OS. The options selected for each are shown in Figures 6.1 and 6.2.

For iOS, follow "Try It Yourself: Creating an iOS Project" in Hour 2. In step 3, do use the Core Data checkbox, as shown in Figure 6.1.

For Mac OS, follow "Try It Yourself: Creating a Mac Project" in Hour 2. In step 3, do use the Core Data checkbox, as shown in Figure 6.2.

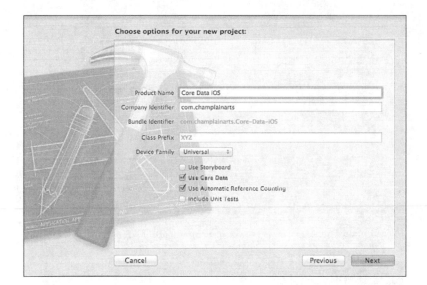

FIGURE 6.1
Create a new
iOS project and
use Core Data.

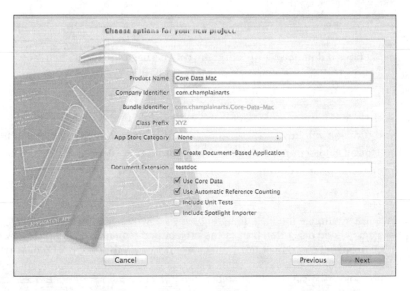

FIGURE 6.2
Create a new
Mac OS project
and use Core
Data.

Adding Entities to the Data Model

From this point on, the Core Data model editor and the steps you take are the same
for iOS and Mac OS. The only difference is in the groups and files shown in the project navigator. They differ from template to template on both platforms, but the data
model is the same. Open the project you have created in Xcode (or go back to Hour
2 and create it). Figure 6.3 shows the project if you have created it for iOS. The project itself (at the top of the project navigator) is selected.

FIGURE 6.3
Take a look at
what Xcode has
built for you.

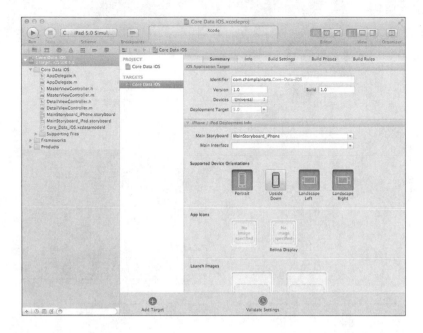

You already have a data model—it's in a file called `<name of your project>`
`.xcdatamodel`. (If your project name has spaces in it, they are replaced by underscores.) In Xcode, this file has been placed in the group named after your project.

On disk, this file is placed inside your app's folder. Note that if your app is named
Core Data iOS, you will have a Core Data iOS folder containing two items: an inter-
nal Core Data iOS folder and, next to it, Core Data iOS.xcodeproj, which is your
Xcode project file. Your xcdatamodel file is inside the internal project folder.

NOTE

If you want to rearrange the files and groups inside Xcode, feel free. Rearranging
the physical files on disk often breaks the project and requires repairs. If you want
to rename a project file, do not use the Finder. Starting with version 3, Xcode helps
you keep class names in sync with their files using the Edit, Refactor, Rename
command. Select the class name in either the implementation or header file,
choose the Refactor command, and accept the options to rename files. This will
keep the filenames in sync with the new class name; the various #import directives will also be changed appropriately.

Select the data model to open the Core Data model editor, as shown in Figure 6.4.

This project was built using the Master-Detail template in Xcode 4 (it replaces the
Split View Controller template from previous versions). This particular template
comes with a data model that has been built with a single entity and attribute.

FIGURE 6.4
Open the Core Data model editor.

When the iOS device is in landscape mode, the app displays a list of data elements in a split view controller; when you select a data element from the list, its details are shown in the other side of the split view controller. In portrait mode, the navigation bar at the top of the window has a button that displays the list of data elements in a pop-over. You can add data to the app as it runs by tapping the +; a item will be added to the list. Its data is set automatically to the timestamp of the time at which you clicked +.

▶ You will find out more about the Master-Detail Application template in Hour 14, "Working with Storyboards and Swapping View," p. 239.

In Figure 6.4, you can see the Core Data model editor in the center of the window. In the sidebar at the left of the Core Data model editor are three sections for entities, fetch requests, and configurations. Most of your basic work is done in the entities section.

Figure 6.5 shows the Core Data model editor for a Mac OS app built with the Cocoa Application template.

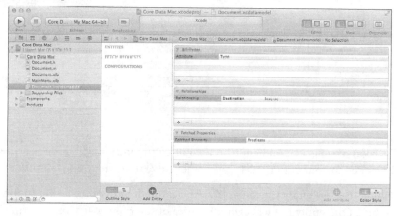

FIGURE 6.5
Examining a template for a Mac OS app.

The biggest difference that you will notice is that this template does not contain any entities—this model is totally empty. This gives you an opportunity to experiment with adding an entity to a data model.

▼ **Try It Yourself**

Adding an Entity to the Data Model

To add an entity to your data model, all you need to know is what you will name it and what kind of data it will contain. Here is the process of adding an entity called Customer to your Mac OS model. This is the beginning of implementing the jobs and customers data model:

1. Start from a new project template, as described previously in "Moving the Data Model from Paper to Xcode and the Core Data Model Editor." Make sure you use the Cocoa Application template in the Mac OS section, and choose the Core Data option.

2. Open the Core Data model, as shown in Figure 6.5. It should not have any entities, fetch requests, or configurations at this point.

3. Click the + Add Entity button at the bottom of the sidebar. A new entity will be created, and you can change its name, as you see in Figure 6.6.

FIGURE 6.6
Create a new entity.

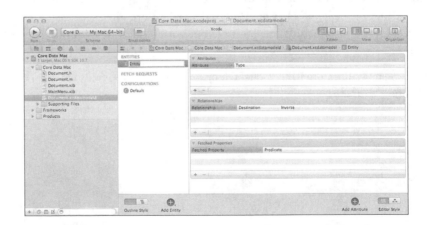

4. As soon as you click Add Entity, a default configuration will automatically be added to your data model. You do not have to do anything with it.

5. Name the new entity Customer. You can name it either by clicking in the name of the entity or by showing Utilities at the right of the window and

choosing the Core Data inspector. The name must begin with an uppercase letter and can contain only letters, numbers, and underscores.

FIGURE 6.7
Name the new entity.

TIP

After you have your first entity, you can add attibutes to it. (An entity without any attributes is usually either a mistake or a work in progress.) In the case of this app, you are modeling an object with direct parallels to the real world, so the list of attributes should not be difficult to create. You probably want a name, an address, and some contact information, such as an email address.

Try It Yourself

Adding an Attribute to an Entity

The process of adding an attribute to an entity is similar to the process of adding an entity to the data model, but it has two additional steps. You need to select the entity to which you are adding the attribute (all entities are simply added to the data model itself). As you add the attribute, not only do you have to name it, but you also have to specify its type:

1. Select the Customer entity.

2. Click the Add Attribute button at the bottom of the Core Data model editor, or click the + at the bottom of the attributes section, as shown in Figure 6.8.

3. As you see in Figure 6.9, the new attribute is named attribute (notice that attributes begin with a lowercase letter) and its type is undefined. Also note that Xcode has immediately shown you an error in the status area and at the upper-right of the Core Data model editor. You can click on the red error circle to review the errors. As shown in Figure 6.9, the error is that you have not created a type for the attribute.

FIGURE 6.8
Add a new
attribute.

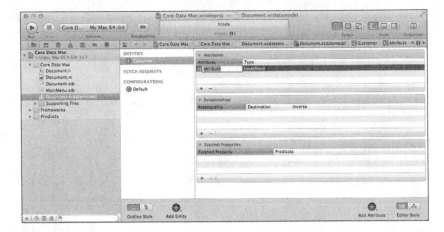

FIGURE 6.9
Review errors
as they arise.

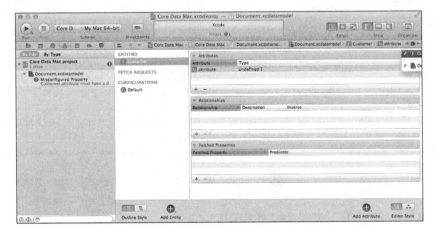

4. You can set the name of the attribute either in the list of attributes or in the
   utility area at the right of the window, as shown in Figure 6.10.

FIGURE 6.10
Name the
attribute and
set its type.

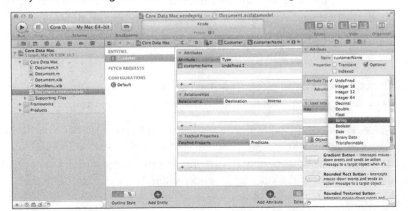

You can set various other settings for attributes. For example, you can make some attributes optional and others required. A customer name, for example, might be required, but some businesses refer to customers by address or phone number. These settings have to be adjusted in the utility area using the Data Model inspector.

Choosing the Editor Style

The Core Data model editor has two styles for its editor: *table* style (that is the style that has been shown so far) and *grid* style. You switch back and forth between them using the button at the lower-right of the Core Data model editor. Which one you use is a matter of personal preference, and many people switch back and forth between them. When you are working with relationships (which is what you will do next), it is easiest to work in the grid style. To get ready for relationships, you will need another table: Job. Create it just as you did the Customer table. Now, choose grid style, as shown in Figure 6.11.

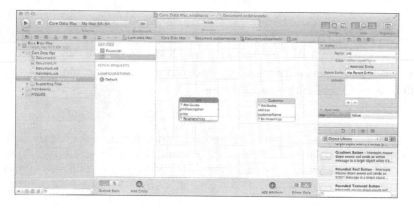

FIGURE 6.11
Use grid editor style.

NOTE

Relationships most often describe the relationships between two tables. It is possible to have a self-join relationship in which a table is related to itself. That is a somewhat special and more complicated relationship than one involving two tables. However, if you have database experience, rest assured that self-joins are alive and well in Core Data.

As you can see, the information is now shown in a diagram. You can move the entities around as you wish.

TIP

Sometimes, when you first enter grid style, the entities are on top of one another. Just drag them apart and rearrange them as you want.

Also, note that in the grid style, although attributes are listed, their types are shown only in the utility area (see Figure 6.12). Also in Figure 6.12, note that the small disclosure triangle on the Add Attribute button brings up a shortcut menu to let you add an attribute, a relationship, or a fetched property.

FIGURE 6.12
Add attributes, relationships, or fetched properties in grid editor style.

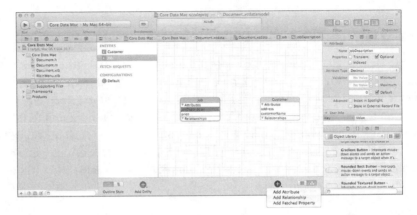

You can also see that more attributes have been added to the two entities in the data model. Add them before you go on. Price can be either a decimal or a float, but it definitely is not a string as the others are.

TIP

As you add entities and attributes, you will find that it makes sense to establish some consistent styles in the naming. For example, the `customerName` attribute could equally have been named `customer_name`. Within a given project, it can be easier to pick one style rather than another if you have a choice.

Adding Relationships to a Data Model

The main relationship that you need relates the Job and Customer entities together. Each relationship in the Core Data model editor links two entities, and each relationship has its rules.

The two most important rules are the following:

▶ **Cardinality**—The number of instances of the relationship that can exist

▶ **Delete rule**—What happens when the relationship is deleted

NOTE

It is important to note that database designers often speak of relationships as being *bidirectional*. In other words, there is a relationship between jobs and customers, and in real life and some database tools, you can look at it from either perspective. In FileMaker, for example, the relationships graph lets you draw relationships between two tables, and you can use it from either table to access the other table.

Core Data takes a different approach. In Core Data, relationships are unidirectional. For example, there can be one relationship from Job to Customer and a second relationship from Customer to Job. The two are combined in the data model by letting you specify an *inverse* relationship for each relationship. Thus, you have the concept of a bidirectional relationship achieved in a different way. You can create relationships by adding them with the Add button; you also will see how to create them by control-dragging from one attribute to another (usually in two different entities). In that case, the inverse relationship is automatically created for you.

You might wonder how relationships are handled in the SQL world. That is done in yet another way. In the world of SQL, relationships are conceptual: You draw them on paper and whiteboards. You implement them in SQL as part of the SELECT statements that you write (specifically part of a WHERE clause).

To sum up:

▶ Relationships are always part of the conceptual design of a database, except for the very simplest single table database.

▶ Relationships in Core Data consist of two unidirectional relationships between two entities that are the inverse of one another.

Specifying Cardinality

Cardinality is a part of every relationship in a relational database. For example, the relationship from a job to a customer is one-to-one: Each job has only one customer. In the other direction, a customer can have many jobs. That is referred to as a *one-to-many* relationship. You can also have *many-to-many* relationships. In the job and customer scenario, this would happen if two or more people shared a job. You can see it being played out in many restaurants as the people at a table (the multiple diners) decide on which wine to order (in this case, the wine is the job).

Many-to-many relationships are very common, but they can be a bit tricky to implement. There is no getting around the fact that you need to have a table between the two ends of the relationship (this intermediate table is technically called a *join table*). This is true with Core Data, but you do not have to worry about it. If you create a many-to-many relationship, Core Data will automatically implement it for you.

Choosing a Delete Rule

There are four types of delete rules, and you must specify one of them for each relationship. Relationships and their delete rules are in the domain of the database owner; this is not a technical decision but a business one. If you are building a database for someone else, you must have this discussion with them.

Here are your choices:

▶ **Nullify**—The inverse relationship is set to null. For example, if you allowed a customer with one or more jobs to be deleted, the relationship from the job to the no-longer-existing customer would be set to null rather than some value that might cause problems at runtime.

▶ **Deny**—The attempt to delete an object will fail if you choose this rule. In the case of jobs and customers, if you set the customer-to-job delete rule, you will get an error if you attempt to delete a customer that has one or more jobs.

▶ **Cascade**—In this case, deleting a customer with one or more jobs will delete the customer and all the jobs.

▶ **No Action**—Users can do what they want. This value empowers users of the database to destroy its *relational integrity*—the logic that holds it together. This is an option to choose for the case in which some action in the real world is needed as part of the relationships.

In general with databases, any time you can push validation and error-checking into the database itself rather than into code that has to be rewritten and rewritten over time, you are better off. Properly chosen delete rules will make your database more robust and will mean you have less code to write. All you do is click a combo box to select the delete rule.

Try It Yourself ▼

Add a Relationship

Now that you have seen the basics of relationships, it is time to try your hand at creating one:

1a. You can create the relationship in either table or grid editor style. In grid editor style, hold down Control while you drag from one entity to another. After you have held down Control for a moment, you will see the pointer change to a crosshair icon and you can draw the relationship. You do not have to be specific about where in each entity you begin and end your relationship. Figure 6.13 shows the line as it is being drawn. You can select the attributes later.

Release the mouse button to complete the relationship. Note that the line extends in both directions now (indicating the inverse relationship), as shown in Figure 6.14.

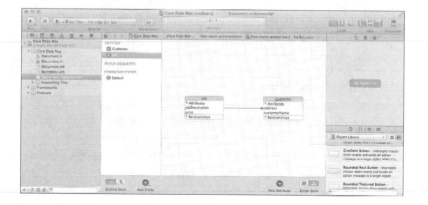

FIGURE 6.13
Draw a relationship.

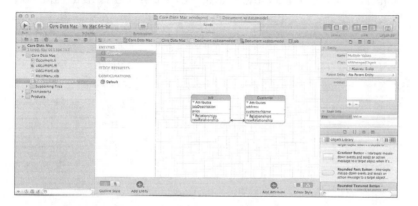

FIGURE 6.14
Release the mouse button to complete the relationship.

1b.   In table editor style, select the entity that will be the start of the relationship. Add a new relationship either with the disclosure triangle next to the Add Attribute button as shown in Figure 6.15 or by using the + at the bottom of the relationships table. (The Add button is "sticky": It actually adds whatever you last used it for, be it an attribute, a relationship, or a fetched property.) Choose the destination entity (the other end of the relationship) from the pop-up menu, as shown in Figure 6.15.

FIGURE 6.15
Add a relationship in table editor style.

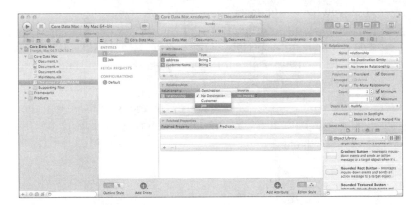

2.   Double-click the name of the new relationship in either table or grid editor style, and change its name to something more meaningful than newRelationship. In the Job entity, the relationship points to the Customer entity, so name this relationship *customer*. In the Customer entity, the relationship points to the Job entity, so name it *jobs*. (Relationships are often lowercase.) Also at this time, use the data model inspector to make the jobs relationship a to-many relationship, as shown in Figure 6.16. (Note that the checkbox is labeled to-many, but the full name is one-to-many.) Also note that in grid view (shown in Figure 6.17), double-arrows are shown at the end of the to-many relationship.

FIGURE 6.16
Name and specify the cardinality of the relationships.

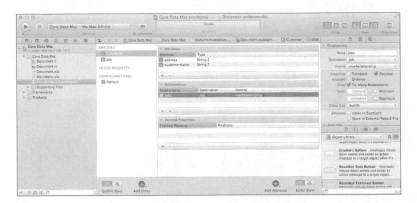

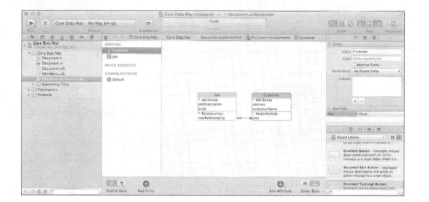

FIGURE 6.17
Double-headed
arrows indicate
a to-many
relationship.

3. Set the delete rule in the utility area, as shown in Figure 6.18.

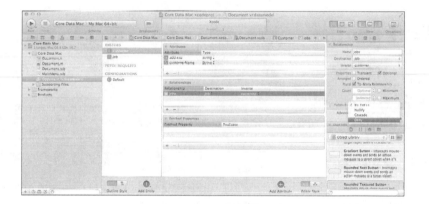

FIGURE 6.18
Set the
delete rule.

Summary

Q&A

Q. *Why do you use database rules rather than into your own code?*

A. Once the database has rules, it does the work for you. All you have to do is check the result of the tests it performs.

Q. *How do you add Core Data to an Xcode project?*

A. It is much easier to create a project from a template that includes Core Data. In fact, if you have to add Core Data after the fact, it might be easier to start from a new project and move your existing code over.

Workshop

Quiz

1. *What is cardinality?*

2. *What are delete rules, and where to do you specify them?*

Quiz Answers

1. Cardinality specifies the number of entities allowed at each end of a relationship, as in one-to-one, one-to-many, or many-to-many.

2. Delete rules determine what happens when one entity in a relationship is deleted. Options include doing nothing, deleting the other entity, and preventing deletion. This helps the database preserve its relational integrity so that, if it relies on relationships, they are there.

Activities

Explore the Xcode templates and check out their data models. You will find data models in some of the iOS examples. Try using the Model Detail template and running it to see how Core Data works. You can also try sample code for Core Data from developer.apple.com.

What Managed Objects Can Do

What You'll Learn in This Hour:

▶ Getting inside managed objects

▶ Putting managed objects in context

▶ Exploring data types—Booleans, BLOBs, and dates

▶ Transforming data

▶ Validating data

Using Managed Objects

Managed objects are one of the primary components of the Core Data architecture. An NSManagedObject represents a record from the database (*persistent store* in Core Data terms). It is managed objects that you deal with in your code: you create, save, modify, and delete them as the user requests.

▶ To use managed objects in your app, you need to have built the Core Data stack as described previously in Hour 4, "Getting the Big Core Data Picture," p. 85, to establish the connection between the data store and your app. You also will have needed to fetch some data; that is described in Hour 9, "Fetching Data," p. 153.

NOTE

Although the fetch precedes the use of the data as your app runs, managed objects—the result of the fetch—are described first so that when it comes time to fetch the data, you will understand what you are working with. If you want to read Hour 9 before this one or even flip back and forth between them, feel free to do so.

Deciding Whether to Override NSManagedObject

When you fetch data, you can fetch it into NSManagedObject objects or fetch it into subclasses of NSManagedObject that you create. Either way, at bottom you are dealing with a managed object.

Using NSManagedObject Directly

Using NSManagedObject directly has one very big advantage—it is much easier than overriding it in many cases. The class contains all the functionality you need for basic operations. You can access the data within the objects using Key-Value Coding (KVC). The two accessors for KVC are the getter (valueForKey) and the setter (setValueForKey).

For example, in the Master-Detail Xcode template for iOS, here is the code that displays data for the timeStamp attribute of the Event entity in a table cell:

```
cell.textLabel.text = [[managedObject valueForKey:@"timeStamp"]
  description];
```

NOTE

The code in this Hour is the Master-Detail Application project with the checkboxes for Core Data checked and the Universal option set.

▼ **Try It Yourself**

Understand valueForKey

This code is typical of code you will use repeatedly, so it is worth stepping through this line of code. The easiest way to do this is to use Xcode and its Quick Help. Figure 7.1 shows a Master-Detail Xcode project. MasterDetailController.m is open, and it is scrolled to configureCell:atIndexPath, which is the code that populates a cell. The line of code shown here is line 279 in Figure 7.1.

1. Open the utility area at the right of the Xcode window, and select Quick Help at the top of the pane.

2. Click textLabel to select it; you'll see what it is in Quick Help. The table cell has a textLabel attribute, and Quick Help shows you it is a UILabel object.

3. Select the text property, and Quick Help shows you it is a NSString.

FIGURE 7.1
Use Quick Help
to look up your
code.

4. On the right side of the replacement operator (the equal sign) is an
Objective-C clause that is easiest to read from the inside out (that is common with Objective-C as well as with parenthesized statements in other
languages). The innermost code is as follows:

```
[managedObject valueForKey:@"timeStamp"]
```

For the managed object that has been fetched into managedObject, the
valueForKey: accessor returns the value for the timeStamp attribute.

5. Select valueForKey:. Quick Help tells your return value is an id—that is, it is,
any object that is a descendant of NSObject. In this case, it is the timeStamp
attribute of the managed object.

6. Moving out to the next level of brackets, the code is as follows:

```
[[managedObject valueForKey:@"timeStamp"] description]
```

7. Select description to see what it is. Quick Help shows you that it is an
NSString and that it is described in the NSObject protocol.

▲

TIP

In Step 7, if you happen to follow the links, you will notice a comment that it is
used in the debugger, and that it is required for all objects that adopt the NSObject
protocol. This means you have a string available to describe every object you deal
with. And, in this case, it will describe the contents of the managed object's content so that you can place it into the table cell for display. NSObject implements a
default method, and NSManagedObject overrides it—as you are free to do.

In MasterDetailController.m when a new Event entity is created, its value is set using key-value coding. Here is the code snippet (it is at line 291 of Figure 7.1):

```
[newManagedObject setValue:[NSDate date] forKey:@"timeStamp"];
```

With these two KVC calls, you can bridge the gap between the persistent store in Core Data and data in your app.

> **NOTE**
>
> Get in the habit of clicking through to the references shown in Quick Help so that you gain familiarity with the framework. UILabel, for example, might sound like a label field to place next to a data entry field, and you can certainly use it for that. But as you will see, it has a number of properties you can set that you will find handy in a variety of circumstances. font, textColor, textAlignment, and numberOfLines are some of the more useful ones. numberOfLines in particular is worth remembering because this is how you place multiline text in what appears to be a text field (UILabel is actually a descendent of UIView).

Overriding `NSManagedObject`

When you consider that NSManagedObject has the major functionality for storage and retrieval built in to it and that it conforms to KVC so you can get data into and out of it, why would you ever want to complicate your life and override it? The answer is that there are certain situations in which you must override it:

▶ **Validation**—NSManagedObject handles basic validation such as making certain that data conforms to the data type you have specified and the other settings in the Attributes inspector. If you have your own validation rules, though, you must implement them yourself.

▶ **Transformation**—If you need to transform the data type returned from the persistent store to another type for use in your app, you need to subclass NSManagedObject. The most frequent transformation involves pictures: You can store a photo as binary data using JPEG, and when it is retrieved from the database, you need to *transform* it back into an image.

  ▶ There is more on validation in Hour 18, "Validating Data," and Hour 22, "Managing Validation."

If either of these cases is true, you need to create your own subclass of NSManaged-Object. There are other reasons you might consider subclassing NSManagedObject, including implementing transient data that is not kept in the persistent store.

CAUTION

There are also performance issues involved in this choice. When you use your own classes, you can refer to the attributes of the Core Data entities as properties of the class that subclasses NSManagedObject. As noted several times throughout this book, be aware of issues that can impact performance, but remember that the only way to determine if there is a performance impact is to test with the actual environment that will be used. Many Core Data apps for mobile devices access web services and shared databases over the Web and the mobile network. Obviously, performance in those cases is likely to be extremely problematic ranging to nonexistent in many places. However, for self contained apps designed for personal use and possible sharing via iCloud or email, the quantity of data involved is often so small that performance issues do not enter into design decisions.

It is a good practice in all cases such as this to document the design decisions you make. That way, if you or someone else comes back to reuse the code in the future, you or she will know which lines of code implement basic functionality and which lines of code bypass or work around performance issues.

Try It Yourself   ▼

Subclass NSManagedObject

If you have decided to subclass NSManagedObject for one of your entities, you have to get ready to write code. With Xcode, you should set aside a block of time to do this arduous task. For beginners, that might be as much as two minutes. The folks at Apple have made it easy for you.

1. You can start from the project you created in Hour 6. Pick up as it was at the end of the hour.

NOTE

Remember that you can download each hour's sample file. For example, for this hour, you want the Hour 6 file. You might want to copy it into a different directory (and perhaps rename it Hour 7) so that you do not get confused.

2. In the Core Data model editor, select one of the entities, as shown in Figure 7.2. Choose Editor, Create NSManagedObject Subclass.

3. Select the directory containing your other project files, as shown in Figure 7.3. You can leave all the other settings as is. Click Create.

4. The header and implementation files are created. The next section of this hour reviews what has been created.

5. For now, you might want to rearrange the Project navigator. Create a new group by selecting the project header and choosing File, New, New Group.

FIGURE 7.2
Begin to create
a subclass.

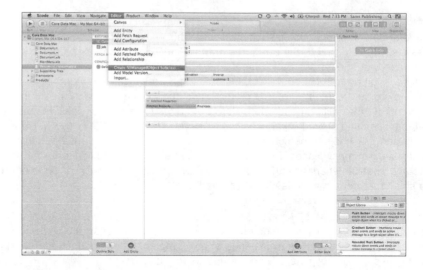

FIGURE 7.3
Create the
subclass.

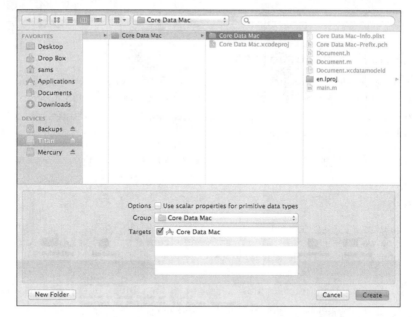

You can name it Data Model. You can drag the two new files into it along
with the data model itself, as shown in Figure 7.4.

6. Xcode has automatically created the two files for you. Notice that in accor-
   dance with modern style, there are no instance variables; instead, declared
   properties (not named) are used. Also, the settings (nonatomic, retain) that
   are appropriate for `NSManagedObject` descendants are set.

FIGURE 7.4
Rearrange the files.

The two string attributes are NSString properties, and the relationship is now an NSSet. Finally, the utility routines to add and delete the entity objects are provided, along with methods to add or remove the sets of objects (that is, the relationships).

7. When you move over to the implementation, as shown in Figure 7.5, you will see that the properties do not use @synthesize; rather, they use @dynamic to indicate that they will be created automatically by Core Data.

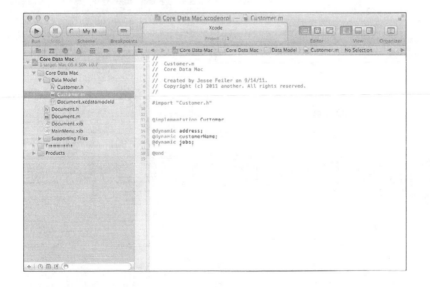

FIGURE 7.5
Review the implementation of your NSManaged Object subclass.

You will find out more about using model classes in the next hour.

TIP

Note that you can mix and match subclasses of `NSManagedObject` with `NSManagedObject` itself. If you have one entity that requires a transformation, it needs to be a subclass, but other entities that do not have that need can remain as they are. You use KVC to access their properties.

▶ Implementing validation is covered in Hour 22, "Managing Validation," p. 393.

Implementing Transformation in an NSManagedObject Subclass

The most common transformation is between an image format and binary data in an `NSData` object. The code in Listing 7.1 does just that (it is based on the `iPhoneCoreDataRecipes` sample). You do not need to customize this code at all for your own use.

The one point you do need to customize is the name of the methods line. You will use this in the Core Data model editor when you specify that the attribute is transformable, as shown in Figure 7.6.

FIGURE 7.6
Include your transformer code in the Core Data inspector.

The name of the transformer in the Data Model inspector matches the name in the first line of the corresponding code in your project. This code is often placed in the implementation file for your class just below the implementation for the class itself. Thus, referring to Figure 7.6, the file would contain the following:

```
@implementation Customer
...
@implementation ImageToDataTransformer
...
```

Because the code in Listing 7.1 indicates that the transformation can be reversed, you do not have to write anything else. When Core Data is transforming the value, it knows in which direction it is going and either calls your implementation of transformedValue or reverseTransformedValue.

LISTING 7.1 Transforming an Image to and from **NSData**

```
@implementation ImageToDataTransformer

+ (BOOL)allowsReverseTransformation {
    return YES;
}

+ (Class)transformedValueClass {
    return [NSData class];
}

- (id)transformedValue:(id)value {
    NSData *data = UIImagePNGRepresentation(value);
    return data;
}

- (id)reverseTransformedValue:(id)value {
    UIImage *uiImage = [[UIImage alloc] initWithData:value];
    return [uiImage autorelease];
}
```

Summary

The entities in your data model are instances of NSManagedObject when your app runs. Whether they are NSManagedObject instances or instances of your subclass depends on whether you need to move beyond the basic functionality of NSManagedObject.

Q&A

Q. *What is Key-Value Coding?*

A. KVC is available for most objects in Cocoa. Instead of referencing an object's data using an instance variable (very bad form) or a setter/getter (better), you can ask the object to give you the value using valueForKey. Among other things, this means you can determine which property you want to obtain at runtime.

Q. *How does Quick Help work?*

A. Select a syntax element in the Xcode text editor, and its reference information appears in the Utility area. The level of detail varies depending on whether this is something that you have created or is part of a framework.

Workshop

Quiz

1. *What is a transformation?*

2. *When do you override* NSManagedObject?

Quiz Answers

1. A transformation data type indicates that at runtime, your subclass of NSManagedObject will transform the raw data from Core Data.

2. You override NSManagedObject if you want to use transformations, if you want to implement your own validation rules, and if you want to be able to connect properties of the NSManagedObject directly to the interface (rather than using KVC).

Activities

Look at iPhone Core Data Recipes in the sample code on developer.apple.com to see how a photo is transformed to and from digital data.

HOUR 8

Controllers: Integrating the Data Model with Your Code

What You'll Learn in This Hour:

- ▶ Understanding controllers in iOS and Mac OS
- ▶ Working with view controllers on iOS
- ▶ Working with data controllers on iOS

Looking Inside Model/View/Controller

Mac OS and iOS are built on the model/view/controller (MVC) design pattern. The concepts are simple: The model is the data, the view is the interface, and the controller mediates between those two objects. This allows the model and the interface to be independent of one another. Both need to know about the controller, but neither needs to know about the other.

This is a fairly common description of MVC. Its disadvantage is that it tends to suggest to many people that the controller object is a second-class part of the picture. This is natural because users can see the interface and work with the data; all that controller stuff might make these things happen, but the controller itself is not visible.

In practice, the bulk of the programming work for many apps is the controller. By treating the data and the interface separately from the controller, their development tools can be highly organized and constructed. It is that mess of the controller where those elegant patterns tend to get a bit muddied.

To be the go-between for the model and the view, controllers need access to both. This access is implemented differently on Mac OS and iOS, with part of the difference being related to the presence or absence of the menu bar.

This hour focuses on the concepts, issues, and tools. In the next hour, you will find hands-on examples you can try for yourself.

> **NOTE**
>
> This hour might be the best example of how programming has moved away from the procedural style of "Hello World." Rather than the lengthy sections of spaghetti-like code that implemented systems decades ago, we are now using a multitude of small procedural steps and declarative programming in the form of checkboxes and connections that are drawn graphically. This does produce more stable code, but it takes some getting used to. In this hour, you will jump from text-based code editors to the graphically oriented Interface Builder editor, with stops along the way in the Bindings inspector, Connection inspector, and Attribute inspector. With the Xcode 4 window displayed in Lion's full-screen mode, this is easy to do. And once you have been through a few Try It Yourself sequences in this book, you will get the hang of it.

Controlling Data

On Mac OS, controlling data is managed by *key-value coding (KVC)*, *key-value observing (KVO)*, and *bindings*. Tools are implemented in the Cocoa framework on Mac OS for you to use to work with bindings. You can access them through the Bindings inspector for an object. On iOS, bindings do not exist, which means you must write code to provide the functionality you have on Mac OS of binding data to interface objects.

Controlling Views

The situation is reversed when it comes to views. Xcode and iOS provide tools for you, but you have to develop your own view management on Mac OS. You can see the difference when you create a new project in Xcode. Figure 8.1 shows the eight application templates for iOS.

Figure 8.2 shows the three application templates for Mac OS; only one of them (Cocoa) is designed for Mac apps.

One of the reasons for this difference is the menu bar. Menu commands have been at the heart of Mac apps since the beginning in 1984. Interface Builder lets you build menus, and you can connect menu commands to windows that you also create in Interface Builder. This is the heart of many Interface Builder demos over the years: You can build an app without writing code as you have to do when you implement other user controls such as buttons.

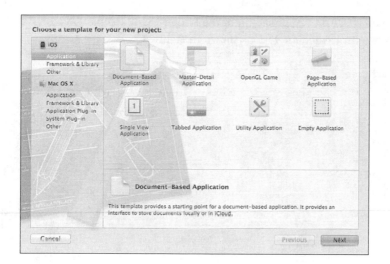

FIGURE 8.1
Choose iOS application templates in Xcode.

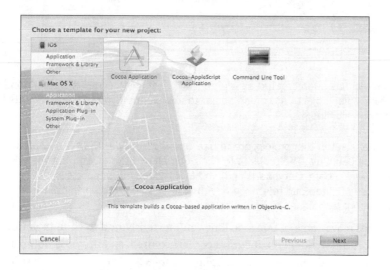

FIGURE 8.2
Choose Mac OS application templates in Xcode.

NOTE

With the advent of larger screens over the years, there is room for additional interface elements like buttons; in addition, new types of interface controls such as floating windows (as they were initially named) and inspectors provide controls in places other than the menu bar. Nevertheless, the menu bar is at the heart of the Mac look-and-feel. Full-screen apps in Lion begin to move beyond the menu bar, which is normally not shown in full-screen mode (you have to hover the pointer over the top of the screen to show it).

Without a menu bar on iOS, the designers at Apple give you tools such as navigation bars and toolbars that often contain buttons that substitute for menu commands.

When you create an iOS project from the Master-Detail template, you have a master view controller created for you, as shown in Figure 8.3.

FIGURE 8.3
Look at connections for an iOS app.

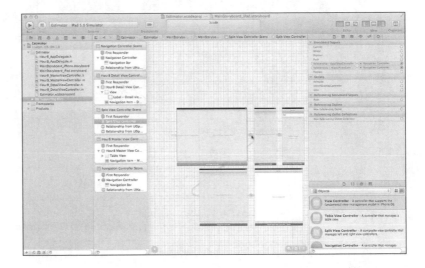

This project has been created as a universal project with code for both iPhone and iPad. Universal projects are much easier to implement if you use storyboards rather than nib files.

The options set in this project are to use Storyboard, Core Data, and Automatic Reference Counting. The projects in this book all use Core Data, but they deliberately show you both storyboard and nib file interfaces in separate projects, as well as the use of automatic reference counting in addition to older memory management techniques.

Storyboards move some of the code that you previously had to write in your own project (particularly in your subclasses of view controllers) into the graphical user interface of Interface Builder. As you see in Figure 8.3, a storyboard consists of scenes that are view controllers that are connected by *segues* (the small circles on the connecting lines.

In the Connections inspector at the right (the right-pointing arrow in the circle), you connect objects in your code to interface objects. As you saw in Figure 8.3, you can connect objects in a segue to the scenes in your storyboard to graphically diagram the control of the user interface.

▶ Hour 14, "Working with Storyboards," shows you the details of using storyboards. Hour 19, "Using UITableView on iOS," shows a project built using nib files instead of storyboards, and the following section of this hour walks you through a Mac OS implementation using nib files (there are no storyboards on Mac OS).

Integrating Views and Data on Mac OS

NOTE

Integrating views and data is the heart of the power of Interface Builder and Cocoa (as well as Cocoa Touch). This is a walkthrough of the process. You will see how to implement it for yourself in Part III of this book, "Developing the Core Data Interface."

In the Departments And Employees sample code for Mac OS, you can also see connections in the Connections inspector. Here in Figure 8.4, each of the items at the right of the Connections inspector is present in the document structure at the left of the Interface Builder pane; the items in the inspector on the left are variables in code from the sample. The connections are for NewObjectSheetController, which is selected in the document structure.

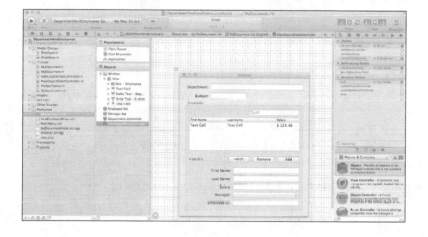

FIGURE 8.4
Look at connections for a Mac OS app.

Bindings come into play on Mac OS. You can see how they are managed by opening the utility area and showing the Object library. Select Objects & Controllers from the pop-up, and you will see the objects you can drag into a nib file using Interface Builder editor. If you look closely at the icons in the document structure at the left of Figure 8.4, you will see that `Employee Set` and `Manager Set` are array controllers, `Department Controller` is an object controller, and `NewObjectSheetController` is an custom-written object in this project. It is implemented in `NewObjectSheetController.h` and `NewObjectSheetController.m`.

For Mac OS, the items in this list fall into two categories. The first is composed of three single objects; the second category consists of five controllers that manage groups of objects—in a Core Data app, these usually are relationships.

The single items are as follows:

▶ **Object**—An object represents a basic `NSObject` subclass. It is designed for you to add it to Interface Builder and then use the Attributes inspector to change its name to `MySpecialObject` (or whatever you want). When the object is created at runtime, the code in MySpecialObject.h and MySpecialObject.m runs to provide that object's functionality. In Interface Builder, it uses this generic icon. You also can set some attributes that apply to all `NSObject` subclasses. You can create connections to subclasses of objects so that, for example, a button might send a message to one or more connected objects.

▶ **View Controller**—This is a view controller or a custom subclass that you implement in your code. You might override it in your code, but you often do not. (Compare this to `UIViewController` in iOS, which you almost always override.)

▶ **Managed Object Context**—This is just what its name suggests: the context for an `NSManagedObject` or its descendants. The managed object context helps you interact with the persistent store.

In the second section are the controllers that manage groups. Each of them is aware of bindings and can be accessed in the Bindings inspector if you add it to a nib file in Interface Builder. You can bind properties of the instance of one of these objects to user interface elements. The group-based controllers are as follows:

▶ **Object Controller**—This controller manages any object.

▶ **Array Controller**—This is a collection of objects that are stored in an array or a set.

▶ **Dictionary Controller and Tree Controller**—These are the standard collection objects that store different configurations of data.

▶ **User Defaults Controller**—This is a special controller that manages user default values.

The Connections inspector at the right of the window shown in Figure 8.5 lets you see how the interface elements connect to the data when Document Controller is selected in document structure at the left of the canvas. In the Referencing Bindings section mid-way down the Connections inspector, a text field, for example, is connected to selection.budget through a binding (this is the Budget field at the top of the window being drawn in Interface Builder). Likewise, another text field (Department) is connected to selection.name through another binding.

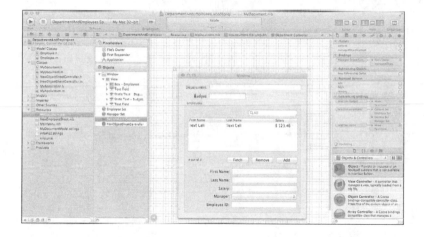

FIGURE 8.5
Trace connections and bindings.

In fact, the connection is actually between the value property of the text field and the data from Core Data, as shown in Figure 8.6. In that figure, the field is selected so you see the connection in reverse (from the text field to the data).

In Figure 8.7, you return to the concept of controllers as you examine the Employee Set controller. It is selected in the document structure, and the Binding inspector is shown on the right. You will see that in the controller content section, the Employee Set is bound to the Department Controller. (contentset is a binding of NSArrayController, which is what Employee Set is.) Here in the Binding inspector, you can see that the binding is established from the contentset property in Employee Set to the key selection and the value employees. As you might expect, selection is the selected item in an array and employees is a Core Data model relationship for this example.

FIGURE 8.6
Trace the opposite direction of the connection.

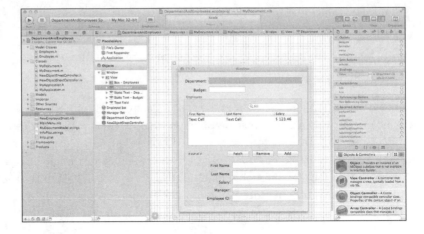

FIGURE 8.7
Examine the binding.

NOTE

And that is how the selected records from the Core Data model wind up being displayed in the table in the middle of the view. The reason for this complication is that there is no problem connecting a field to a single data value, but when you have an array of an unknown number of objects that must be used to populate a table, things get complicated very quickly.

As you walk through several of these examples, you will start to see how they fit together, so do not panic if the details are not yet clear.

Integrating Views and Data on iOS

With iOS apps, you do not have key-value binding, so you need to work with what you have—and that is usually connections. As you saw in the previous section, connections work perfectly well for binding a single data value to the value property of a text view. The complication comes when you want to bind a collection of objects to an interface element that can manage that set. In practical terms, that means a table. The function of binding in Mac OS is performed by code you write.

If you explore the Object library of an iOS project, you will see a different set of objects and controllers for Cocoa Touch apps compared to the Mac OS objects described previously in this hour.

In this case, there are two objects and six controllers.

The iOS objects are as follows:

▶ **Object**—This serves the same purpose as the same item in Mac OS.

▶ **External Object**—This is a placeholder for an object that is outside the app's world. There is more on this in Hour 24, "Migrating Data Models," p. 423.

The controllers are as follows:

▶ **View Controller**—This serves the same purpose as the controller with the same name on Mac OS in general, but it conforms to the iOS view management structure.

▶ **Table View Controller**—This frequently-used controller incorporates much of the bindings functionality, particularly in its UITableViewDataSource protocol, which is frequently added to your subclass of a UITableViewController. UITableViewDelegate is also frequently added to the subclasses to implement features of display and functionality, such as setting row height and managing selections and edits. These are available as separate protocols because, in many cases, your subclass of UITableViewController needs both of them to function (it might need to check data values for a specific cell to calculate its row height, for example), but in other cases, they may be adopted by separate objects.

▶ **Split View Controller, Navigation Controller, Tab Bar Controller, and Page View Controller**—These implement functionality that is common on iOS. These are more complex than the basic UIViewController, and they illustrate the differences noted previously with regard to the roles of controllers in the two environments. Much of the specialized code in these controllers is devoted to managing a set or sequence of separate views—just as menu commands can do on Mac OS.

Summary

This hour has explored the roles of controllers in Core Data. On Mac OS, controllers typically mediate between data structures such as arrays and your interface elements. On iOS, they typically do that but also provide the functionality for view management with navigators and toolbars. The difference reflects the fact that, without a menu bar, on iOS you need to implement view management that menu commands can handle on Mac OS.

Q&A

Q. *Because bindings don't exist on iOS, how do you provide that functionality?*

A. You provide binding-like functionality in the code you write for an iOS controller. That is why you almost always override the basic view controllers in your iOS code but do so less often on Mac OS.

Q. *When do you use Object from the Object library?*

A. Any time you need to add an object to your storyboard or nib file for which there is no object in the library, use Object and then immediately change its name in the Identity inspector. Then you will be able to connect elements in the interface to and from properties in your custom class.

Workshop

Quiz

1. *How are Core Data relationships represented at runtime?*

2. *What do bindings rely on to work?*

Quiz Answers

1. At runtime, relationships are typically represented as collection objects— arrays, trees, dictionaries, and sets.

2. Bindings rely on KVC.

Activities

Look at the code for the iPhoneCoreDataRecipes sample code (iOS) or Department and Employees (Mac OS). Find the controllers and follow the logic as they manage views and data.

HOUR 9

Fetching Data

What You'll Learn in This Hour:

- ▶ Identifying the Core Data paradigms
- ▶ Learning how Core Data fetches data
- ▶ Using managed object contexts
- ▶ Creating fetch requests

Choosing the Core Data Architecture

In Hour 4, "Getting the Big Core Data Picture," you learned how the Core Data stack can be initialized. The basic components are

- ▶ **Data model**—This is the data model you create with Xcode. It is normally stored inside your app as a resource that is loaded at runtime.

- ▶ **Persistent store**—This is the data itself. It often is stored in the built-in SQLite library on Mac OS and iOS, but it can also be stored in memory on either system or in XML on Mac OS. You can also create your own type of persistent store.

- ▶ **Managed Object Context**—This object is created at runtime from the data model and the persistent store. Your app can have multiple managed object contexts.

TIP

Runtime objects representing the data model and the persistent store must be created before the managed object context can be created because it needs to refer to both of them. After you have a managed object context, your Core Data stack is ready for action.

In Hour 4, you also saw how these objects are initialized in a standard iOS app, but that is not the only way in which they can be created. There are two basic architectures for Core Data apps. They differ in the ownership of the Core Data stack:

▶ **Library/shoebox apps**—These apps manage their own Core Data stack that is more or less out of sight of the user. When you launch the app, you gain access to this behind-the-scenes data store. (As described in Hour 7, "What Managed Objects Can Do," p. 133, this is often located in a file in the user's Library directory on Mac or in the app's sandbox area on iOS.) Examples of this type of app are iCal, Address Book, and Bento. In these apps, the Core Data stack is often initiated in the app delegate. The Core Data stack must be available from the moment the app starts up in most of these cases.

NOTE

The terms *library* and *shoebox* refer to the common store for all a user's data just as if it were stored in a shoebox or library rather than in individual documents under the user's control. The term *sandbox* is used in the technology world to describe a self-contained area in which apps can run without having access to system-wide resources. Many people first heard the term in the context of Java.

▶ **Document-based apps**—These apps have one or more documents that users can create, open, close, and save. Each document has its own Core Data stack—that is, its own data model, persistent store, and managed object context. If multiple documents are open, each has its own managed object context, but they might run off the same data model and even the same persistent store. The managed object contexts are what keep each document's data separate.

Neither architecture is better than the other; they are different. One point that can influence your choice is that, with a document-based architecture, users can see their documents (each of which contains its own database). If a user might want to share a document with a friend, this architecture can be your choice. With the shoebox/library architecture, you need to implement an exporting process to create a sharable copy of part of the common shoebox/library.

Exploring the Core Data Fetching Process

Databases are all about organizing data so that it can be retrieved and updated easily as needed. This section reviews the basics of data retrieval and explores the specific Core Data features and their implications.

Comparing Data Retrieval Paradigms

For more than half a century (since the late 1960s), database designers and software engineers have settled on several basic design patterns that are designed to provide optimal database performance. You might recognize these patterns from your own database experiences. As you will see, Core Data adds a pattern that might be new to you:

▶ **Load-then-process**—Because databases often manage large quantities of data, the time required to fetch that data can be significant. A common strategy is to begin by loading all the relevant data into memory so it will be there when it is needed. This is the pattern that is used in many productivity apps: You load the entire spreadsheet or word processing document into memory and then go to work. With traditional databases, the data load might follow on user interaction that determines the scope of what is needed, such as which class, which date range, and so forth.

▶ **Load-a-chunk**—As part of the interaction with the user that scopes out the data to be loaded, the user might specify values such as the number of items per page. The app code is then written to retrieve the chunk for a page. When the user asks for another page (the next one or a distant one), that page's data is loaded and then displayed. This can wind up taking longer than the initial load, but because the user controls the chunks, it might have a feel of being faster. In most cases, the time to load any single page is less than the time to load the whole data set. A disadvantage of this method is that the app has to implement the pagination and chunk retrieval code. In addition, if user actions require switching around from one chunk to another, response time can be sluggish; in such cases, the start-up cost of loading everything into memory is counterbalanced by faster performance of the rest of the app.

▶ **Core Data faulting**—Core Data implements *faulting*. Managed objects can be created without having their data retrieved for them. This incomplete object can be used without having that data retrieved. Only when the data becomes necessary does the object cause a *fault*, which causes Core Data to go out to the persistent store and retrieve the data. This design is similar to load-a-chunk, but rather than having individual apps implement pagination and loading, that service is provided by Core Data.

With Core Data's faulting mechanism, you can generally write code as if it were to be loaded all at once (in the load-then-process paradigm), but the data will actually be loaded on demand. This changes the architecture of your apps; it also has implications for the interface design.

Data Retrieval Performance and Metrics

Everyone knows that database performance can be highly variable depending on the volume of data being accessed and other demands on the computing environment. In this case, "everyone knows" is true, but you can take measures in testing and design to improve the chances of your database performance being as responsive as possible.

Regardless of the platform or the database management system, you can speculate and estimate what database performance will be like. These exercises can give you an idea of what real-life performance will be, but there is no substitute for stress testing with live data on the actual run-time environment.

Such stress tests do not just let you benchmark the time to store or retrieve specific data sets, but also let you get an idea of how variations in the environment affect database performance. For example, uploading an enormous video file while you are attempting to access a database or do anything else can degrade system performance.

This section is an overview of issues, but even with the best and most controlled testing, the proof of the performance comes only from ongoing experience with the systems in production.

Today's Core Data evolved from Enterprise Objects Framework in WebObjects in 1994. In that guise, its architecture included *adaptors* that allowed it to access commonly used databases such as Oracle, Sybase, Informix, and ODBC-compliant servers.

The architecture and performance features, including faulting, were initially designed for databases such as these in shared environments—often in large enterprises. That infrastructure remains basically in place today, and you can construct your own interfaces to persistent stores that function in this type of environment.

However, most Core Data apps today use the built-in SQLite libraries in Mac OS or iOS. (XML on Mac OS and in-memory persistent stores on both platforms are also widely used.) The SQLite libraries are not shared in the way that Oracle and even FileMaker databases are shared. Most of the time, concurrency and contention for database resources are issues that arise among different threads in your own app. When data is shared in real time by several apps or several users, that sharing is normally accomplished by messaging between the apps rather than direct database sharing.

NOTE

FileMaker Pro provides a good example of this type of architecture. Its Open Remote command establishes a connection from one copy of FileMaker Pro to FileMaker Server or to another copy of FileMaker Pro. The communication to the database is provided by FileMaker Server or the copy of FileMaker Pro that acts as a server. The client copies of FileMaker Pro talk to the database only through the server.

In practical terms, this means that the Core Data code you write can as easily function in a multiuser environment sharing a database using Oracle, DB2, or FileMaker Server as it can function with the built-in single-user SQLite library. If you have a background in traditional databases, you might find that your mental adjustment to working with Core Data consists of recognizing that, for the most part, you are in a single-user environment on a single computer. Many of the adjustments to handle concurrency and performance issues are unnecessary in this simplified environment.

On the other hand, if your background is in the world of non-database software such as simple calculation apps with no need to store any data beyond a few preferences and, perhaps, a past game's high score, you need to think about larger data storage issues and performance tuning.

Furthermore, when you throw in the issues involved in working with devices powered by batteries, you have an entirely different set of performance issues. It is not simply the time it takes to perform a database access that you need to worry about.

NOTE

Every database access and every network access needs to be considered in the context of whether that access will deplete the power supply sufficiently so that some future process will not be able to be performed. Other tasks also take power, but database and network accesses can take significant amounts of it.

You simply have to evaluate the specific circumstances and the environment of your app, evaluating the costs and benefits of everything you do both in the running of your app and in its design and maintenance. You can become so careful with system resources that your app will barely drain the battery even with heavy use, but the implementation and maintenance of the app will be so complex and expensive that you will be dealing with self-imposed hardships all the time.

TIP

The only hard-and-fast rule for dealing with performance and design issues is to question everything repeatedly during the design process and keep an open mind. There are conflicting sets of rules of databases in general, and Core Data in particular depending on the circumstances.

Remember that Core Data is heavily tuned for the operating systems and hardware that it runs on. Before working around a potential performance problem, confirm that it exists in practice and not just in theory

This suggestion goes back many years to mainframe database systems. Many developers denormalized their databases to improve performance only to discover that the database developers had been there first. Relational databases handle normalized data in many cases without the theoretical performance penalty that some developers assumed existed.

Representing Fetch Results

The result of a fetch request is an array consisting of the managed objects that have been fetched. Objective-C provides a number of collection objects you can use in addition to arrays. As you will see in Hour 10, "Working with Predicates and Sorting," p. 171, you might actually move the objects returned from a fetch into one of the other collection objects. The basic collection objects are NSArray and its descendant NSMutableArray; NSSet and its descendant NSMutableSet; and NSOrderedSet, which are ordered and unordered collections of objects; and NSDictionary and its subclass NSMutableDictionary, which are lists of key-value pairs.

> ▶ See the sidebar "Using Dictionaries for Key-Value Pairs in Objective-C" in Hour 10, "Working with Predicates and Sorting," p. 171, for more on dictionaries and key-value coding.

Using Managed Object Contexts

A managed object context combines the persistent store with your data model. When it is created at runtime, it manages the data in the database. It mediates between the managed objects themselves and the persistent store, keeping track of what needs to be read and written.

You deal directly with a managed object context in your code, although that inter-action is often minimal, consisting of simply creating a managed object context and passing it on to objects in the framework that need its functionality. For library/shoebox apps, the managed object context is usually in the app delegate. For document-based apps, there is a managed object context in each document; this allows each document to have its own entire Core Data stack.

TIP

The model and persistent store can appear in several documents, but the man-aged object context is unique to a single document.

NOTE

In older iOS apps, templates, and sample code, the managed object context might be stored in a view controller rather than the app delegate.

No matter where you place the managed object context, you create it in the same basic way. The code is shown in Listing 9.1.

LISTING 9.1 Creating a Managed Object Context

```
NSPersistentStoreCoordinator *psc = <#Get or create the coordinator#>;

// create the moc
NSManagedObjectContext *myContext = [[NSManagedObjectContext alloc] init];

// set the persistent store
 [myContext setPersistentStoreCoordinator:psc];
```

Given a managed object context, you can reverse the process and get its persistent store with the following method:

```
- (NSPersistentStoreCoordinator *)persistentStoreCoordinator;
```

With a persistent store coordinator, you can go back to the managed object mode with this method:

```
- (NSManagedObjectModel *)managedObjectModel;
```

That is basically all you need to know about working with a managed object context in most cases.

Creating and Using a Fetch Request

In traditional database programming, you create fetch requests (or their equivalents in other languages and frameworks) when you need to interact with the database. As noted previously, Core Data's faulting mechanism means that you often create the fetch request when you create the object that will do the fetching. This means, for example, that the fetch request might be created and set as a property of a table view. The fetching happens as the table is displayed (and that includes as it is scrolled from one set of records to another).

You can create fetch requests programmatically as described in this section. You also can create them with Xcode as part of your data model.

> ▶ Because the fetch request can include both the basic request and the predicate that selects specific data records, the process of creating both of them with Xcode is described in Hour 10, "Working with Predicates and Sorting," p. 171.

Listing 9.2 shows a basic fetch request being created. First, you need to have a managed object context. In many cases, you already have one for the object that is creating the fetch request, but in some special cases, you need to create a new managed object context. In Listing 9.2, you see that the existing managed object context is being used.

Next, you need an NSEntityDescription for the entity to be fetched. An NSEntityDescription is an object representing an entity in a managed object model. With an NSEntityDescription, you can get the managed object model, its name, its attributes, its properties, and a variety of other items. You get an NSEntityDescription using a class method into which you pass the name of the entity and its managed object context.

Then you create the fetch request and add the entity description to it.

LISTING 9.2   Creating a Fetch Request

```
//get the managed object context
NSManagedObjectContext *moc = [self managedObjectContext];

//get the entity description object
NSEntityDescription *entityDescription =
  [NSEntityDescription entityForName:@"MyEntityName" inManagedObjectContext:moc];

//create the fetch request
NSFetchRequest *request = [[[NSFetchRequest alloc] init] autorelease];

//add the entity description
[request setEntity:entityDescription];
```

You can sort the results of a fetch request, and you can also add conditions in a *predicate*.

▶ You will find information about using predicates in Hour 10, p. 171.

It is a managed object context that you call upon to execute a fetch request after you have created it. Usually, this is the same managed object context you created and have been using in a document or in the app delegate for a library/shoebox app.

You call executeFetchRequest on the managed object context using the following method:

```
- (NSArray *)executeFetchRequest:
  (NSFetchRequest *)request
  error:(NSError **)error;
```

This returns an array of fetched managed objects as its result. Separately, the error parameter contains an NSError object with properties describing in some detail what happened. This is a much richer structure than a simple integer error number.

Your code might look like the code in Listing 9.3.

NOTE

The & in the second line of code is the standard C address indicator—in this case, the address of the error object.

LISTING 9.3   Executing a Fetch Request

```
NSError *error = nil;
NSArray *array = [moc executeFetchRequest:request error:&error];

if (array == nil)
{
  // no objects returned — this might or might not be an error
  // you may want to check the error result as well
}
```

Stopping the Action to Add New Data

A common issue you must address when you add new data to any database is demonstrated in Figure 9.1. It shows what happens when you click the Add button in the Departments and Employees sample code. The Add button in the main document window brings up a sheet, as shown in Figure 9.1. This lets users provide information about a newly created object. Sheets are modal; this means that the only way out of the sheet is to either cancel it or to provide the information (in this case, the name of the new employee).

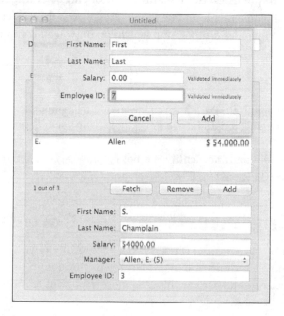

FIGURE 9.1
Use a sheet to collect informa tion about a new employee.

This interface demonstrates a key choice you have to make in adding data to your database. If certain fields are required (a name, for example), do you halt the update with a modal interface element to force the user to provide the necessary data? The alternative is to provide a default name and allow the user to change it. Here are your choices:

▶ **Use a hidden primary key and a possibly non-unique user identifier**—It is common (and a good practice) in databases to use the name as a descriptive attribute for a given record. A unique primary key (generated automatically to ensure uniqueness) is the actual identifier. This means you can have non-unique names in your database. Names do change for people, cities, and concepts along with just about everything else you can think of. Not allowing for name changes in a database can turn out to be a problem.

▶ **Generate user-visible identifiers to be changed**—You can generate a name for new records automatically. It might be something like New Record. The suggestion is that users should then use the modification feature of the interface to change the name in the same way that they would change any other data value. This avoids the need for a separate interface that interrupts the process of adding a new record. On the other hand, the new record name (New Record, for instance) means you have non-unique names in the user interface.

▶ **Generate unique user-visible identifiers that can be changed**—You can automatically generate a unique name for new records; that commonly is a name that includes a timestamp which, on any given computer, is likely to be unique.

NOTE
Remember that most Core Data apps today are not using multiuser shared databases, so within a single database, a given timestamp value is unique.

The choice of a name for a new entity is a basic database choice that applies equally to Mac OS and iOS, Core Data, FileMaker, and Oracle.

Optimizing Interfaces for Core Data

As is the case with much of Core Data, using it successfully means you can forget about some of the contortions you might have gone through in the past to build effective and efficient database systems. The most important feature to remember is faulting: the fact that Core Data takes care of providing data on demand after you have set up the data model and initialized it.

The other key point to remember is the architecture you are using. It can be a libraryshoe box architecture in which the database is stored somewhere in the user's directory but is basically out of sight. On the other hand, it can be a document-based architecture in which the database is stored in a user-visible document that can then be moved, renamed, or sent to another user.

▶ There is more information about architectures in Part V, "Managing Data and Interfaces."

Taking Advantage of Mac OS Interface Features for Core Data

Figure 9.2 shows the basic interface from Apple's Departments and Employees sample code (available on developer.apple.com or directly at https://developer.apple.com/library/mac/samplecode/DepartmentAndEmployees/DepartmentAndEmployees.zip). This sample dates from 2007, and it was designed to demonstrate the use of NSPersistentDocument. For that reason, it is a document-based app.

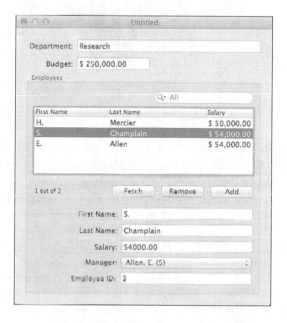

FIGURE 9.2
Department and Employees is a Core Data sample for Mac OS.

As shown in Figure 9.2, Department and Employees uses a primary window with a number of buttons along with data entry and display tools.

This is a compact interface ideally suited to the Mac. Everything is in a single window. To expand the sample beyond the basics, you might add more windows providing reports and summaries of individual employees and departments, but the basic functionality is all provided in Figure 9.2.

Without modification, the sample provides common menu commands, as shown in Figure 9.3. The menu commands are the very basic commands (New, Save, Print, and so forth), and they are connected to methods in First Responder. There is no customization in this sample beyond the basic menu commands and the standard functionality provided in Cocoa.

FIGURE 9.3
Explore the built-in menu commands in the sample code.

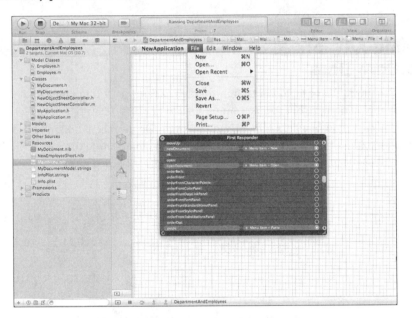

The generic menu bar is typical of the direction in desktop-based software over the last several years. The functionality is provided by contextual commands in buttons located in the window right where the relevant data is displayed. Years ago, the in-window buttons shown in Figure 9.1 would probably have been menu commands.

NOTE

The buttons in the window shown in Figure 9.1 do not include a Save button. Save and Save As are standard menu commands, as shown in Figure 9.3. They are implemented in Cocoa. They are also triggered by default if you attempt to close a window with unsaved changes. In Mac OS X 10.7 Lion, Autosave handles this automatically if you enable the feature.

The functionality of this sample app is provided by the Cocoa framework as well as bindings to the fields and views. There is very little code for you to write. The link between the application itself and its documents is provided in the Info tab, as shown in Figure 9.4.

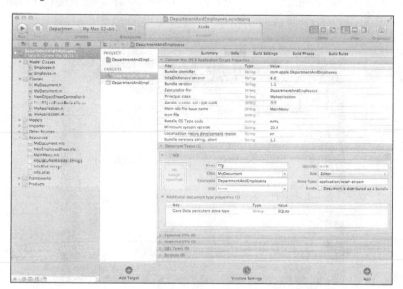

FIGURE 9.4
Specify the document class in the Info tab.

After you have bound your data model to fields (including the NSTableView shown in the center of Figure 9.1), user interaction with the interface causes Core Data to store or retrieve data. You do not have to explicitly write any code.

Taking Advantage of iOS Interface Features for Core Data

You can use the built-in Master-Detail template in iOS to see what is available with Core Data. By comparison to the Mac OS sample code and templates, there is a big difference in that bindings are not provided on iOS. However, most of the other features and design choices are available.

The main point to remember is that after your data model is created and you have connected to it, Core Data uses its built-in faulting and other features to provide data on demand. On iOS, those demands do not to come from menu commands (there are none on iOS) or even from buttons embedded in the view. On iOS, the commands are most frequently triggered by buttons on navigation bars or toolbars.

These include buttons that are primarily for navigation and that, as you navigate, cause new data to be displayed.

Figure 9.5 shows the Master-Detail template in action. You can use the + to add new instances of the Event entity. Event has a single attribute—the timestamp at which it was created. This is a basic structure you can easily expand.

FIGURE 9.5
Master-Detail Xcode template in action on iPad.

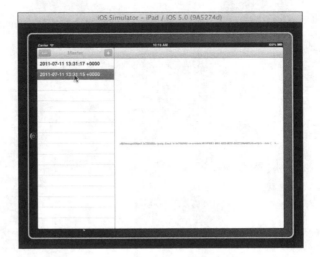

NOTE

The Master-Detail template replaces the Navigation-based Application and Split View-based Application templates starting with Xcode 4.2 and iOS 5.

You can choose to build the Master-Detail template for iPad, iPhone, or universal use. If you choose the universal option, it is built for both devices. Depending on which simulator you select in the Xcode window or which device you are running on, the appropriate interface is provided, as shown in Figures 9.5 and 9.6.

If you examine the code carefully, you will see that the differences between the split view version for iPad shown in Figure 9.5 and the navigation version for iPhone shown in Figure 9.6 consist primarily of a different storyboard. That is one of the objectives of the storyboard feature available in Xcode 4.2 and later.

FIGURE 9.6
The Master-Detail template can be built for universal use so that it runs on iPhone as well as iPad.

Summary

This hour has shown you how to fetch data from your persistent store in Core Data. The heart of the technology is a fetch request that specifies the entity to be fetched. You can add a sort descriptor to the fetch request so that the data is sorted when it is returned. You also can add a predicate so that only some of the instances rather than all of them are returned. Those are the topics of the following hour.

Q&A

Q. *What is the required component of a fetch request?*

A. You must specify the entity to be fetched.

Q. *What is the purpose of a managed object context?*

A. A managed object context keeps track of a group of objects that have been fetched. It monitors their changes (if any) and, when it comes time to save data, the managed object is what performs the saving.

Workshop

Quiz

1. *What is faulting?*

2. *How can you set values such as the name for a new entity instance?*

Quiz Answers

1. Faulting is the process by which Core Data creates managed objects that can be manipulated and moved around but that do not contain data. Thus, the actual data store access occurs on an as-needed basis.

2. You can provide a constant default value (New Customer) or a dynamic default value (New Customer created at <date/time>), or you can stop and query the user with a dialog box so that the user-specified value is set as the instance is created.

Activities

During the course of an hour when you are doing a variety of computer activities, from sending/receiving email to browsing the Web, keep track of how the various software products handle the issue of setting required values. Mail, for example, lets you create a message with no addressee, but it will not let you send it. The Finder lets you create an untitled new document, but it adds serial numbers (Untitled, Untitled 2, etc.) so that each name is unique.

HOUR 10

Working with Predicates and Sorting

What You'll Learn in This Hour:

- ▶ Selecting data the Core Data way
- ▶ Constructing predicates
- ▶ Sorting data two ways

Understanding Predicates

A *predicate* is a logical operator that evaluates to a Boolean value—*true* or *false*.
Many people think of a predicate as the WHERE clause in a SQL statement, but that
is only one particular case. In SQL, you can write the following:

```
SELECT name, address FROM employee WHERE department = 'research';
```

department = 'research' serves as the predicate. For each record that might be
returned by the SELECT statement, department = 'research' is evaluated based
on that record's data and the result is either true or false. The records where the
result is TRUE are returned by the SELECT statement.

> **NOTE**
>
> This describes the procedural process but not the actual process in most data-
> base management systems (DBMSs). Where possible, the predicate is applied to
> indexes so that instead of retrieving data and then testing the predicate, the DBMS
> checks in the indexes to find all the records that fulfill the predicate (that is, all
> records where department = 'research'). At that point, the data is retrieved,
> making the process the reverse of the procedural method you might be thinking of.

The word *predicate* has been used in this sense since the nineteenth century, although most of the time it is descriptive rather than prescriptive as it is in database terminology. (In other words, instead of defining the records to be returned from a database, it describes the data that has been returned from a database or collected from a manual process.) This last point is important because you can use predicates with Core Data fetch statements (the primary consideration in this book), but you can also use predicates to filter arrays, key paths, Cocoa bindings, and controller data.

NOTE

Predicates and their uses are described in this section. Later in this hour, you will find "Constructing Predicates," which explains how to create them. Some people find it easier to learn how to use them first and then how to create them; others prefer the reverse order. You can use whichever sequence you prefer and can jump back and forth if you want.

Using Dictionaries for Key-Value Pairs in Cocoa

Key-value coding is used extensively in Cocoa. This is a simple mechanism in which a value is paired with a key. Key-value pairs can be stored in a *dictionary* (NSDictionary); each such pair is referred to as an *entry*. For key-value coding, each key is a unique string in that dictionary. (It is possible to create dictionaries where the keys are not strings, but for most purposes, dictionaries contain keys that are strings.)

The supporting code for dictionaries in Cocoa's runtime implementation has been highly optimized over time; it is some of the most efficient code found anywhere in Mac OS and iOS. Dictionaries provide simple and efficient ways of passing collections of parameters and data to operations instead of using sequences of parameters that might be identified by nothing more than their sequence in a list of many such items.

You can get a value for a key by using the NSDictionary method:

```
- (id)objectForKey:(id)aKey
```

There are two common ways to create a dictionary with values and keys. If you have values and keys in separate arrays, you can use the following:

```
- (id)initWithObjects:(NSArray *)objects forKeys:(NSArray *)keys
```

For small dictionaries, it is sometimes easier to enter the key-value pairs in a nil-terminated list, as in the following:

```
NSDictionary *dict = [[NSDictionary alloc] initWithObjectsAndKeys:
  @"value1", @"key1", @"value2", @"key2", nil];
```

You can also create and initialize dictionaries from other dictionaries and from resources in your app's bundle.

Just as with other collections such as arrays, the basic objects are read-only. This works well for the common cases such as parameter-passing. Sometimes, however, you need to be able to modify a dictionary (or any other collection, such as an array). For this reason, there are mutable versions. Because they are read/write structures, they are a little less efficient, but you get important functionality if you need it. If you are dealing with an NSMutableDictionary, you can add entries using the following:

```
- (void)setValue:(id)value forKey:(NSString *)key
```

In special cases, you can use a non-string key, as in the following:

```
- (void)setObject:(id)anObject forKey:(id)aKey
```

Most of the time, you will be using setValue: forKey.

Looking at Predicate Syntax

Predicates are going to wind up looking like various selection criteria, including regular expressions and WHERE clauses. They have their own string parser that converts those expressions to code. They are combinations of two components:

▶ Literals and variables

▶ Comparison operators

Literals and Identifiers

Literals can be quoted strings such as "committee" or defined values such as TRUEPREDICATE or FALSEPREDICATE, which evaluate to TRUE and FALSE, respectively. (Note that in the world of predicates and databases, TRUE and FALSE are used; Objective-C uses YES and NO.)

Variables are your own variables preceded by $, as in $lastName.

Comparison Operators

These are many of the same logical operators you are used to in C and other programming languages, as shown in Table 10.1.

TABLE 10.1 Comparison Operators for Predicates

Operator	Meaning
Basics	
=, ==	Equal.
>=, =>	Greater than or equal.
<=, =<	Less than or equal.
>	Greater than.
<	Less than.
!=, <>	Not equal.
BETWEEN	Between two values expressed as an array, such as {$LOWER, $UPPER}.
Strings	
BEGINSWITH	One or more characters.
CONTAINS	One or more characters.
ENDSWITH	One or more characters.
LIKE	One or more characters. Use ? for a one-character wild-card character and * for any number of wildcard characters, as in LIKE ca*t, which matches *cast*, *cart*, and *cannot*.
MATCHES	Regular expression.
Aggregate Operators	
ANY, SOME	As in ANY employee.salary < 35000.
ALL	As in ALL employee.salary < 35000.
NONE	Equivalent to NOT (ANY...).
IN	Like the SQL IN operator; the right side can be a Cocoa dictionary, array, or set.
Array Operators	
index	
FIRST	
LAST	
SIZE	
Logical Operators	
AND, &&	
OR, ¦¦	

TABLE 10.1   Comparison Operators for Predicates

Operator	Meaning
NOT, !	

For predicates, FALSE and NO are treated the same as TRUE and YES are, as well as NULL and NIL.

Using Predicates with Arrays and Other Objects

After you have constructed a predicate (an NSPredicate object), you can use it to evaluate any object. The method is shown here:

```
- (BOOL)evaluateWithObject:(id)object
```

Note that the object is an id, which means it can be any Objective-C object. If the predicate successfully evaluates against the object, the result is YES; otherwise, it is NO.

TIP

Remember that Objective-C uses YES and NO rather than TRUE and FALSE. Core Foundation also defines TRUE and FALSE, so you can use them, too. It is best not to mix the styles, and most of the code you will download from developer.apple.com uses YES and NO.

Certain types of objects have their own predicate handling methods. For example, given an NSArray, you can use filteredArrayUsingPredicate to return an array of those elements of the array that match the predicate:

```
- (NSArray *)filteredArrayUsingPredicate:(NSPredicate *)predicate
```

Thus, with a predicate called myPredicate and an array called myArray, you would write the following:

```
NSArray *myNewArray = [myArray filteredArrayUsingPredicate:myPredicate];
```

With an NSMutableArray, filterUsingPredicate returns the matching objects (not a new array of objects):

```
(void)filterUsingPredicate:(NSPredicate *)predicate
```

You would write the following:

```
[myArray filterUsingPredicate:myPredicate];
```

You can use predicates with Cocoa bindings in Xcode as well as with your own code.

NOTE

Using predicates with Cocoa bindings in Xcode is beyond the scope of this book, but it is important to realize that predicates go beyond Core Data and certainly beyond the built-in SQLite library. In part, it is those features of predicates that provide additional functionality and, in some cases, changes to the syntax that would exist if predicates were simply a Core Data or SQLite construct.

Using Predicates with Core Data

Bear in mind that, although SQLite is perhaps the most commonly used database library for Core Data, Core Data can run against XML documents, in-memory data stores, and other types of data stores you create. (Remember that the Enterprise Objects Framework original implementation of what is now Core Data ran against Oracle, OpenBase, and other data stores, and nothing prevents data stores such as them from being used today.)

Today, Core Data is also used on Mac OS to implement Spotlight. Because a Core Data predicate might be translated to or from SQL, XML, or another format, you need to consider Core Data predicate syntax independently of the particular data store. That is why Core Data predicates are not simply SQL WHERE clauses.

That being said, it is worth pointing out that in many cases, whether you are using SQLite, Oracle, or another DBMS, your predicates and WHERE clauses are likely to be fairly simple. Sophisticated database users often use complex logical structures, but many other database users stick to the basics even if it means using more statements or more complex statements to avoid constructs such as inner and outer joins that are more complicated for many people.

Predicates are added to fetch requests if you want to use them (they are optional). If you do not add a predicate to a fetch request, all the data is returned.

NOTE

If you do not use a predicate and retrieve all the data, you can place it in an array as is done in a number of the sample code projects on developer.apple.com. Then you can work through the array to determine which data you want to process or display. Although this might appear to be more work than a predicate, remember that Core Data's faulting mechanism minimizes database accesses. Furthermore, although it is impossible to give hard and fast rules for performance, unless the Core Data entity objects are particularly large, retrieving dozens or scores of objects might not produce a significant performance hit either for the processor or for memory use.

Listing 9.2, "Creating a Fetch Request," in Hour 9, "Fetching Data," p. 153, shows you how to create a fetch request. To add a predicate, construct the predicate you need and then add it to the fetch request with this line at the end of the code shown in Listing 9.2:

```
[request setPredicate:predicate];
```

This line of code assumes that the predicate you have created is named predicate, but it can be named anything you want. The next section of this hour shows you how to construct the predicate.

Constructing Predicates

There are several ways of constructing predicates. Each has its pros and cons, and each is shown with examples in this section. As you will see, when it comes to constructing predicates (as in many other cases), Xcode is one of the simplest ways of getting the job done:

▶ **Xcode and predicate templates**—Xcode has a built-in predicate editor that can handle many basic situations for you. This will let you create a predicate template in Xcode that you can then use at runtime.

▶ **Format strings**—This method uses a standard C format structure for the predicate. The syntax uses the class method predicateWithFormat: and its companions, such as predicateWithFormat :arguments, predicateWithFormat :argumentArray, and the like. The main disadvantage of using format strings is that they can get fairly unwieldy rather quickly, particularly for programmers without a strong background in C.

▶ **Code**—You can construct predicate and parts of predicates using code. NSExpression can be the heart of a predicate, and those objects can be combined into an NSComparisonPredicate and then further combined into an NSCompoundPredicate. This can produce more verbose but easier to read code than a format string does.

NOTE

Learning how to construct predicates using code is beyond the scope of this book. However, you can find more information about this topic in "Predicate Programming Guide" on developer.apple.com (just search on the title). In that document, you'll find more than thirty pages of description and code samples.

Creating a Fetch Request and Predicate with Xcode

You can see how predicates can be created when you create a fetch request with Xcode. For many people and many fetch requests, this is the fastest and simplest way to work.

Before you begin, you need to create a data model with the entity you want to retrieve. You also need to have defined any of the attributes you will want to use in selecting the data. If you have not done this already, do not worry: You can move back to the data model to modify it and then return to the fetch request. It is very common to get into a fetch request and then realize that an attribute you want to display or to use for selection is missing. Follow these steps:

1. The simplest way to begin is with a data model, as shown in Figure 10.1. Select one or more entities on which to build the fetch request. (You can change it later.)

FIGURE 10.1
Start to create a fetch request in Xcode.

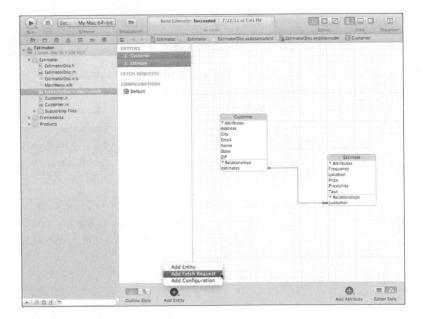

2. Click and hold the Add Entity button at the lower-left of the data model editor to bring up the shortcut menu that lets you choose to create a new fetch request.

3. A new fetch request is created in the editor, as shown in Figure 10.2. You can select or change the entity you want to retrieve.

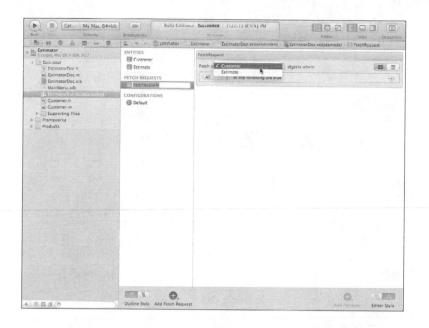

FIGURE 10.2
Choose the entity to retrieve.

4. Begin to build your predicate, as shown in Figure 10.3. Decide if you want all or any of the predicate components to be true. If you choose none, then all of them must fail. This is sometimes simpler than specifying the various positive conditions.

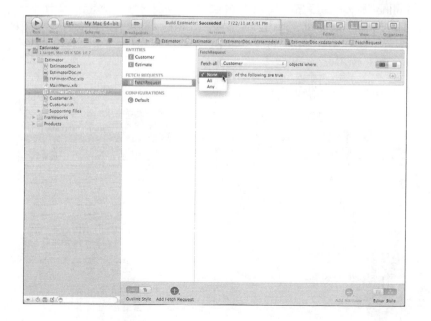

FIGURE 10.3
Start to create a fetch request in Xcode.

5. In Figure 10.4, you see how you can choose the attribute, the comparison operator, and the value to be used in the predicate test.

FIGURE 10.4
Build your predi-
cate graphically.

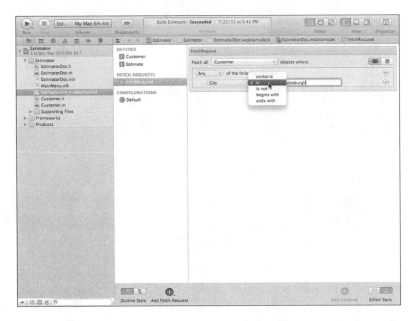

6. You can switch from the table view shown in Figure 10.4 to a text version, as shown in Figure 10.5, by using the control at the right of the predicate builder. If you start from scratch in the text version, you will see that the default first predicate is NOT FALSEPREDICATE, which evaluates to true for every record. This is the same behavior you get with no predicate: every record is retrieved.

No matter which view you are in, use + to add another rule.

FIGURE 10.5
You can view
the predicate in
text rather than
a table.

7. You can switch back and forth between the views. This is an easy way to convert the graphically generated predicate to a text version. Figure 10.6 shows a more complex predicate in the table view. This is easier for many people to create than a text version.

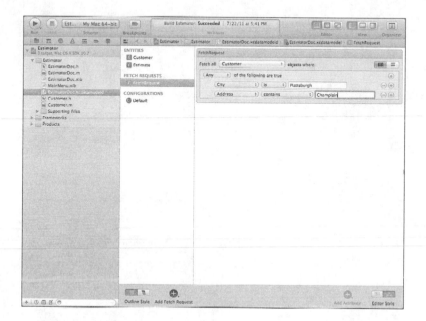

FIGURE 10.6
You can build complex predicates in table view.

8. Continue building a predicate in text view if you want, as shown in Figure 10.7.

9. Show utilities to see the Data Model inspector and set the fetch request name. You can also set other options there, as shown in Figure 10.8. You can also set the fetch request name by double-clicking it in the list of fetch requests at the left of the editor window and changing its name there.

FIGURE 10.7
You can switch
back and forth.

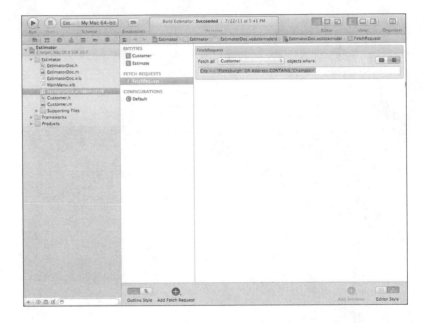

FIGURE 10.8
Use the Data
Model inspector
to set the fetch
request name.

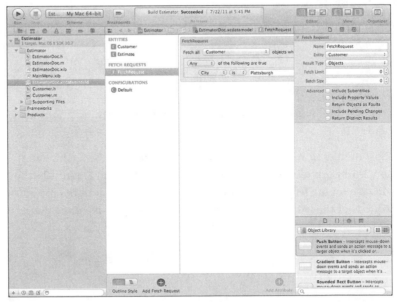

Your fetch request might or might not contain data that needs to be created at run-time. For example, if the fetch request contains a clause along the lines of

```
salary < 45000
```

that can be hard-coded when you create the template, as shown in the Try It Yourself. To use a template like this where any comparison values are hard-coded, you use the code shown in Listing 10.1.

LISTING 10.1 Use a Predicate Template with Hard-Coded Data

```
// get the data model — perhaps from the persistent store coordinator
NSManagedObjectModel *model = myModel;

// create the error object and set to nil
NSError *error = nil;

// create the fetch request from the template using the name you set
// in the data model inspector in utilities
// pass nil for the substitution variables
NSFetchRequest *fetchRequest =
  [model fetchRequestFromTemplateWithName:@"myFetchRequest"
          substitutionVariables:nil];

// execute the fetch request
NSArray *results =
  [aManagedObjectContext executeFetchRequest:fetchRequest error:&error];
```

However, if you want to use a clause in which the comparison number is drawn from runtime data (perhaps from a data value that has just been retrieved for another entity), you need to pass that value in at runtime.

> ▶ To pass a value at runtime, you must use a dictionary as described previously in this hour in "Using Dictionaries for Key-Value Pairs in Cocoa."

Listing 10.2 shows you how to do this. It is basically the same code as in Listing 10.1, but you create a dictionary and pass it in to fetchRequestFromTemplate.

LISTING 10.2 Use a Predicate Template with Runtime Data

```
// get the data model — perhaps from the persistent store coordinator
NSManagedObjectModel *model = myModel;

// create the error object and set to nil
NSError *error = nil;

// create a dictionary for the runtime data
NSDictionary *substitutionDictionary = [NSDictionary dictionaryWithObjectsAndKeys:
  manager.salary, @"salaryComparison", nil];

// create the fetch request from the template using the name you set
// in the data model inspector in utilities
// pass in the dictionary you just created
NSFetchRequest *fetchRequest
  [model fetchRequestFromTemplateWithName:@"myFetchRequest"
    substitutionVariables:substitutionDictionary];

// execute the fetch request
NSArray *results =
  [aManagedObjectContext executeFetchRequest:fetchRequest error:&error];
```

Using Format Strings for Predicates

You can use a C-style print format string to create a predicate. Here's one such string:

```
printf ( "Hello, %s  and hello to you, too %s.", "Nicole", "Giovanni" );
```

The format tags within the first argument (%s in this case) are replaced by the subsequent arguments. In this case, the output would be the following:

```
Hello, Nicole, and hello to you, too Giovanni.
```

Just as is the case with format strings for printing, it often is easiest to start from the result that you want to create—in other words, the actual wording of the predicate.

One quick way of doing this is to use the techniques in the previous Try It Yourself and create a predicate with hard-coded values, as previously shown in Figure 10.7. Then translate that predicate so that it uses dynamic values at runtime.

For example, the predicate constructed graphically in Figure 10.7 can be created with a format string using the code in Listing 10.3.

LISTING 10.3   Create a Predicate with a Format String

```
NSPredicate *myPredicate =
  [NSPredicate predicateWithFormat:@"City == Plattsburgh
    OR Address CONTAINS Champlain"];
```

You could also do it with runtime data inserted into the format string, as shown in Listing 10.4.

LISTING 10.4   Create a Predicate with a Format String and Runtime Data

```
NSPredicate *myPredicate =
  [NSPredicate predicateWithFormat:@"City == %
    OR Address CONTAINS %@", @"Plattsburgh", @"Champlain"];
```

You now have a predicate that you can add to a fetch request.

You can expand on this structure with clauses such as

```
%K LIKE %@
```

where you substitute NSString objects for %K and %@, thereby creating a dynamic condition based on user actions or other circumstances.

Sorting Data

Asked to identify the most resource-consuming and unnecessary process performed with databases, many experienced developers would quickly identify sorting. In part because databases can easily deal with large amounts of data, people quickly jump to the conclusion that the way to tame all that data is to sort it one way or another.

In fact, what databases do incredibly well is to locate and retrieve data on demand. People have trouble doing that, and so it is best to provide sorted and indexed lists of data to people who need to find something. But with the various techniques for locating data that are available in a database, those lists are not necessary in many cases. (One case in which sorting is essential is in the preparation of printed reports people will be using: People need the sorted data.)

CAUTION

There is one important case in which sorting data matters very much—in the case of data that is ordered by users according to an arbitrary sequence. Computers can sort alphabetically or by numeric values easily, but it is always a challenge to implement an interface in which users can reorder the items in a list. This is one of the problems where a touch interface excels because users can simply drag the list items up or down as they wish.

▶ You will find out how to reorder items in a list in Hour 21, "Rearranging Table Rows on iOS" p. 375. Although sorting enters into the picture, in this book (and in most documentation), the issue of rearranging rows in a table is considered a separate topic.

Although sorting is used more than necessary overall, it is essential for many operations. The Cocoa frameworks include the NSSortDescriptor class that lets you create an object that encapsulates sorting functionality. Instances of that class can be used to sort arrays, elements in a table or controller, and the items retrieved in a fetch request.

Sorting is yet another case in which key-value coding is used. In creating the sort descriptor, you specify the key to be used. You can use a number of methods to create a sort descriptor, but the class method shown here is one of the most common:

```
+ (id)sortDescriptorWithKey:(NSString *)key ascending:(BOOL)ascending
```

CAUTION

Because the sort descriptor contains the string for the key to be used in sorting, you do have to modify it each time you use it, but that is a simple change to make. The only complication that occasionally arises is if attributes in the data model are not clearly identified; in that case, you can sort on the wrong attribute. This is another reason for being careful with your naming conventions. Some people even go so far as to indicate which attributes are designed for sorting by giving them names such as `date_forSorting`. This could be used to clearly differentiate between a date attribute that always contains a date and another date attribute that is a text field and can contain data such as `next week`.

Create and add a sort descriptor to a fetch request, as shown in Listing 10.5. (Note that this is an alternative to using the class method shown previously. Use whichever you prefer in a specific case.)

LISTING 10.5   Using a Sort Descriptor

```
// create a sort descriptor
NSSortDescriptor *sortDescriptor = [[NSSortDescriptor alloc]
  initWithKey:@"employeeID" ascending:YES];

// add it to the fetch request
[myFetchRequest setSortDescriptors:[NSArray arrayWithObject:sortDescriptor]];
```

> **NOTE**
>
> Many developers believe that sorting done in the database manager can be more efficient than sorting done in the app code itself. It is hard to make a definitive statement on this matter, but it does seem as if it might be the case. Adopting a standard convention in an app may make maintenance easier because future developers will know where sorting occurs.

Summary

You can add predicates and sort descriptors to fetch requests so that the data is sorted and only some instances are returned by the fetch request. The fetch request can be executed as needed.

Q&A

Q. *Why are predicates not exactly like a SQL* WHERE *clause?*

A. Core Data is designed to work with SQLite (built in to Mac OSX and iOS), Spotlight (Mac OS X), XML (Mac OS X), and other data stores that you might create or use. The WHERE clause is a particular implementation of SQL and is not applicable to Spotlight and XML.

Q. *What is a dictionary (in the context of Mac OS X and iOS)?*

A. A dictionary is a collection of key-value pairs. It can be used to store large and small amounts of data in an organized and easy-to-store-and-retrieve fashion. Within a dictionary, keys are unique.

Workshop

Quiz

1. *How do you construct predicates?*
2. *Why is sorting overused in many computer programs?*

Quiz Answers

1. You can construct predicates with format strings, with Xcode's predicate builder, and by using code.
2. Sorted data is easier for people to use than unsorted data. Database managers are very good at finding data using searches that would be tedious or impossible for people (checking values on each of several thousand records, for example).

Activities

Create an Xcode project that uses Core Data. Build a data model and experiment with building a fetch request. Switch back and forth between the structured request and its text representation to understand the syntax.

Finding Your Way Around the Interface Builder Editor: The Graphics Story

---

What You'll Learn In This Hour:

- ▶ Exploring the Interface Builder editor
- ▶ Using the canvas
- ▶ Working with placeholders and objects

Starting to Work with the Interface Builder Editor in Xcode

As described in Hour 1, "Introducing Xcode 4," p. 7, what is now Xcode used to be a pair of programs: Project Builder and Interface Builder. Now they are combined into a single, powerful interface.

Just as is the case when you are starting to write code, there is one way that definitely is not the way to start building an interface: Do not start from a blank canvas and build your interface from scratch. First of all, this is rarely the real-world scenario. Most of the time, you work from one of the built-in Xcode templates, from sample code, or from code that you or someone else wrote in the past. The concept of starting from scratch makes a nice scenario for basic demos, but it is not the most common practice.

In this part of the book, you will see how to put the pieces together from the basic programming building blocks in Part I, "Getting Started with Core Data," and the Core Data information in Part II, "Using Core Data." The code examples and snippets in those parts of the book illustrate specific features. Now, as you combine basic programming and Core Data with an interface, you can build realistic apps.

A Note About Versions and Platforms

Most of the examples and screenshots in this part of the book use iOS 5 and Mac OS X 10.7 Lion—the current versions of both operating systems as this book was written. Furthermore, the then-current version of Xcode (4.2) is used. You might be using later versions; you also might be using earlier versions in the form of sample code or apps that you or someone else wrote in the past. There are some notes in this hour and Hour 12, "Finding Your Way Around the Interface Builder Editor: The Code Story," p. 209, that point out how the syntax differs from version to version. Those notes are not repeated in other hours that focus simply on the current versions of the software, so you might want to bookmark the notes if they apply to you.

Also, note that in this hour and the next one, the examples are built primarily with iOS. Mac OS comes into the picture in the following hour. With the exception of binding for Mac OS and storyboard for iOS, both operating systems function very much the same way. Where there are significant differences, they are pointed out.

Creating a Universal App and Interacting with the Device

In this hour, you build a universal app using Xcode 4.2 and iOS 5. A universal app is one that can run on both iPhone and iPad (the iPhone version also runs on iPod touch). This is accomplished by having alternative interface files and controllers for the two environments. You choose the appropriate controller or interface by checking the device on which you are running.

You do this by calling the class method currentDevice and testing it, as shown in the following snippet of code:

```
[[UIDevice currentDevice] userInterfaceIdiom] == UIUserInterfaceIdiomPhone
```

The other constant for which you might test is UIUserInterfaceIdiomPad. UDevice Class Reference gives details on other properties of UIDevice that you can interrogate at runtime. It is common to want to check some of these to make your app behave appropriately, so the list of properties is provided in Table 11.1. Many of them are self-explanatory; for the others, search on developer.apple.com.

TABLE 11.1   Properties for **UIDevice**

Property	Commonly Used Values or Type
multitaskingSupported	BOOL
name	NSString *
systemName	NSString *
systemVersion	NSString *
model	NSString * (this would be something such as iPhone or iPod touch)
localizedModel	NSString *
userInterfaceIdiom	UIUserInterfaceIdiomPad or UIUserInterfaceIdiomPhone
orientation	UIDeviceOrientationUnknown,
	UIDeviceOrientationPortrait,
	UIDeviceOrientationPortraitUpsideDown,
	UIDeviceOrientationLandscapeLeft,
	UIDeviceOrientationLandscapeRight,
	UIDeviceOrientationFaceUp,
	UIDeviceOrientationFaceDown
generatesDeviceOrientation Notifications	BOOL
batteryLevel	float (0–1)
batteryMonitoringEnabled	BOOL
batteryState	UIDeviceBatteryStateUnknown,
	UIDeviceBatteryStateUnplugged,
	UIDeviceBatteryStateCharging,
	UIDeviceBatteryStateFull,
proximityMonitoringEnabled	BOOL
proximityState	BOOL

Using Storyboards

In Xcode 4.2, a new feature called *storyboards* is implemented. The previous structure of interface files, views, and controllers is still supported, but storyboards make it much easier to implement a universal app in which alternative controllers and views are used based on the device that is being used.

At the time that this book is written, storyboards are used as an option for new built-in Xcode templates. For most of the existing sample code projects on developer. apple.com, storyboards are not used (over time, they will probably be converted to the new interface). Rather than throw the complexity of storyboards/non-story-boards at you in this, the first hour where you build an interface, for this hour and the next, the traditional method of building interfaces is used. In Hour 14, "Working with Storyboards and Swapping Views," you will see how to reimplement the code from this hour.

Finding Your Sandbox for iOS Apps in the Simulator

When you work with Xcode to develop your iOS apps, the simulator is a key part of the process. The simulator simulates the look and feel of the app on an iOS device; it also simulates storing data to the device's local storage. Each app on an iOS device has its own *sandbox* where it can store its data in folders. Some of the folders exist for each app, and you can add your own folders and subfolders as you see fit.

> **NOTE**
> The iPhone simulator runs both the iPhone and iPad versions.

Particularly with Core Data, you sometimes need to access the sandbox files during testing. A common reason for doing this is to adjust to a new database structure or to use one of the SQLite apps from the App Store and Mac App Store to inspect your data (it is good to use a separate app sometimes to see exactly what is stored and what your app is presenting). As you will see in Hour 24, "Migrating Data Models," p. 423, you can build in automatic migration so that your database can adjust to changes in its structure. During basic testing, as you change the database, it is often easiest simply to remove the old database and let the app create a new database with the new structure. That code—code to create a new database if one does not exist—is needed in most Core Data apps and is included in many of the templates.

Your app's sandbox is located in your Library folder. There is a Library folder at the root level of the boot disk, but within each user's home folder, there is another Library folder, and that is where the sandbox files are located. (This means that if there are several accounts on a single Mac, each of those users can have a separate set of sandbox files.)

In Mac OS X Lion, the Library folder within a user's Home folder is normally hidden. (The Library folder at the root level of the boot disk is not hidden.) To show the Library folder for your Home folder, use the Go menu, as shown in Figure 11.1. Hold down the Option (or Alt) key while the menu is visible, and the Library folder will appear. Select it to open the Library.

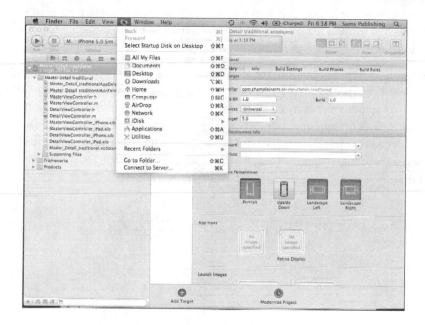

FIGURE 11.1
Use the Option key to add the Library folder to the Go menu.

After you are in the Library folder, navigate to Application Support, iPhone Simulator, the folder for the iOS version number (5.0 in this case), Applications, as shown in Figure 11.2.

Inside Applications is a folder for each of your apps. You will see the name of the app inside that folder along with the basic folders—Documents, Library, and tmp.

NOTE

The app shown in Figure 11.2 is named Master Detail traditional. You will build this app later in this hour.

FIGURE 11.2
Explore the
sandbox.

If you are using the default location for your SQLite file, it will be in the Documents
folder, as shown in Figure 11.2. When you have made a change to your database
structure and want to remove the previous version, just delete the sqlite file; the
default code in the Core Data template will create a new file with the new structure.

When you start from a built-in Xcode template or from sample code downloaded
from developer.apple.com, it is always a good idea to build and run the code without any alterations just to make certain that everything is running properly. If you
do that for a Core Data app, in most cases the app will create its own Core Data file
in the Documents folder, as shown in Figure 11.2. To find the code that creates the
database, copy the file name from the Finder and use the Xcode Search navigator to
find the string in the code, as shown in Figure 11.3.

FIGURE 11.3
Find the Core
Data file cre-
ation code in
your app from
the filename.

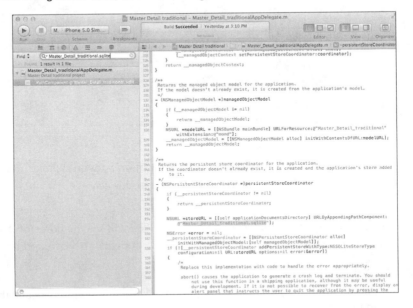

Try It Yourself

Creating Your Core Data App

To start working with both Core Data and the user interface, create a new project.

▶ You might want to review the task "Creating an iOS Project" in Hour 2, "Creating a Simple App," p. 49.

1. Start from the built-in Master Detail template for iOS, as shown in Figure 11.4. (If you are using an older version of Xcode, use the Split View-Controller template that is similar in its structure and functionality.)

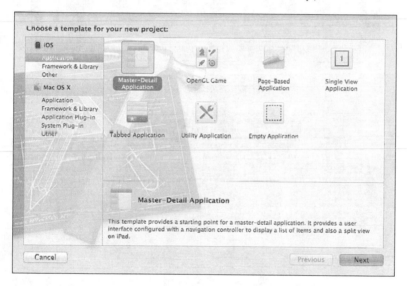

FIGURE 11.4
Create a new project.

2. Click Next and, as shown in Figure 11.5, name the project. You can choose any name you want, but you might want to indicate that this uses the traditional interface structure rather than the storyboard structure that you will use for the same template in Hour 14.

3. If necessary, enter your company name. It is used to identify your bundle.

4. Set the device family to Universal, and use the checkbox for Core Data. Make certain that the checkboxes for Storyboard and Unit Tests are *not* checked.

5. The project should look like Figure 11.6.

6. Set the scheme to build for the iPad simulator, as shown in Figure 11.6.

FIGURE 11.5
Name the new
project and set
options.

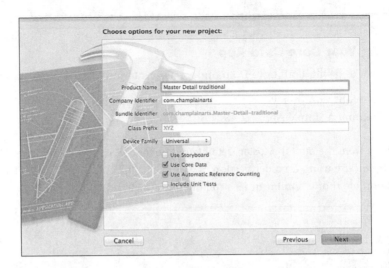

FIGURE 11.6
Check out the
project.

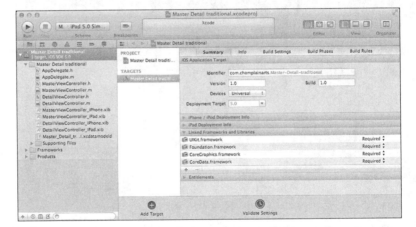

7. Click Run to build and run the project. It should look like Figure 11.7.

8. Using the simulator's Hardware, Rotate commands (or the keyboard Command-arrow combinations), rotate the device. Explore the pop-over as you rotate the device. Add new data with the +; delete data with the Edit button.

9. Stop the simulator (use the button next to Run in Xcode). Change the scheme to build for iPhone, and rerun the project, as shown in Figure 11.8.

Because this is a single universal app, the same data model and data files are used for both iPhone and iPad. You can add data in the iPhone simulation and view it in the iPad simulation.

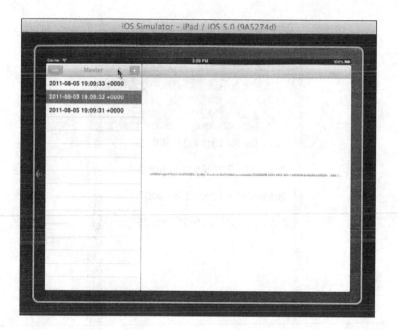

FIGURE 11.7
Build and run
the project.

▶ In real life, this would not happen because each device's data is stored on the device itself. However, iCloud can help you implement this functionality if you want. You will use the document model for the Core Data persistent store. There are more details on northcountryconsulting.com in the Downloads section for Core Data.

Working with the Canvas

In the center of the Xcode window is the editor. For code, it is the powerful text editor; for a data model, it is the data model editor you saw in Hour 6, "Working with the Core Data Model Editor," p. 117. Now, you use the *canvas* in the editor to lay out your interface graphically. This editing environment can trace its roots back to Interface Builder (on NeXT), but in Xcode 4, it is more powerful and flexible than ever before.

TIP

Many people like to lay out their Xcode window in a standard format to which they get accustomed. When you start really getting into the Interface Builder editor, you will probably find that you want to work in full-screen view (if you are running Lion) and that you will regularly show or hide the utility, navigator, or debug panes depending on where your focus is. If you are used to leaving your Xcode window in a single configuration, explore the options to show and hide the various panes.

FIGURE 11.8
Change the
scheme to build
for iPhone.

Exploring the Interface Builder Editor

Begin your exploration by selecting a nib file in the Project navigator. (Remember that nib started as NeXT interface builder files. Their format was changed to rely on XML, and at that point, the extension was renamed xib, but they are still referred to as nib files.)

As shown in Figure 11.9, when you select a nib file, the Interface Builder editor opens in the center of the Xcode window. The interface is shown with schematic versions of the runtime elements. You can use Editor, Simulate Document to open the current view in the simulator to get a better approximation of its runtime appearance.

You can show or hide the document structure area with Editor, Show/Hide Document Structure Area, or with the arrow at the lower-left of the canvas.

Figure 11.10 shows the document structure area for the master view controller on iPhone. If you look at the iPad nib file, you will see the same basic design arranged for the iPad. (The iPhone version is used in these figures because it is more compact.)

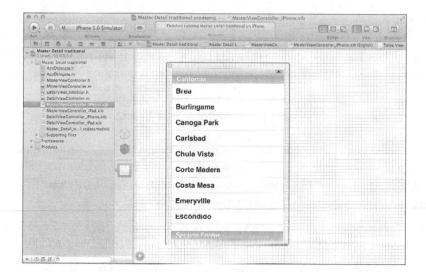

FIGURE 11.9
Start to work with the Interface Builder editor.

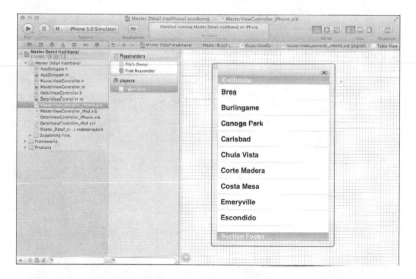

FIGURE 11.10
Open the document structure area.

NOTE

The document structure area in Xcode 4.2 was referred to as the dock in previous versions of Xcode.

The main view that you see is a UITableView. Table views are used extensively with Core Data because their integration on both Mac OS (with bindings) and iOS (with data sources) gives you a great deal of functionality with very little programming effort. When you have a table view on the canvas, it automatically is populated with the data shown in these figures. When it is combined with your own data, you will see your own data at runtime, but in Interface Builder, it uses the placeholder data.

▶ Hour 19, "Using UITableView on iOS," p. 337, and Hour 20, "Using NSTableView on Mac OS," p. 363, provide more information on this topic.

If you choose another nib file such as the detail view controller shown in Figure 11.11, you see a slightly different type of display. Whereas the master view controller consists of a table view, the detail view controller consists of a single object that contains text. The structure and nomenclature are consistent and common:

▶ A table view lists the items that can be displayed. This is the master view. (In older versions of Xcode and its templates, it was often called the root view.)

▶ The user taps or clicks on an item in the table view, and its data is displayed. This is the detail view.

FIGURE 11.11
Detail views display the data.

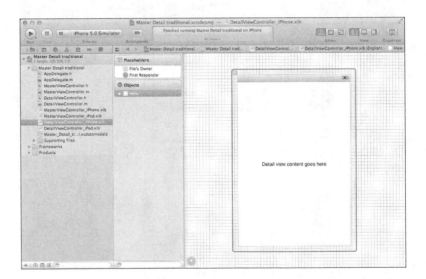

A tap or click on a table view can bring up another table view so that you have several lists through which to navigate until you arrive at the detail information you are searching for. On iPhone, this is a common interface. On iPad, it is common to flatten the navigation hierarchy. You can do this because the screen is larger, and you can get several levels of navigation onto a larger and more complex display.

On Mac OS, you can use multiple windows or panes to provide yet another style of navigation: One window can display the top-level navigation options, while another displays a second level of navigation options. A third window or pane can simultaneously display the selected data.

As shown in the Master-Detail Application template, you can share a single data model and just switch nib files to implement the appropriate interface for iPhone and iPad. You can do much the same thing yourself on Mac OS.

▶ Hour 14, "Working with Storyboards," p. 239, shows you how to use storyboards to make the transitions and alternative nib files easier to manage. Hour 15, "Saving Data with a Navigation Interface," p. 257, explores the navigation interface used frequently on iPhone and in a master view controller on iPad. Hour 16, "Using Split Views on iPad," p. 279, explores the iPad way of working with multiple views.

Working with the Document Structure Area

The document structure area represents the structure of the nib document when it is closed. When it is opened, it represents the structure of the nib document as well as the objects within each of the structural elements. When you select an element of the nib in the canvas, it is highlighted in the opened document outline area. If it is visible in the document outline area, it also is highlighted. The Editor, Reveal in Document Outline command opens the document structure area if necessary and highlights the selected object.

In Figure 11.9, the closed document outline area displays three objects. In the opened document outline area of Figure 11.10, they are displayed and identified. In the closed version, a small horizontal line separates the top two objects; in the opened version, that distinction is identified by name. The top objects are *placeholders*, and the others (if any) are *objects*.

Understanding Placeholders

Placeholders (sometimes called *proxy objects*) are objects that are present at runtime for every nib file. The first one, *file's owner*, is the object that controls the nib file. It is typically a descendant of UIViewController (iOS) or NSViewController (Mac OS); in a document-based app, it is typically a descendant of UIDocument (iOS) or NSDocument (Mac OS).

That object is instantiated at runtime and, when it needs to display the nib file, it executes calls to one of the following methods (or one of several similar methods):

On Mac OS:

```
- (id)initWithNibNamed:(NSString *)nibName bundle:(NSBundle *)bundle
```

On iOS:

```
- (id)initWithNibName:(NSString *)nibName bundle:(NSBundle *)nibBundle
```

The method declarations indicate that an ID is returned, and that could be any object. In fact, on Mac OS, an NSNib is returned; on iOS, a UIViewController is returned. This distinction is important at the lower levels of the Cocoa and Cocoa Touch frameworks. All that matters to you is that the nib file is loaded at runtime by some instantiated object in the app, and when it is loaded, File's Owner is set to that instantiated object that loaded it.

TIP

When you are working in Interface Builder editor, select the File's Owner object and use the Identity inspector in the utility area to inspect or set the File's Owner class, as shown in Figure 11.12.

FIGURE 11.12
Set File's
Owner.

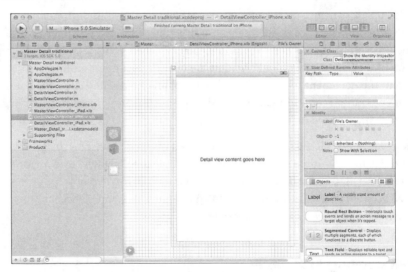

NOTE

The class name that you specify in the Identity inspector is the name of the class to be used by Interface Builder editor. At runtime, the class that is actually used might be a descendant of that class, but that should not matter to you.

After you have specified the class for File's Owner, Interface Builder editor can locate that class's interface. You can control-click or right-click on File's Owner to bring up a list of the class's interface properties that can be connected to Interface Builder editor objects, as shown in Figure 11.13.

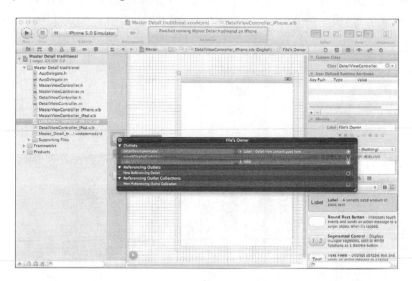

FIGURE 11.13
You will be able to connect interface elements to their corresponding code objects.

▶ See Hour 12, "Finding Your Way Around Interface Builder Editor: The Code Story," p. 209.

Below the File's Owner object, the other placeholder is the *First Responder*. Your app receives messages on which it can act. These can be generated by the framework itself or by user actions. Some of these messages are handled by the frameworks, and some are handled by your code. The messaging architecture for Mac OS and for iOS (as well as for many other graphical user interfaces) relies on a chain of responders.

When an action takes place, a message is sent to the most immediate object—for example, the button directly beneath the mouse. If that object does not act on the message, the message is passed on to the next responder in the chain. This architecture relies on a responder chain, and the item at the front of the chain is the first responder. The responder chain is modified by events—usually in response to user actions. The button that was first responder before you moved the mouse might not even be in the responder chain at all after you have moved the mouse or clicked in another window.

The first responder placeholder in Interface Builder editor is actually a list of all the actions that are defined for all the objects that are allowed to become first responders. As with the file's owner, a control-click opens that list, as shown in Figure 11.14.

FIGURE 11.14
View the list of first responder actions.

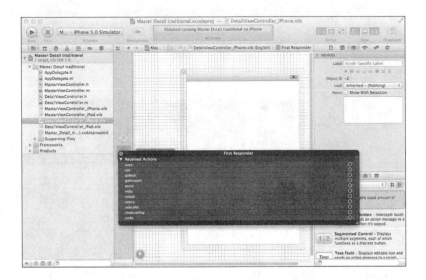

▶ As with file's owner actions, you will be able to connect these events to your code in Hour 12, p. 209.

Working with Objects

Beneath the placeholders are the objects that you add to the interface. You drag these from the library in the utility area as described in Hour 1, "Introducing Xcode 4." Use the Objects tab and the filter at the bottom of the Library pane to find the object you are looking for. Drag the object onto the canvas or into the document outline area. In either case, you can place an object inside many other types of objects. Not all objects can accept objects within them, but a remarkable number can. When placing an object within another one, be certain to check the document outline area to make certain that it is within the object and not merely on top of it.

Get in the habit of immediately using inspectors as soon as you have dragged an object from the Library onto your canvas. Here are some of the settings you might make or modify most of the time:

▶ **Identity Inspector**—Always set the class of the object unless the default class is correct. For example, if you drag a button object from the Library, you might want to change its class to MyButton if that is what you intend because you have subclassed the standard button class to add new behavior. If you drag an abstract object (such as Object) from the Library, definitely change its class. Except for the smallest interfaces, also set the Label attribute, as shown in Figure 11.15. This string will appear in the document structure area instead of a generic name such as View. ("Label" is used in the sense of the name of the object and not in the sense of a companion label field to a separate field containing data.)

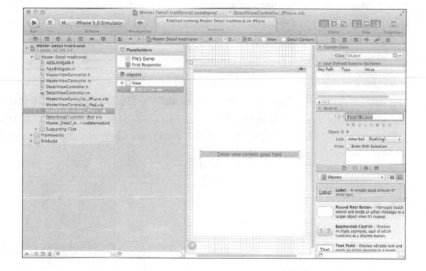

FIGURE 11.15
Use the Identity inspector.

▶ **Attributes Inspector**—Here is where you set background, default text, and just about everything else associated with the object's appearance.

▶ **Size Inspector**—Set size and autosizing options here.

▶ **Connections Inspector**—This inspector summarizes the connections that you can make with File's Owner and First Responder so you can see them all in one place for an interface object.

▶ **Bindings and View Effects Inspectors**—These Mac OS–only inspectors are discussed in Hour 20, "Using NSTableView on Mac OS," p. 363.

Summary

Xcode's Interface Builder editor lets you create and edit your interfaces using a graphical user interface itself. You can simulate the interface on its own (without the rest of the app). Inspectors at the top of the utility area let you inspect and modify attributes of the interface elements including their size, identity, and connections to code and other objects.

Q&A

Q. *How many times does an interface object appear in the Interface Builder editor?*

A. If you have added it to the canvas, it is shown in the canvas in a schematic view that suggests its appearance in the runtime interface. It is also shown in the document structure area in its hierarchy of objects (for example, text field and button within a view).

Q. *What are placeholders?*

A. Placeholders are objects related to the nib file. File's Owner represents the owner of the nib file: This relationship is established at runtime. First Responder is a placeholder that collects all the actions from any class that can become a first responder. The File's Owner placeholder is an object at runtime. There is no First Responder object.

Workshop

Quiz

1. *What is a universal app?*

2. *What is the sandbox?*

Quiz Answers

1. A universal app contains common code for both iPad and iPhone device families. In practice, this means separate nib files along with relatively small sections of code that switch between the two nib files depending on the device in use. Many people build apps with the universal setting on, but they do not add to the default implementations for one of the devices. This means that when

they want to move ahead to implement the other implementation, they do not have to start from scratch.

2. The sandbox is the area of storage assigned to a specific app. With the simulator, it is found inside ~/Library/Application Support/iPhone Simulator.

Activities

Browse the Mac App Store for SQLite. You will find a number of apps that let you browse SQLite databases. Occasionally, you might want to browse the actual SQLite database behind your app. One of these will let you do so. Be careful to always work in a copy of the database, and NEVER change its structure. Because you will use this only for occasional debugging and research, limit your choices to the apps that cost less than $10. Do not bother with an app that converts a format such as CSV to SQLite; instead, look for SQLite viewers. Then copy one of your sandbox `sqlite` files and take a look.

HOUR 12

Finding Your Way Around the Interface Builder Editor: The Code Story

---

What You'll Learn in This Hour:

▶ Working with connections
▶ Creating and connecting IBOutlets
▶ Creating and connecting IBActions
▶ Making connections programmatically

Using the Connections Inspector

The heart of the linking between the code in your app and the objects in your interface is the connections you draw in Xcode. (You also sometimes create them programmatically, as you will see later in this hour.) Control-clicking an object in the document outline area or on the canvas brings up a list of connections, as shown in Figure 11.14 in Hour 11, "Finding Your Way Around the Interface Builder Editor: The Graphics Story," p. 189. The Connections inspector lets you do the same thing using standard inspector behavior. As you are analyzing and debugging your app, inspectors are often a faster way to work.

With the list of connections shown in Figure 11.14, you select an object and control-click it to show the connections. You can use the close box to close the list; also, if you simply select another object with a click, that object is selected and the list disappears. (Of course, you can open another one with control-click.)

Inspector behavior leaves the inspector open and displays the data for whatever object you have selected. Thus, if you want to compare the connections of two objects, use the Connections inspector and alternate between selecting the two objects.

Whichever technique you use, it is important to differentiate between *outlets* and *referencing outlets*, as described in the following section.

Understanding Outlets

An outlet is an interface object that is connected to a runtime object in your code. Outlets are identified by the keyword IBOutlet, which is recognized by Interface Builder editor but is not part of the Objective-C language. After you have connected the interface object to an object in your code, they function as a single object that combines code and interface.

Outlets are often simple interface elements such as text fields or labels. They also can be other elements that might not even be visible. For example, a table view can have a data source object and a delegate—they help control the table view and manage its data. Neither the data source nor the delegate is visible, but the results of their work can be visible.

The connections between your interface (in a nib file) and your code can be drawn using the Connections inspector. You also can make connections between objects directly by holding down the Control key and dragging from one object to another. Typically, when you release the mouse button to end the drawing of the connection, a small pop-up lets you specific details of the connection.

In this hour, you learn how to use the Connections inspector because that is the heart of the connections. In later hours, we explore direct connections drawn between two objects in Interface Builder editor (including in its document outline area or between the canvas and the document outline area). All these techniques do the same basic things; they are often interchangeable depending on what you are trying to do and your preferences.

File's Owner and the table view created for you in the Master Detail Application template demonstrate connections. The only modification to the project that has been made is that the Table View object has been renamed My Table View, as described in Hour 11 and shown in Figure 11.15. (In Hour 11, you created your own project based on that template. You may want to continue with that project rather than creating a new project.)

Once you have a project to work with, start to explore connections. Show the utility (if necessary) and then select the Connections inspector. Start by selecting the File's Owner placeholder, as shown in Figure 12.1.

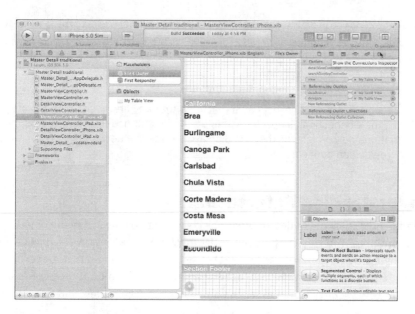

FIGURE 12.1
Look at outlets
for File's
Owner.

The Identity inspector tells you that the class for File's Owner is `MasterViewController`.
Listing 12.1 shows the interface for `MasterViewController.h`, and you can now compare that code with the Connections inspector.

LISTING 12.1 `MasterViewController.h`

```
#import <UIKit/UIKit.h>

@class DetailViewController;

#import <CoreData/CoreData.h>

@interface MasterViewController : UITableViewController
  <NSFetchedResultsControllerDelegate>

@property (strong, nonatomic) DetailViewController *detailViewController;

@property (strong, nonatomic) NSFetchedResultsController *fetchedResultsController;
@property (strong, nonatomic) NSManagedObjectContext *managedObjectContext;

@end
```

There are three declared properties in this interface: `detailViewController`,
`fetchedResultsController`, and `managedObjectContext`.

But what of the other two outlets shown in Figure 12.1 (`view` and
`searchDisplayController`)? If you follow the hierarchy up, you will see that

MasterViewController is a subclass of UITableViewController, which in turn, is a subclass of UIViewController. UIViewController is where these two outlets are declared.

> **NOTE**
>
> Just as First Responder collects all the actions that any first responder can call, so, too, the Connections inspector scans up the inheritance hierarchy to find outlets that can be connected. They are displayed in the Connections inspector, which is where you can connect them.

Understanding Referencing Outlets

Referencing outlets are outlets in other objects that are connected *to* the object you are examining. You can compare the outlet to view in MasterViewController (actually inherited from UIViewController) to the referencing outlets dataSource and delegate in MasterViewController (actually inherited from protocols adopted by UITableViewController) to see the difference between outlets and referencing outlets.

Although it can seem a bit tangled, it is a common structure to have a single object that in some contexts contains an outlet (view in MasterViewController) and in other contexts is referenced by another object, as is the case with dataSource and delegate in MasterViewController's adopted protocols. UITableView is a frequent example of this, and that is how it works with Core Data.

▶ There is more on this in Hour 19, "Using UITableView on iOS," p. 337.

Figure 12.2 lets you look at the other side of the connections. Select My Table View, and the Connections inspector changes to what is shown in Figure 12.2. From the point of view of My Table View, the outlets are dataSource and delegate while the referencing outlet is view.

> **NOTE**
>
> For some people, this is a difficult concept to grasp. If it is murky for you, do not worry at this point. As you work through the examples in this book, you will come across many samples of connections and outlets and gradually you will become more comfortable with them.

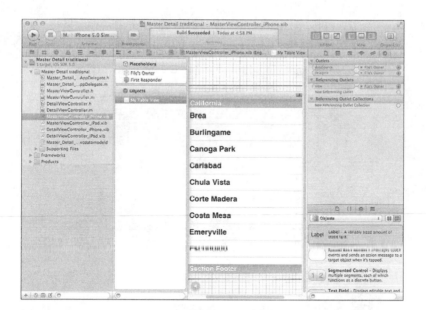

FIGURE 12.2
Look at connections from the other side.

Try It Yourself

Create, Break, and Debug Connections

You have seen how to examine connections from the point of view of the object's outlets and from the opposite viewpoint of the referencing object(s). In this task, you actually work with those connections.

As is often the case with Cocoa and Cocoa Touch, there can be a hefty bit of preparation work both in terms of understanding and in terms of laying the groundwork for later action on your part. Here you will see how to create, break, and debug connections.

One of the reasons that they are all covered together in this task is that, after you have your interfaces created, each of those steps is done with one command. Follow these steps:

1. Select File's Owner, as shown previously in Figure 12.1.

2. Break the connection to view by clicking the small *x* in the lozenge labeled My Table View. You will see the connection line disappear.

3. Objective-C is a dynamic language, and these connections happen at runtime. With the connection broken, build and run the app (you can just click Run at the upper-left of the workspace window). (Make certain you run the app in the simulator for the device you have chosen. If you have made changes to the iPhone nib file, make sure to simulate the app on iPhone.)

4. This step is a non-step. Observe that you get no compile or build errors.

5. As the app runs, it will crash. Depending on your settings in Xcode's Preferences, your display might respond to the error in varying ways. The standard behavior at this point is shown in Figure 12.3.

FIGURE 12.3
Without the connection, the app will crash.

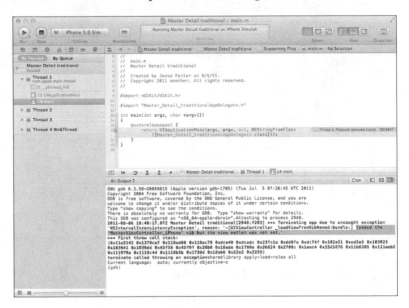

What you see is this information:

▶ The Debug navigator is shown. It locates where the crash occurred.

▶ In the editor, the SIGABRT message is shown and the offending line of code is marked with the green arrow.

▶ At the bottom of the editor, the Debug pane is shown with the error message. If you do not see it, use the controls at the top of the Debug pane to view the right side of the Debug pane rather than the left side or the combined view.

The panes in Figure 12.3 have been rearranged a bit, and the critical part of the error message is highlighted. The view outlet is not set (that is because you just deleted it).

6. Reconnect view to My Table View. Drag from the circle next to view in the Connections inspector to My Table View in the document outline area.

Alternatively, you can drag from the circle to My Table View, as shown in the center of the canvas (with the default list of Brea, Burlingame, and so forth).

7. Run and observe the non-event: no error message.

Congratulations! You now know how to make, break, and debug connections. ▲

Using IBOutlets for Data Elements

You have seen how to connect your code to interface elements, but one of the most common situations you need to address is adding a new interface element as well as a code element. In the Master Detail Application template, the master view controller provides a list of all the detail items you have created in the app. When you create a new detail item (with the + at the upper-right of the master view controller), its timeStamp property is set to the current date. That is the behavior that is built in to the template, but you can easily expand it.

The code in the template uses a UILabel field to display the current timestamp when you create a new Event record. What is displayed is the description property that is common to all objects adopting the NSObject Protocol—which is all NSObjects. You can rely on the description property to give you a string for every object that you can display. (You can also override it to give specific information about your subclass.) It often displays some data, so it is the easiest way to display an object's value. This combination of UILabel and the description property is a fast and simple way of demonstrating the creation and display of a new object.

While this is fine for debugging, it is not always optimal for moving on to an incremental development process. In this section, you learn how to add a new field to the interface and how to connect it to a new attribute in the data model. The data for this attribute will be filled in automatically using the current date—just as happens with the timeStamp attribute in the template. However, instead of using a Date type for the attribute (that is, an underlying type of NSDate), this new field will be a String type in the data model (that is, an underlying type of NSString). This will make it easier to move on to the next step, which includes editing the automatically generated string and saving the results.

Converting Dates to Strings

Converting dates to strings (and vice versa) is very common, particularly in languages such as Objective-C that are strongly typed. If you are used to languages other than Objective-C, you might be expecting a single function that does the job for you, but that is not the case. You can argue back and forth for hours as to whether the Objective-C structure is overly complicated or blessedly flexible. Rather than argue, it is easier just to understand and use the features you have.

The heart of date/string conversions in Objective-C is a formatter that combines options and styles for handling the conversion. Formatters are available for numbers, dates, and other types of data. All of them function more or less in the same way.

Here is the code you use to convert a date to a string using a formatter. You will probably use it over and over:

```
// get a date — in this case the current date
NSDate *date = [NSDate date];

// create a date formatter
NSDateFormatter *dateFormatter = [[NSDateFormatter alloc] init];

// set the style for the date using a constant from the framework
[dateFormatter setDateStyle:NSDateFormatterLongStyle];

// set the style for the time using a constant
[dateFormatter setTimeStyle:NSDateFormatterLongStyle];

// you can use both date and time styles or only one

// format the date to a string
NSString *dateString = [dateFormatter stringFromDate:date];
```

TIP

Remember that attributes in the data model become properties in your code.

To implement this change, you need to modify insertNewObject in MasterViewController.m. Listing 12.2 shows the code as it exists in the template. You might want to refer to this listing as you carry out the task that follows.

LISTING 12.2 insertNewObject As It Is in the Template

```
- (void)insertNewObject
{
  // Create a new instance of the entity managed by the fetched results
    controller.
  NSManagedObjectContext *context = [self.fetchedResultsController
    managedObjectContext];
```

```
NSEntityDescription *entity = [[self.fetchedResultsController fetchRequest]
  entity];
NSManagedObject *newManagedObject =
  [NSEntityDescription insertNewObjectForEntityForName:[entity name]
    inManagedObjectContext:context];

// If appropriate, configure the new managed object.
// Normally you should use accessor methods, but using KVC here avoids the need
//  to add a custom class to the template.

[newManagedObject setValue:[NSDate date] forKey:@"timeStamp"];

// Save the context.
NSError *error = nil;
if (![context save:&error])
  {
    /*
    Replace this implementation with code to handle the error appropriately.

    abort() causes the application to generate a crash log and terminate.
    You should not use this function in a shipping application, although it
      may be useful during development.
    */
    NSLog(@"Unresolved error %@, %@", error, [error userInfo]);
    abort();
  }
}
```

Try It Yourself

Add a New Data Field to the Model and a New Text Field to the Interface

Now that you know how to modify insertNewObject in MasterViewController.m, it is time to modify the model and the interface.

This is the basic recipe for adding a new data field to the model and a new text field to the interface. You need to do both to complete this task, but you can do them in either order. Note that this task uses the iPad nib file.

NOTE

As you work through this task, you might notice that you've switched back and forth from one file to another several times. That is common as you are connecting items. Before long, the various events will blur into one sequence that you can almost perform in your sleep.

1. Because you are going to be modifying the data model, the simplest way to start is by removing the existing file from the simulator. That way, the built-in template code will create a new file for you with the new data

model. Use the steps described in the "Finding Your Sandbox" section in Hour 11 to do this.

▶ You will learn how to handle model migration in Hour 24, "Migrating Data Models," p. 423. For now, simply removing the old file will do the trick.

2. Open the data model, as shown in Figure 12.4. Select the Event entity, and add a new attribute to it. Name it **newField** and set its type to String.

FIGURE 12.4
Add a new field
to the data
model.

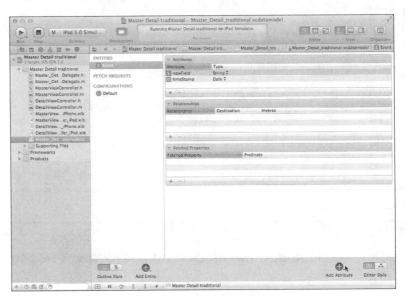

3. Locate insertNewObject in MasterViewController.m (refer to Listing 12.2). newManagedObject is the new Entity object that is created. Now that you have added the newField attribute to it in the data model, when you insert a new object, that attribute will be present. Following the line of code that sets the old timeStamp attribute, add code to get the current date, format it (as shown in the sidebar, "Converting Dates to Strings"), and set newField to that formatted string. That section of the method should look like Listing 12.3.

LISTING 12.3   Add a New Field to insertNewObject

```
// existing code to set the timeStamp field
[newManagedObject setValue:[NSDate date] forKey:@"timeStamp"];

// use a date formatter to convert the current date to a string
NSDate *date = [NSDate date];
```

```
NSDateFormatter *dateFormatter = [[NSDateFormatter alloc] init];
[dateFormatter setDateStyle:NSDateFormatterLongStyle];
[dateFormatter setTimeStyle:NSDateFormatterLongStyle];
NSString *dateString = [dateFormatter stringFromDate:date];

// set the new field to the formatted string
[newManagedObject setValue:dateString forKey:@"newField"];
```

4. Select DetailViewController_iPad.xib to show the Interface Builder editor.

5. Show utilities if necessary. From the library, drag a new text field into the canvas, as shown in Figure 12.5.

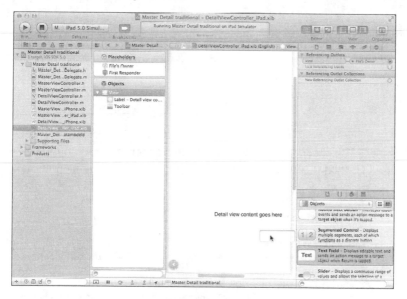

FIGURE 12.5
Add a new text field to the canvas.

6. Use the Identity inspector to provide a meaningful label for the new field. As shown in Figure 12.6, this label appears both in the Identity inspector and in the document structure area.

7. Add a UITextField to DetailViewController.h with this line of code:

```
@property (strong, nonatomic) IBOutlet UITextField *textField;
```

8. Add the synthesize directive to DetailViewController.m:

```
@synthesize textField;
```

FIGURE 12.6
Create a meaningful label for
the new field.

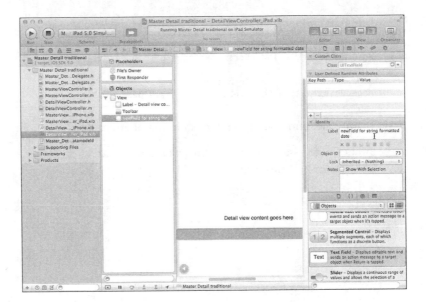

9. In DetailViewController.m, change `configureView` to fill in the new
    interface field. The code should look like this:

```
- (void)configureView
{
  // Update the user interface for the detail item.

  if (self.detailItem) {
    self.detailDescriptionLabel.text = [self.detailItem description];

    // ADD THIS LINE OF CODE FOR THE NEW FIELD
    self.textField.text = [(NSManagedObject *)self.detailItem
      valueForKey:@"newField"];

  }
}
```

10. Connect File's Owner in DetailViewController_iPad.xib to the new text field.
    As you control-draw the line from File's Owner to the new field, the label
    for the field will appear, as shown in Figure 12.7. This is very helpful when
    several objects are adjacent in a small area.

11. When you release the mouse button, you can choose which outlet in the
    code you want to connect to. In this case, it is `textField`, as shown in
    Figure 12.8.

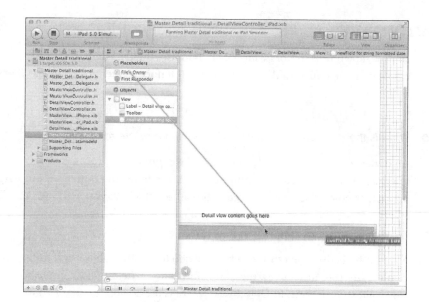

FIGURE 12.7
Control-drag
from File's
Owner to the
new field.

FIGURE 12.8
Choose the
outlet.

12. Make similar changes to DetailViewController_iPhone.xib.

You should be able to run the app now and see the formatted string as you create
new objects with + in the master view controller.

Summary

This hour has shown how to work with code in Interface Builder editor. You have learned how to create outlets and connect them to interface elements such as text fields.

Q&A

Q. *What is the difference between an outlet and a referencing outlet?*

A. An outlet is a property in an object's interface that can be connected to an interface element or another runtime object. A referencing outlet is a property in another object that is connected to the object at which you are looking.

Q. *What is a formatter, and why is it used?*

A. A formatter is an object that can be attached to another object and transform its data. In other languages, these transformations are often accomplished with built-in functions. In Objective-C, there is a trade-off for slightly more complexity in some simple cases but much more power in many other cases.

Workshop

Quiz

1. *How do you create a connection?*

2. *How do you break a connection?*

Quiz Answers

1. Control-drag from an object such as a view or File's Owner to an interface object.

2. Control-click on a view or File's Owner to bring up all connections. Click the small *x* at the left of the connection you want to break.

Activities

Practice adding new fields, properties, and connections to your app. Watch what happens if you remove a property from the interface file—note how Xcode shows the connection is invalid. Use the *X* to delete an invalid connection or redraw it to the correct property. Broken connections are a common cause of runtime problems.

HOUR 13

Control-Dragging Your Way to Code

What You'll Learn in This Hour:

▶ Switching data models for the master-detail application template

▶ Building IBOutlets for the new data model with your mouse

▶ Building IBActions for the new data model with your mouse

Repurposing the Master-Detail Application Template

The Master-Detail Application template, when built as a universal app, gives you a split view controller interface for iPad and a navigator interface for iPhone, with both of them running off the same data model. This is a powerful structure that gives you a big leg up on development.

NOTE

The steps in this hour are summarized in Hour 15, "Saving Data with a Navigation Interface," as you continue work with this template. That summary omits the steps that help you explore the template as you are working; if you want to replicate the task in the future, you might prefer that shorter list of steps. It also reverses the sequence of creating connections and fields so that you see both ways of working. In addition, the figures illustrating the use of the Assistant editor use two different alignments of the panes of the editor so that you can take your pick.

Creating a New Project

Begin by creating a new project based on the Master-Detail Template (Split View-Controller in older versions of Xcode). As shown in Figure 13.1, provide a name for the project, provide your company name, and choose to use Core Data. Although it is not strictly required, the example in this hour uses Automatic Reference Counting, the modern way of managing memory. If you do not use it or if you are using an earlier version of Xcode that does not support it, your template code may be slightly different from the code shown here. Because it handles memory with much less effort on your part, it is worthwhile converting to using Automatic Reference Counting in your new projects.

FIGURE 13.1
Create a new universal project.

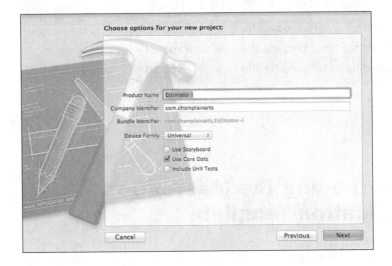

Choose options for your new project:

Product Name   Estimator I
Company Identifier   com.champlainarts
Bundle Identifier   com.champlainarts.Estimator-I
Device Family   Universal

☐ Use Storyboard
☑ Use Core Data
☐ Include Unit Tests

Cancel   Previous   Next

TIP
Use the universal device family, but do not use storyboards or unit tests.

Create the files for the new project and just test that it works. You should really do a pair of tests on the simulator—one for iPhone and the other for iPad.

The heart of the template is a master view controller (the class is called `MasterView Controller`) and a detail view controller (called `DetailViewController`). `MasterView Controller` is a subclass of `UITableViewController`, and `DetailViewController` is a subclass of `UIViewController`. The various objects contain appropriate links and connections. In particular, you can count on these connections being declared and set up in the template. For the master view controller, there is a table view that functions the same way in both the pop-over (iPad) and navigator (iPhone). The detail view controller differs on the two devices because it has more data fields on the iPad.

NOTE

In versions of Xcode before 4.2, master view controllers were often called root view controllers.

Outlets in MasterViewController and DetailViewController

▶ `MasterViewController_iPad.xib` and `MasterViewController_iPhone.xib`—File's owner is `MasterViewController` in identity inspector.

  ▶ Outlets in Connections inspector.

    ▶ `detailViewController` not connected.

    ▶ `searchDisplayController` not connected.

    ▶ `view` connected to Table View.

  ▶ Referencing outlets in Connections inspector.

    ▶ `dataSource` in Table View.

    ▶ `delegate` in Table View.

▶ `DetailViewController_iPad.xib`—File's owner is `DetailViewController` in Identity inspector.

  ▶ Outlets in Connections inspector.

    ▶ `detailDescriptionLabel` connected to Label—Detail view content goes here.

    ▶ `searchDisplayController` not connected.

    ▶ `view` connected to View.

  ▶ No referencing outlets connect to `DetailViewController`.

▶ `DetailViewController_iPhone.xib`—File's owner is `DetailViewController`.

  ▶ Outlets in Connections inspector.

    ▶ `detailDescriptionLabel` connected to Label—Detail view content goes here.

    ▶ `searchDisplayController` not connected.

    ▶ `view` connected to View.

  ▶ No referencing outlets connect to `DetailViewController`.

This is what you have in the template. If you want to repurpose it, you have two sets of changes to make:

▶ In the master view controller, change the table so that it picks up the new entity in your data model rather than the default Event entity. Then change it to pick up the appropriate attribute from your data model instead of timeStamp.

▶ In the detail view controller, pick up the appropriate entity and attribute for the label object. Alternatively, use a text field or other element. Furthermore, you can use other elements to display new attributes for your new data model.

Creating a New Data Model

You can create a brand-new data model or work with the existing one. If you do that, you will need to rename the Event entity and adjust the timeStamp attribute. The data model is so small in the template that modifying it might even be faster than creating a new one from scratch.

This data model will eventually consist of two tables: Customer and Job. It will contain estimates and eventually prices for a variety of jobs, each of which will be associated with at least one customer. For now, it just needs a Customer table. You can take the data model from the template and modify it:

▶ Change the Event entity to Customer. Just double-click on the title to change it.

▶ Add the necessary attributes. Either delete the one old attribute (timeStamp) or change its name. Make certain the attributes have the appropriate data types set. The data model should look like Figure 13.2 when you are done.

TIP

As noted in Hour 17, "Structuring Apps for Core Data, Documents, and Shoeboxes," the simplest way to avoid data model errors is simply to remove the old sqlite file from the Documents folder in the sandbox. Make sure you do that now.

Adjust the Code for the New Data Model

This template is easy to reuse not only because it is well-designed, but also because its references to the data model are few and far between. The original data model has an Event entity with a single attribute—timeStamp. Using the Search navigator, search for Event.

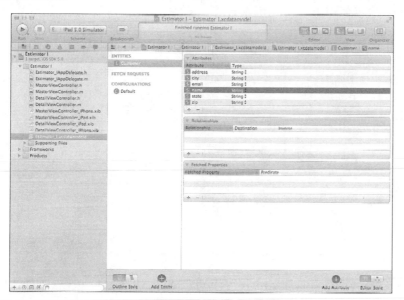

FIGURE 13.2
Build your new data model (or revise the old one).

You will find two instances: one is the entity in the data model (unless you have already changed it), and the other is a reference to the entity for the Controller. This is typical for basic Core Data apps. Exactly where in the controller the reference is varies.

NOTE

The Document-Based Application template is worth exploring in the iOS templates. It builds in iCloud syncing for a document that contains a Core Data stack. Compare it to the document-less Master-Detail Application in which a Core Data stack belongs to the app itself and rather than to one (or more) documents within it.

Figure 13.3 shows the search. Line 184 contains the highlighted text.

Listing 13.1 shows the line of code to change in MasterViewController.m. There is even a helpful comment showing you what to change in the template. The code is in fetchedResultController.

LISTING 13.1   Change the Entity for the Fetched Result Controller

```
// Edit the entity name as appropriate.
NSEntityDescription *entity = [NSEntityDescription entityForName:@"Event"
  inManagedObjectContext:self.managedObjectContext];
```

FIGURE 13.3
Search for
Event.

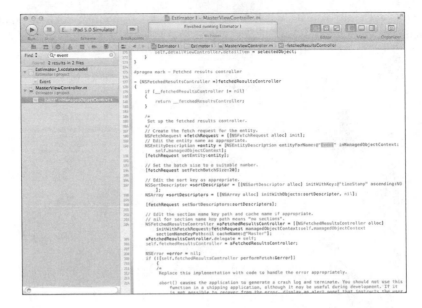

Change Event to Customer or whatever name you are using for your new data model.

Next, search for the attribute name used in the old entity—timeStamp in this case. As shown in Figure 13.4, there are four occurrences (if you have already changed the name in the data model, there will be three).

FIGURE 13.4
Search for
occurrences of
the old attribute
timeStamp.

The first occurrence is in `fetchedResultController`. You will need a sort descriptor. For now, sort on name rather than `timeStamp`. Just change the code to use name, as shown in Listing 13.2. As you can see, there is even another helpful comment for you.

LISTING 13.2   Change the Attribute for the Sort Descriptor

```
// Edit the sort key as appropriate.
NSSortDescriptor *sortDescriptor = [[NSSortDescriptor alloc]
  initWithKey:@"name" ascending:NO];
```

The second is in the `configureCell` method, as shown in Listing 13.3. It is used to set up a cell in the table of the master view controller. Just change the name from `timeStamp` to name. Now the table will list the names of the customers rather than the timestamps of the events.

LISTING 13.3   Change `valueForKey` in `configureCell`

```
- (void)configureCell:(UITableViewCell *)cell atIndexPath:(NSIndexPath
*)indexPath
{
  NSManagedObject *managedObject = [self.fetchedResultsController
    objectAtIndexPath:indexPath];
  cell.textLabel.text = [[managedObject valueForKey:@"name"] description];
}
```

The third and final occurrence is in `insertNewObject` where the current date is placed in the `timeStamp` attribute. There is another helpful comment. For now, replace the initialization with the string New Customer rather than the date. Listing 13.4 shows the old code.

LISTING 13.4   Change `setValue:` forKey

```
// If appropriate, configure the new managed object.
// Normally you should use accessor methods, but using KVC here avoids the
// need to add a custom class to the template.
[newManagedObject setValue:[NSDate date] forKey:@"timeStamp"];
```

Change the last line to:

```
[newManagedObject setValue:@"New Customer" forKey:@"name"];
```

As the comment mentions, using key-value coding can be a little more expensive than creating a custom class.

▶ You will see how to create a custom class later in Hour 15, "Saving Data with a Navigation Interface," p. 257.

Run the App

Try things out. The changes you have made so far are in the code, and not in the nib files. That means you should be able to switch the schema to iPhone and back again as you run and rerun the app. Figure 13.5 shows the iPhone version.

FIGURE 13.5
Test the app.

Adding New Fields as IBOutlets

In Hour 11, you learned how to add fields to the data model add new fields to the interface, and link them together. In this hour, you have revised a (or created a new) data model to contain additional fields for the Customer entity, so the first step is done.

Interface Builder Type Qualifiers and Macros

When you declare a property (or when you declare an instance variable), you can specify a type qualifier that Interface Builder editor can use. To indicate that a specific property (or variable) can be an outlet (that is, that it can be connected from a graphical element on a nib file's canvas to a code construct in the corresponding file), you use the IBOutlet type qualifier. This is defined as blank, so it has absolutely no effect on the declaration (because, at compile time, it has disappeared). It is only used by Interface Builder editor.

Beginning in iOS 4.0, a variation on IBOutlet has been introduced. You use it to make a connection to an NSArray or NSMutableArray object. You specify the type of object that will be placed in that collection so you might use it, as in this sample:

```
@property (strong, nonatomic) IBOutletCollection(UIView) NSArray *views;
```

IBOutletCollection is actually a macro rather than a type qualifier, but that should not matter to you.

To be able to connect a declared action in the interface file to an interface element on the canvas (perhaps a button), you use the type qualified IBAction. IBAction is defined to void. This means that when you declare an action in your interface file, you write something like the following:

```
- (IBAction)myAction:(id)sender;
```

At compile time, that line is interpreted as follows:

```
- (void)myAction:(id)sender;
```

However, Interface Builder editor is able to recognize it as an action because Interface Builder editor is looking at your source code and not the compiled code.

You can add the fields to the detail view by following the steps in the "Add a New Data Field to the Model and a New Text Field to the Interface" task from Hour 11. However, that is a tedious process. In this section, you learn how to automate that process with Xcode. DetailViewController is the controller that manages the detail view (DetailViewController_iPad.xib or DetailViewController_iPhone.xib).

NOTE

Remember that although there are two xib files, a single DetailViewController manages both of them. This is one of the virtues of using a universal app controlled by UIUserInterfaceIdiom tests in the controller code.

▶ You will see other ways to automate this process in Hour 15, p. 257. You will also see how to use table views in Part V so that you do not have to manage individual fields in the interface.

▼   **Try It Yourself**

Build the Interface with Control-Drag in Xcode

Because you already have the new fields (attributes) in the data model, what you need to do is

▶ Create `IBOutlet` properties in `DetailViewController.h`.

▶ Add new fields to the xib files from the Library in Xcode (`UITextField` for now is the most likely choice).

▶ Connect the `IBOutlet` properties to the appropriate xib file objects.

▶ At runtime, set the data appropriately as shown in step 9 of "Add a New Data Field to the Model and a New Text Field to the Interface":

```
self.textField.text = [(NSManagedObject *)self.detailItem
   valueForKey:@"newField"];
```

These are the steps you take to accomplish that task:

1. Start by opening the `DetailViewController_iPhone.xib` file in Xcode. The canvas is smaller than `DetailViewController_iPad.xib`, so it is a bit easier to work with. Eventually, you will also need to modify the other file.

2. You will need to work with both the `DetailViewController_iPhone.xib` file and `DetailViewController.h` at the same time. The simplest way is to use the Assistant editor, which lets you look at them side by side. Use View, Assistant to change the layout of the multiple panes. As shown in Figure 13.6, use the jump bar above the editors to open those two files. If you are running Lion, consider using full-screen mode.

3. Add a text field from the library to the interface as you saw in step 5 of "Try It Yourself: Add a New Data Field to the Model and a New Text Field to the Interface" in Hour 12.

4. Control-drag from the text field to the declaration of `DetailViewController` in `DetailViewController_iPhone.xib`, as shown in Figure 13.7. At this point, it does not matter which object you choose. (Compare Figure 13.6 with Figure 13.7: You can do it with the document outline shown or hidden. If the document outline is hidden, drag from the object on the canvas.)

5. When you are in a place where an outlet can be created, Xcode will tell you, as shown in Figure 13.7. You can place the new outlet anywhere that is syntactically correct within the interface.

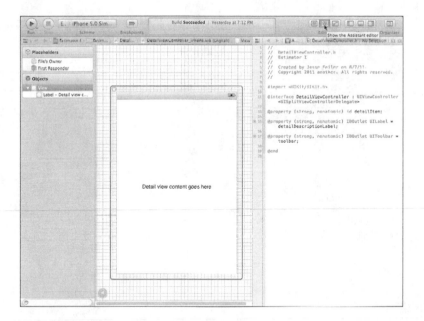

FIGURE 13.6
Use the Assistant editor to work on two files at the same time.

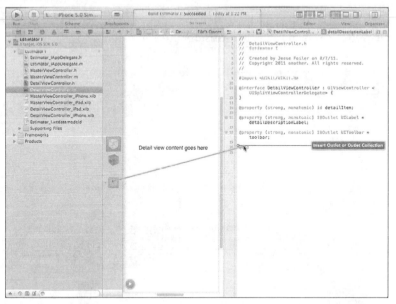

FIGURE 13.7
Control-drag to start to create a new outlet or outlet collection.

6. Release the mouse button, and a small dialog box appears, as shown in Figure 13.8. Select the type of the outlet you want (the default IBOutlet is fine in cases such as this), and provide the name for the outlet. As shown in Figure 13.8, that name need not be the same as the name of the attribute, but it should be related.

FIGURE 13.8
Provide details
of the new
outlet.

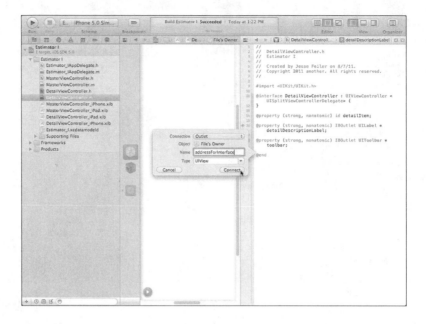

7. Click Connect, and you will see that the property has been added to the interface, as shown in the left Assistant pane in Figure 13.9.

FIGURE 13.9
Review the gen-
erated code.

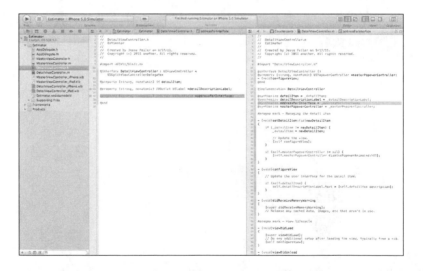

8. When you declare a property, you must remember to synthesize it in the implementation file. Xcode has already done that for you: This code has been added at the top of `DetailViewController.m`. Note that it uses the private instance variable that it created:

`@synthesize addressForInterface = _addressForInterface;`

This is shown in the right Assistant pane of Figure 13.9, and it provides a good illustration of how your can use multiple Asssistant panes with the counterpart setting.

9. You have to remember to dispose of the objects you create. Again, Xcode is ahead of you, having added the appropriate line to `viewDidUnload`, as shown here (the added line is shown in italics). Because Automatic Reference Counting is turned on in this example, you do not have to worry about `dealloc`.

```
- (void)viewDidUnload
{
    [self setAddressForInterface:nil];
    [super viewDidUnload];
    // Release any retained subviews of the main view.
    // e.g. self.myOutlet = nil;
}
```

10. If you look at the Connections inspector for File's Owner in `DetailViewContoller_iPad.xib`, as shown in Figure 13.10, you will see that Xcode has connected the outlet to the view object, which is where the line was first drawn from in step 4.

11. Repeat steps 3 through 9 for the other controller (iPad or iPhone).

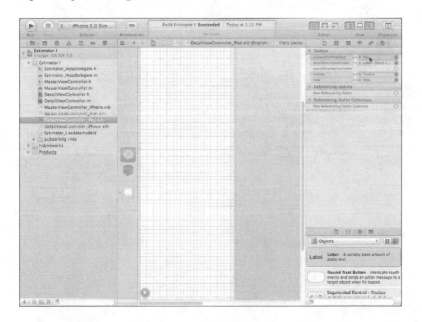

FIGURE 13.10
A connection is already made for you.

If you review this process, you will see that most of the steps involve reviewing what Xcode has done for you. There is very little work for you to do. You can eliminate a step if you create the fields in Interface Builder editor before you create the connections. In that way, you will be able to draw the connection (as in step 3) to the right place at the start. Some people like to create all the fields in the interface first; other people like to create all the outlets first (that is the process done here). It really does not matter because in either case, most of the work is done for you by Xcode.

▲

Summary

This hour has shown you how to use Xcode to automatically create properties and connections. This means less typing for you; it also means that the generated code is not subject to typing errors.

Q&A

Q. *Why is it often easier to repurpose a template than to start over from scratch?*

A. There are very few changes to make to the template, and it is often easier to modify template code rather than writing your own from scratch.

Q. *When do you use the Assistant editor?*

A. The Assistant editor lets you work on two files at the same time in the same window. You can manually configure it so that you specify the file for each pane of the assistant, but you can also set it up to automatically display related files (such as the .h for a .m file, and vice versa).

Workshop

Quiz

1. *What determines if a class is key-value compliant for a specific property?*

2. *How do you dispose of an object when you are finished with it using Automatic Reference Counting?*

Quiz Answers

1. If a class implements setValue:forKey and valueForKey for a property, that property on that class is KVC-compliant.

2. Set the property to nil. You must know that you are truly finished with it and will not be accessing the nil value as if it were an object in the next line of code.

Activities

Now that you have seen a good deal of Cocoa code, take an hour and sit down with the "Coding Guidelines for Cocoa" at http://developer.apple.com/library/ios/documentation/Cocoa/Conceptual/CodingGuidelines/CodingGuidelines.pdf. This provides guidelines and some options so that your code will be easier to read and maintained. Keep the guidelines handy. (As a PDF file, it is a good one to download through iTunes to your iPad or iPhone.)

Working with Storyboards and Swapping Views

What You'll Learn in This Hour:
- ▶ Creating storyboard projects
- ▶ Swapping views with nib files or with storyboards
- ▶ Creating the Estimator app project with a storyboard

Creating a Project with a Storyboard

This hour provides an overview of using storyboards as you encounter them in the Xcode templates. In many cases, you can work with the default code and merely add your own view objects such as text fields. The hour starts with a new project based on the Master-Detail Application template that has been used previously to build the Estimator example. In this hour, that example is rebuilt using the storyboard infrastructure rather than nib files.

Storyboards are a new (Xcode 4.2) way of building your interfaces and apps. They are available only for iOS and are primarily a new user interface to the existing structures. As you will see, your storyboards contain the same elements you are used to creating in your nib files, and you manipulate them in exactly the same way you have always done. In Xcode, this means dragging objects from the library pane into the canvas and then connecting them to code in your programs in any of the ways described previously.

- ▶ By far, the easiest techniques for most people are those described in Hour 13, "Control-Dragging Your Way to Code," p. 223.

Although the basic techniques are the same, storyboards are different enough in their developer interfaces that it makes sense not to convert existing nib files to storyboards. Apple's advice to developers is to either adopt storyboards for a new project or adopt storyboards for a major new segment of an existing project.

Existing code examples on developer.apple.com tend not to use storyboards; new examples will use them where appropriate. As a result, you will probably find yourself working with the old-fashioned nib file structure on some projects and with storyboards on your new projects. Take the time to read through this hour to see what you get with storyboards. They address issues that have long been problems for developers.

Table 14.1 can help you get started. It lists the iOS templates in Xcode 4.2 and for each one indicates the options you can set with checkboxes as you create the project. Starting with Core Data and with storyboards gives you a big leg up when it comes to developer productivity. Attempting to retrofit either Core Data or storyboards can be a difficult process.

TABLE 14.1   Options for iOS Templates in Xcode 4.2

Template	Storyboard	Core Data	Automatic Reference Counting	Unit Tests
Document	*	x	x	x
Master-Detail Application	x	x	x	x
OpenGL Game	x		x	x
Page-Based Application	x		x	x
Single-View Application	x		x	x
Tabbed Application	x		x	x
Utility Application	x	x	x	x
Empty Application	*	x	x	x

x checkbox to use/not use feature

* feature always used

NOTE

Before you get depressed at being stuck with an unfinished app that uses old-style interfaces, take a step back and look at where you have invested your time in that app. If it is your first iOS app, most of your time has been spent getting familiar with Cocoa Touch and, perhaps, even with Xcode if you have never used it before. The code you have written to implement your app is mostly about the app and its functionality. Your view controller code can usually be moved to storyboards with few if any changes. If you choose to rewrite the app using storyboards, you may find that the major effort will be redrawing the views in the storyboard editor and reconnecting the outlets you already have in your view controllers. For even a good-sized app, just redrawing the views is only the work of a few hours. It is worthwhile taking a day off to experiment with this ground-up rewrite because it turns out to be just a matter of redrawing views and reconnecting your outlets in many cases.

Swapping Views on iOS Devices

Swapping views is something that happens on iOS devices but not on Macs and other desktop-style computers. The reason is simple: The screen on an iOS device displays what is in effect one window at a time. There might be multiple views (think of split view controllers on iPad, for example, and the navigation bar–based interface to Settings on iPhone), but you do not have multiple windows as you do on a desktop computer. With multiple windows, you move them around, minimize and maximize them, and otherwise change their appearance. On an iOS screen, none of this applies.

As a result, it is common to automatically move views and their view controllers onto an iOS screen. In the case of split view controllers on iPad, the detail view controller can be swapped in and out as you navigate; often that is done with a navigation bar interface at the top of the detail view. On iPhone as well as iPad, detail views are often swapped in and out in response to taps on a table row.

In a split view controller, the master (root) view controller can also have a navigation bar interface that swaps those views in and out. When the iPad is vertically oriented, the master view controller appears in a pop-over, but the interior view is the same whether it is in the left size of a split view controller or in a pop-over.

NOTE

It is generally a bad idea to use navigation bars in both views of a split view controller, particularly when it is in a horizontal position and both views are shown side-by-side. You can confuse your users as they try to figure out which back button is appropriate.

You can experiment with swapping views by creating a new project using the Master-Detail Application template, as shown in Figure 14.1. Opt for a universal project, storyboards, and Core Data.

FIGURE 14.1
Create a new
iOS project
from the
Master-Detail
Application
template.

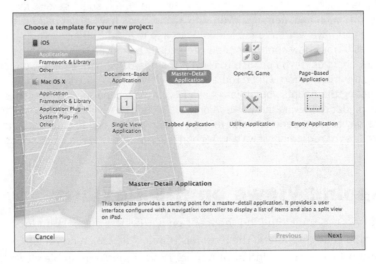

When you build and run the project for iPhone, a navigation interface appears, as shown at the left of Figure 14.2. Tap a row in the interface (it is the master view controller) and you see the detail view as shown at the right of Figure 14.2.

The same project built for iPad is shown in Figure 14.3.

With both interfaces, what happens is that the detail view is swapped in. On iPhone, it replaces that master view in the navigation interface, and on iPad, it replaces whatever view is currently shown in the detail view (it starts with default data). As always, the view is what you see; the view controller is what presents it and what is swapped in and out.

NOTE
The default text in the detail view for iPad is very small. To see that it has actually changed, you may need to rotate the simulator to horizontal.

Storyboards abstract a lot of this functionality and appearance, so as you will see in the following sections, the same universal code is used for both iPhone and iPad. There are separate storyboards for the two environments, but there is almost no difference in the code beyond the storyboards. That will become clear in the following two sections, which explore the old (non-storyboard) technique with the new (storyboard) technique.

FIGURE 14.2
On iPhone, you have a navigator interface.

FIGURE 14.3
You have a split view controller on iPad.

Swapping Detail Views (the Old Way)

As discussed in the "Using the Model/View/Controller Concepts" section of Hour 3, "Understanding the Basic Code Structure," many people think of the three components of the design pattern by drawing a mental picture of the model and the view with a subsidiary object connecting the two. This is natural because the model (basically the data model) is easy to understand and place in context, and the view (basically the interface) is equally easy to understand and place in context. The controller for many people is best described as "all the other stuff," and as you find out after a while, "all the other stuff" is a great deal of stuff indeed. With graphical tools in Xcode to help you design the Core Data model and the interface, your task in developing the controller is to write code. The controller is where traditional programming is done.

With experience, you learn that if you think of model/view/controller as a diagram with three objects in it, the controller object is not some subsidiary link: It is the bulk of your work and most of your app. In many ways, storyboards redraw the mental image of model/view/controller, placing the controllers at the heart of the app.

This has always been the case, although it has not been quite as obvious as it is with storyboards. For example, the Multiple Detail Views example on developer. apple.com provides code that lets you swap detail views in a split view controller.

NOTE

By the time you read this, Multiple Detail Views might have been converted to storyboards, so the critical code from the non-storyboard version is provided here.

At the left of Figure 14.2, a table view displays a table with two rows—one for each of the objects in the persistent store. As you will learn in Hour 19, "Using UITableView on iOS," you implement `didSelectRowAtIndexPath` to handle a tap in a table row. That method is part of the `UITableViewDelegate` protocol. In the Master-Detail Application template using nib files (that is, not using storyboards), it is implemented in `MasterViewController.m`, as shown in Listing 14.1.

As the code in Listing 14.1 shows, the three steps to switching a view controller (and, with it, a view) are

> ▶ **Create a new view controller**—Typically, this will be either a subclass of a framework class, such as `UIViewController` or `UITableViewController`, or a view that adopts a custom protocol, such as `SubstitutableDetail ViewController` protocol in the Multiple Detail View example. The newly created view controller is assigned to a local variable you create.

▶ Put the newly created view in a split view controller, navigator, or other place where it is displayed.

▶ Clean up any stray settings (such as reflecting that a new detail item has been selected), adjust popovers, and so forth.

This has been the standard way of changing views: You actually change view controllers, and the views come along with the controllers.

LISTING 14.1   Swapping the View

```
- (void)tableView:(UITableView *)tableView didSelectRowAtIndexPath:
  (NSIndexPath *)indexPath
{
  if ([[UIDevice currentDevice] userInterfaceIdiom] == UIUserInterfaceIdiomPhone) {
    if (!self.detailViewController) {
      self.detailViewController = [[DetailViewController alloc]
        initWithNibName:@"DetailViewController_iPhone" bundle:nil];
    }
    NSManagedObject *selectedObject = [[self fetchedResultsController]
      objectAtIndexPath:indexPath];
    self.detailViewController.detailItem = selectedObject;
    [self.navigationController pushViewController:self.detailViewController
      animated:YES];
  } else {
    NSManagedObject *selectedObject = [[self fetchedResultsController]
      objectAtIndexPath:indexPath];
    self.detailViewController.detailItem = selectedObject;
  }
}
```

NOTE

This code is found all through iOS apps that change views. You use the code in Listing 14.1 or a variation on it with segmented controls.

Understanding the Storyboard Concept

Storyboards have been used to plan time-dependent projects, such as Stanislavski's production of *The Seagull* (1898), Walt Disney cartoons ("Three Little Pigs" in 1933), *Gone with the Wind* (1939), and many other projects along the way. The frames in a storyboard typically represent a single scene or camera shot in a movie, commercial, or play. Originally, each scene was drawn as a pencil sketch, but now each scene can be shown as a photo or even a key frame from a movie clip. Storyboarding has become an important tool in the development of games and software; as this use has increased, storyboards have added an emphasis on the transitions between scenes.

Storyboards in Xcode adopt this model of a sequence of scenes, each of which is typically one view in the sense of UIView or a descendant. The transitions between storyboard scenes become important in games and interactive software as they provide a mechanism for changing the linear sequence of a typical storyboard. In addition, the particular animation in the transition can subtly guide the user to understand what should happen next (for example, is the app waiting for user input). In Xcode, transitions are referred to as *segues*, which is the term for transitions typically used in music and, now, other areas.

Looking at the iPhone Storyboard

Refer to Figure 14.2, which shows the iPhone version of Estimator (Master-Detail Application template). It uses a navigation interface with a master view controller containing a table view that displays a list of the items in the persistent store; tap one, and a detail view controller slides in to display the detail data. The navigation view controller maintains its stack of view controllers; as the user interacts with the navigation view controller, new view controllers are pushed onto and popped off from its stack.

Now, translate the previous paragraph into a storyboard, shown in Figure 14.4. There are three *scenes* in the storyboard. From left to right, they are the navigation view controller, the master view controller, and the detail view controller. The name of each controller is shown beneath its view. Click it and its title will be replaced by its placeholders—File's Owner (now filled in with the name) and First Responder. (If the editor is zoomed out, you may need to double-click.)

Between the scenes are the *segues*. Select one and use the Attributes inspector in utilities to see the settings. (Note that from the navigation controller to the master view controller, the connection is actually containment, and there are no segue details.) Figure 14.5 shows the segue from master view controller to detail view controller.

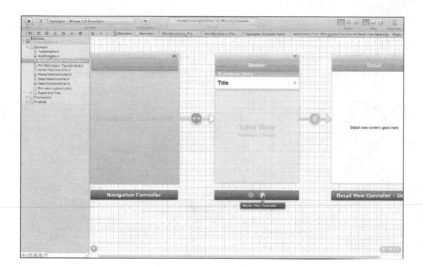

FIGURE 14.4
Review the storyboard for Figure 4.2.

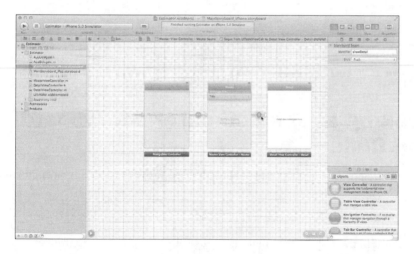

FIGURE 14.5
Look at the segues.

You connect scenes by control dragging from one to the other; the segue is automatically created, and you can customize it with the Attributes inspector. Note that for the iPad version of Estimator, both the master view controller and detail view controller are contained in the navigation controller.

Looking at the iPad Storyboard

Figure 14.6 shows the storyboard for the iPad version of Estimator.

Now you can see one of the significant benefits of storyboards. These are the same view controllers that you saw in the iPhone storyboard. What differs are the segues.

Instead of being contained with a navigation controller, the view controllers are now contained in a split view controller. One of the benefits of a split view controller is that it can flatten a data structure. Notice that the connections in Figure 14.6 are just connections; there are no segues in which things appear to move.

FIGURE 14.6
Review the iPad storyboard.

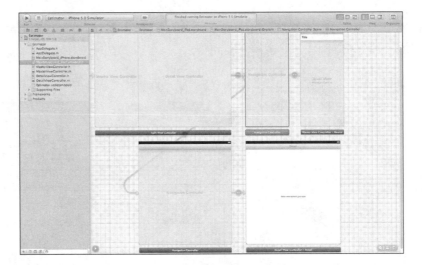

Looking at the Estimator Storyboard and Code

Listing 14.1 showed the technique frequently used to swap views. To recap, these are the three common steps:

▶ Create the appropriate view controller.

▶ Put it in the appropriate place (such as within a split view controller).

▶ Clean up and finish by adjusting popovers, toolbars, and the like.

As you learned in the previous section, "Understanding the Storyboard Concept," the storyboard contains references to the view controllers as well as to the segues that link them together in the storyboard. In the nib-file structure, the controllers are identified as the class of the File's Owner placeholder in Interface Builder editor (you set the class in the Identity inspector). With storyboards, the controllers are more tightly integrated. Given the listings and figures in the previous section, you can see that the storyboard identifies its view controllers not merely as objects of a specific class, but as the view controllers on which the storyboard depends.

Looking Inside `UIStoryBoard`

If you look up the class reference for the `UIStoryBoard` class in Xcode's organizer or on developer.apple.com, you will see that it has only three methods declared. The first is common to many classes. It is a class method that creates and returns an object of the class—in this case, a storyboard. The second instantiates the initial view controller in the storyboard's view controller graph. From this first view controller, segues lead to subsequent view controllers in the storyboard.

Now comes the heart of the matter: The third method of the `UIStoryBoard` class, `instantiateViewControllerWithIdentifier`. Here is the declaration of that method:

```
- (id)instantiateViewControllerWithIdentifier:(NSString *)identifier
```

You set the identifier for the view controller in Interface Builder by selecting the view controller in a storyboard and setting the identifier in the Attributes inspector, as shown in Figure 14.7.

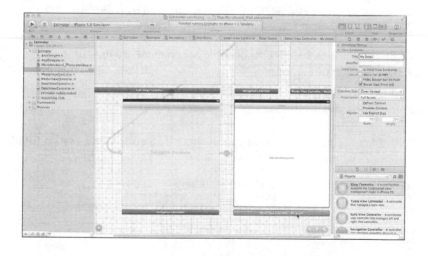

FIGURE 14.7
Set the identifier for a view controller in Interface Builder.

Now refer to the three steps needed to manage views. The first two, which are creating the appropriate view controller and putting it in the right container, can be managed by the storyboard using its own methods. This means that steps one and two in Listing 14.1 are removed from your code. These sections of code were typically standard and repetitive, differing only by the names of the view controller in question. Storyboards dramatically simplify the process of creating views.

Looking Inside the View Controller Storyboard Methods

In place of the repetitive code you used to have to write (such as Listing 14.1), you do have to provide support in your code for storyboards. Three methods are added to UIViewController to manage storyboards. The first is simply a property to return the storyboard that contains a view controller. For view controllers created from nib files instead of storyboards, the property value is nil.

prepareForSegue

In addition to creating the view controllers, there is often some housekeeping to be performed as part of the process. You do that in prepareForSegue. The declaration of that method follows here:

```
- (void)prepareForSegue:(UIStoryboardSegue *)segue sender:(id)sender
```

The segue is defined in the storyboard and is instantiated at runtime. This method is called on the view controller when the segue is about to be performed. The default method is empty, but you commonly override it.

For example, Listing 14.2 shows the override of prepareForSegue in the MasterViewController.m of Estimator (remember this is the Master-Detail Application template) when it is created for iPad. This code typically checks for the identifier of the segue, which you saw being set in Figure 14.5.

LISTING 14.2   prepareForSegue in MainViewController.m (iPad)

```
- (void)prepareForSegue:(UIStoryboardSegue *)segue sender:(id)sender
{
  if ([[segue identifier] isEqualToString:@"showDetail"]) {
    NSIndexPath *indexPath = [self.tableView indexPathForSelectedRow];
    NSManagedObject *selectedObject = [[self fetchedResultsController]
      objectAtIndexPath:indexPath];
    [[segue destinationViewController] setDetailItem:selectedObject];
  }
}
```

Working in a Split View Controller on iPad

You may notice that prepareForSegue relies on the showDetail identifier for a segue. That is the case only on iPhone for this project. On iPad, both parts of the split view controller are present at all times, even though the master view controller may not be shown. Because both objects are accessible, the detail item for the detail controller can be set directly. Listing 14.3 shows the code that does that. Compare it with Listing 14.2, and you will see that they do the same thing (set the detail item).

LISTING 14.3   didSelectRowAtIndexPath

```
- (void)tableView:(UITableView *)tableView didSelectRowAtIndexPath:
  (NSIndexPath *)indexPath
{
  if ([[UIDevice currentDevice] userInterfaceIdiom] == UIUserInterfaceIdiomPad) {
    NSManagedObject *selectedObject = [[self fetchedResultsController]
      objectAtIndexPath:indexPath];
    self.detailViewController.detailItem = selectedObject;
  }
}
```

Creating a Storyboard

Now that you have looked at storyboards that come with a template, you may well want to create your own. The process is simple. You add a new view controller by dragging it into the storyboard from the pane. If necessary, use the Identity inspector to change its class to your subclass.

Within that view controller, you construct your view just as you have always done in Interface Builder. Add objects from the library pane and set their attributes as needed. Any object that has an IBOutlet lets you link it to another view controller. If you want a button in one view controller to show another view, control-drag from the object to the view controller.

Setting the Project Storyboard

When you create a new project with a storyboard, it will automatically be set up with the appropriate storyboards for iPod, iPhone, or both in the case of a universal project. The project itself must identify the storyboard for each environment; that is done for you when the project is created, but if you need to change it later on, the settings are in the project information, as shown in Figure 14.8.

The first view controller in the storyboard is set as you create it. All view controllers you add later are normally connected to other interface elements. You can rearrange them as you see fit.

FIGURE 14.8
Set the story-
boards.

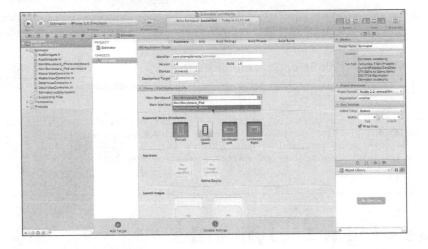

Adding and Deleting View Controllers

You can delete any or all of the view controllers from a storyboard. When you delete the last one, the arrow at the left disappears. That arrow indicates the initial view controller, and now there is none. To add a view, drag one from the library pane, as shown in Figure 14.9.

FIGURE 14.9
Add a view from
the library
pane.

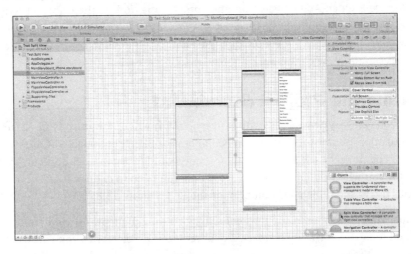

In Figure 14.9, a split view controller is being added. As you can see, that object is a complex object containing the split view controller, a navigation controller, a table view controller, and a view controller. Everything is already set up and configured for you. Furthermore, note the small arrow at the left. As soon as you add the first view to a storyboard, it is automatically flagged. You can drag the arrow to another view to change the sequence of view controllers.

You can command-click on any view controller in the storyboard to see its segues, outlets, referencing segues, and referencing outlets and outlet collections. Of course, you can change them. Figure 14.10 shows the initial segues for a navigation controller.

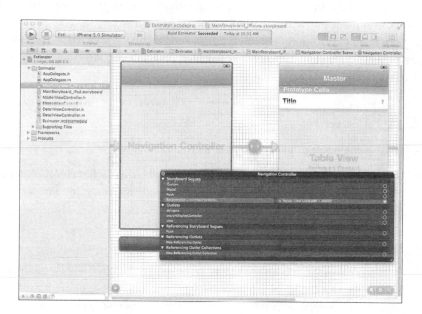

FIGURE 14.10
Review segues and outlets for a navigation controller.

Figure 14.11 shows the initial settings for a split view controller.

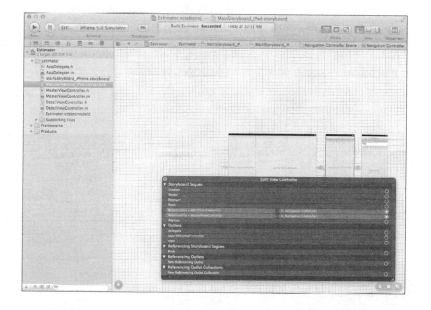

FIGURE 14.11
Review segues and outlets for a split view controller.

Summary

In this hour, you have learned how storyboards provide a new way of looking at nib files. The traditional nib files are there underneath the new storyboard interface, but you work with them through storyboards both as a designer and as a developer of code. Compared to traditional nib files, storyboards require you to write less code because they include the most commonly written code to swap views so you do not have to rewrite it.

Q&A

Q. *What is the point of using storyboards?*

A. Instead of designing each view on its own, storyboards include a collection of views together with the segues that power their transitions; it lets you see how they flow together from one to the other.

Q. *How do storyboards work on Mac OS compared to iOS?*

A. Storyboards are an iOS-only concept. Perhaps one day they will be ported to Mac OS, but for the moment, the need for them there is not so great as it is on iOS. That is because with movable and resizable windows as well as a menu bar to centralize commands, you have more options for your users to manipulate their data.

Q. *How do storyboards work with universal apps?*

A. By abstracting the segues and the device-specific view layouts, your universal apps require less customization for each device family.

Workshop

Quiz

1. *How many views can a segue manage?*

2. *How do you convert a nib file interface to storyboards?*

Quiz Answers

1. Two.

2. At the moment there is no way to do this. However, consider restarting with a storyboard-based project and moving your custom code. Typically, it is only the nib layouts and, perhaps, the view controllers that need attention. For modification to an existing app, sometimes it is not difficult to use storyboards for that new section.

Activities

Explore one or more of the storyboard templates. See what happens as you change the style of the segue in the Attributes inspector. Look at the transitions under the Modal style and experiment with them. Notice how the appearance of your entire app can change. Notice also how distracting it can be to use different transitions for every segue.

HOUR 15

Saving Data with a Navigation Interface

What You'll Learn in This Hour:

- ▶ Walking through a navigation app
- ▶ Using the debugger for basic analysis
- ▶ Enhancing the code to save data

Using a Navigation Interface to Edit and Save Data

So far, you have seen the basics of how to use Xcode, how to build apps from the built-in Xcode templates, and how to build Core Data stores. You have seen the key sections of code that make things happen, but now it is time to put it all together. In this hour, you learn how to build a basic iPhone app to let you add, delete, and change data in a Core Data persistent store.

> ▶ In Hour 16, "Using Split Views on iPad," p. 279, you learn how to make the minimal changes required for this app to run in a split view controller on iPad.

As you have seen, there is a lot of background information to learn and process. Becoming familiar with the frameworks of Mac OS and iOS as well as the Objective-C language, which is new to many developers, is not something you can do in a spare hour or two.

NOTE

If you happen not to be an experienced user of Mac OS or iOS, you also have to develop a good hands-on feel for how things fit together from the user's point of view.

Many people have noted that the learning curve for these technologies is long and steep, but once you have climbed up that curve, the development process is faster and more efficient than most people have ever experienced in other environments. There are many reasons for this, but the main one is that the development process for iOS and Mac OS is highly automated. What you know about writing code is valuable background, but much of that experience is not necessary because there is relatively little traditional code to write. With Mac OS and iOS, it is a matter of understanding the very large structures of the frameworks with which you are dealing and then, based on that understanding, writing or changing a few lines of code for each feature you want to implement.

You find out how to do that in this hour by building on the app you worked on earlier in this part of the book. Adding new interface fields, new database fields, and the code to display and save the data is not complex. Thus, in this hour (and many of the hours that follow), you will have less and less to do because it all builds on what you have already done and, more importantly, what the frameworks have already done for you.

Figures 15.1A–15.1G show the app you will have by the end of this hour.

FIGURE 15.1A
Start from an empty data store and the empty master view.

Without modification, the built-in Xcode Master-Detail Application is shown in the iPhone simulator in Figure 15.1A. It has been built as a universal app and will be built into an app to keep track of customers.

Across the top of the screen, a *navigation bar* contains controls and, usually, a title in its middle. You will see how to modify it. The faint horizontal lines across the screen in Figure 15.1A indicate that it is a table view that is capable of displaying a number of lines of data. For now, all you see are the faint lines because there are no entity instances in the list.

Tap + to add a new item to the master view, as shown in Figure 15.1B. For this app, it will be a new instance of the Customer entity, and you will provide a default name: New Customer.

FIGURE 15.1B
Add a new
instance.

Use the gray disclosure indicator at the right of the New Customer row to move to the detail view, as shown in Figure 15.1C. You will see the name at the top in the navigation bar. In this hour, you will add new fields for the customer name and address and add a label for each one.

Tap in a field and the keyboard will appear so you can type in new data. (In Figure 15.1C, the name of My Customer is changed to My First Customer.) Most of this behavior is built into the frameworks automatically.

FIGURE 15.1C
Tap in a field to
enter data.

TIP

Note that the faint horizontal lines shown in Figure 15.1A and 15.1B are not present here. That is because beneath the navigator bar in Figure 15.1C, you have a simple view rather than a table view. A view can contain other views such as the labels and text fields shown here. The organized list structure of a table view does not exist so you can place things wherever you want them in the view.

Return to the master view by tapping Master at the left of the navigation bar. As shown in Figure 15.1D, changes entered on the detail view have been saved and appear in the master view's list.

Just to make certain that everything is working properly, tap the arrow to look at the data for the detail view, as shown in Figure 15.1E. Yes, the data you changed now shows up in the text field for data entry. You can change it again if you want to.

On the master view, tap Edit at the left of the navigation bar. This starts editing of the persistent store, as shown in Figure 15.1F. As you will see, the navigation bar paradigm separates edits to the structure (adding, removing, and rearranging entity instances) from editing to the data (changing a name, for example).

Delete the instance and tap Done to exit from edit mode. The data is gone, and you return to an empty master view list, as shown in Figure 15.1G.

FIGURE 15.1D
Changes are propagated to the master view.

FIGURE 15.1E
Check that the modified data is shown on the detail view.

FIGURE 15.1F
Start to edit the
structure.

FIGURE 15.1G
The entity
instance has
been removed.

Starting from the Master-Detail Template

In Hour 13, "Control-Dragging Your Way to Code," p. 223, you saw how to build a basic app based on the built-in Xcode Master-Detail template. It has basic functionality (most of it thanks to the template). Along the way, you learned how to use various options; you also saw some of the choices you have to accomplish similar results in different ways. For those reasons, there are some inconsistencies in the finished app that reflect these variations. It will make your life easier to start over with a new template.

Try It Yourself ▼

Create a New Master-Detail Application

This task walks you through the process of creating a new universal app based on the Master-Detail App template.

You will probably use these steps more than once (maybe many times) as you create new apps. (Refer to Hour 13 for the details.) The sequence of creating fields and connections is deliberately reversed from Hour 13 to show you the two ways of handling these tasks:

1. Create a new iOS project from File, New Project.

2. Choose iOS, Application, and Master-Detail Application.

3. Provide the details, as shown in Figure 15.2. You might want to use the new Xcode class prefix if you are building the same project in several different contexts (as in several different chapters of this book).

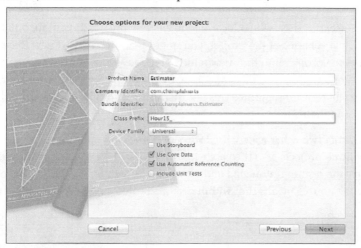

FIGURE 15.2
Create the new project.

Because the class prefix is used, all the files in this hour begin with it, as in `Hour15_MasterViewController_iPad.xib`. When you use a class prefix, new files you create with File, New also begin with it. However, as you create those new files, you can change the prefix for each file, so you might have `Hour16_MasterViewController_someotherdevice.xib`. This can help you keep the evolution of your project under control. However, as files are referred to in this book, the prefix is omitted unless it matters. This means that in the text, `Hour15_MasterViewController_iPad.xib` is referred to as `MasterViewController_iPad.xib`. (This is how most people refer to it in practice.) Figure 15.3 shows the files as automatically named with the class prefix.

FIGURE 15.3
The files are named with the class prefix.

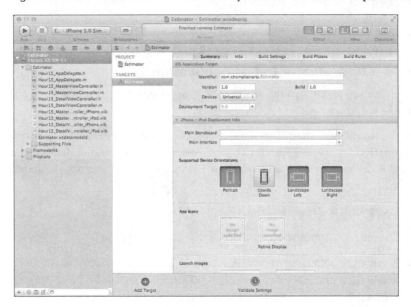

4. Click Next and provide a location for the new project. If you are building multiple versions of the project, you might want to create a new folder and place the project into that new folder. That way, you can have several versions of the project at the same time. By placing them in separate folders, they will remain separate. This is easier than renaming the internal projects and their files.

There are two other widely used ways of managing files. If you are creating duplicate projects as is the case with the various hours of this book, you can leave the names untouched and place each one in a new folder. This organizes the files, but it means that within a single project, the names do not change from one version to another. This is good and bad because you may forget which version you are working with.

The other way of managing source code is to use version control such as Git for which Xcode provides a built-in interface. For real projects rather than hour-by-hour examples, nothing beats source code version control. Xcode implements interfaces to the basic controls, so that although Git has many more features than you can access through Xcode, you can access the powerful subset that are most frequently used.

5. Create or modify the data model so that it looks like Figure 13.2.

6. Seach for Event in the project. There is one occurrence: Change it to Customer, as shown in Listing 13.3. (If there are two occurrences, review step 5.)

7. Search for timeStamp in the project. There are three occurrences (four if you have not done step 5 properly).

8. Make the three code changes shown in Listings 13.2, 13.3, and 13.4.

9. Open the Assistant editor so you can see two files at the same time. Set it to show DetailViewController_iPhone.xib and DetailViewController.h.

In Hour 13, you opened them next to one another; you can use View, Assistant Editor to change the configuration. Figure 15.4 shows the two files stacked vertically. Depending on your screen and the files in question, you might choose one layout rather than another or switch back and forth.

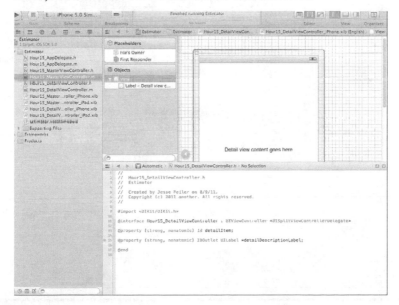

FIGURE 15.4
Arrange the assistant panes as you see fit.

10. Delete the label from the nib file. (The label's default data is "Detail View Content Goes Here.") Either expand View in the document structure area to expose the label object and delete it from there or delete it from the canvas.

Also delete the property and the synthesize directive.

11. Show the Library in utilities if necessary. With the Objects pane visible, drag a text field into the canvas of `DetailViewController_iPhone.xib`. It is always good practice to set the label of a library object as soon as you create it. Use the Identity inspector to do so. (Name `field` is a good label for this field.)

12. Control-drag from the text field in the canvas or in the document structure area to the interface in `DetailViewController.h` to create a new outlet, as shown in Figure 15.5. It will be created as a property.

FIGURE 15.5
Create a new
property for the
name field.

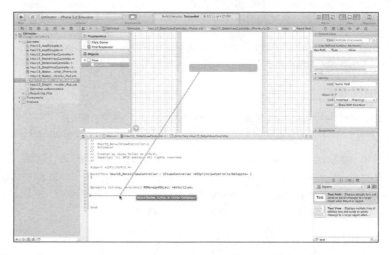

Name the new property name, as shown in Figure 15.6.

FIGURE 15.6
Name the new
property.

NOTE

Note that this sequence is deliberately different from that in Hour 13 so that you can see both ways of accomplishing the same task.

Similarly, add a text field for the address, and create the property for it, as shown in the previous steps. It is a good idea to add labels to both fields.

Test the app to make certain it functions the way you expect.

Using the Debugger to Watch the Action

Your data model now has attributes for the data you want to save (such as the name and address). You have implemented code to set the name for a newly created entity instance. You have already added a text field to display the name. You can type data into the text field. All you have to do now is to save that data and restore it when the app runs or when you switch from one entity instance to another.

TIP

If you try it now, you will see that entering text into the text field works but that text remains there no matter what entity instance you go to. If you quit the app in the simulator and run it again, the data will be gone from the name field.

Implementing Saving in a Navigation-Based App

The app you have built so far is a universal app, and you have been working in the code for iPhone. Sometimes you use a universal app with the idea that at some point in the future you will implement the other device family code. Other times, you start from the beginning to develop both versions.

You might want to check back and forth periodically to make certain that both versions work properly. Fields you add to one nib file need to be added to the other and sized appropriately. The properties you are creating in the code files apply to both environments.

This is relevant at this point because the navigation based iPhone template on which you are working has a significant difference from the iPad template. This section walks you through the iPhone version that has served as the basis for many apps.

TIP

You might want to look at the Core Recipes sample code on developer.apple.com, but it might no longer match the code described here. See the next section in this hour, "Checking Out the Split-View Version," for a discussion of the differences with iPad and how to deal with them.

▷ There is more information on working with the split-view version in Hour 16, "Using Split Views in iPad," p. 279.

To implement saving data, here is what you need to do:

1. When displaying the detail view, move the data from the name attribute into the text field.

2. When leaving the detail view, move the data from the text field into the name attribute.

3. Save the managed object context.

This is already happening with the master view, but it is hard to tell because so far, every customer has the same name: New Customer. After you have implemented editing in the detail view, you will see that you do not have to do anything else for the master view to behave properly.

For each of your app's screens, there are two entities and three files that you have to worry about:

▶ The view itself is described in the nib file (with suffix .xib).

▶ The view is managed by a view controller object that is implemented the way any class is implemented with a header (.h) file and an implementation file (.m).

You have already updated the nib file and DetailViewController.h with the text field, so all that remains is changing the code in DetailViewController.m to do the work.

As is the case with most of the Xcode built-in templates, a number of methods in the template either are commented out or are just shells. These include viewWillAppear and viewWillDisappear, which are automatically called at the appropriate moments. They are in your app now and have been functioning in their basic stripped-down versions all along as you have been testing.

Using Breakpoints in the Debugger

You can prove this by using the debugger and breakpoints, and this is a good time to look at that process because you will need to use it as you develop apps. Figure 15.7 shows the section of code in DetailViewController.m that has the view lifecycle code. As you can see, most of this code is just shells: calls to super.

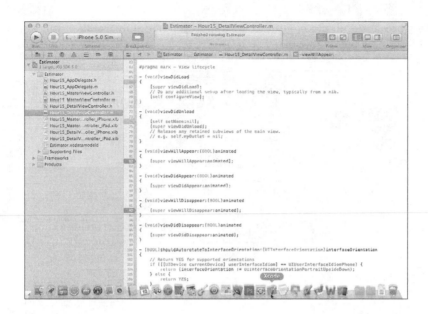

FIGURE 15.7
Place break-
points in the
view lifecycle
code.

The viewWillAppear and viewWillDisappear methods are where many apps move data between the text field in the interface and managed object. To verify this, you can click in the gutter to place breakpoints in those methods.

TIP

Remember that the breakpoint is activated—execution stops—just *before* the line of code is executed. You can disable a breakpoint by clicking on it; it will be dimmed somewhat but will remain in the gutter where you can activate it again if you want. In Figure 15.7, inactive breakpoints are dimly shown in viewDidLoad and viewDidUnload. You can remove breakpoints by dragging them out of the gutter, and you can temporarily disable all breakpoints with Breakpoints in the toolbar.

The inactive breakpoints demonstrate a common question you might have—what is the difference between viewWillLoad and viewWillAppear (and their correspon-ding unload and disappear versions)? After a while, you will become quite familiar with methods such as these, but for now, you can find out the difference with break-points. What you will find out is that viewWillLoad is called the first time that view is loaded into the app. Thereafter, as you navigate between the master and detail views and possibly from one customer instance to another, viewWillLoad is typical-ly not called again. viewWillAppear is called each time, so that is where you want to adjust the data in the view.

With a breakpoint in place, just run the app as you normally would. It will stop at the first breakpoint, as shown in Figure 15.8.

FIGURE 15.8
Breakpoints fire
just before the
line of code is
executed.

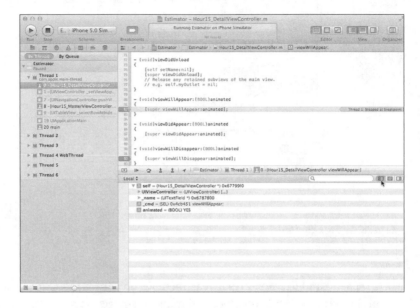

Displaying the Debug Pane

When execution stops, you might need to show the Debug pane at the bottom of the editor. At the upper-right of the Debug pane, you can choose to show the right side (the console with messages), the left side (variables), or both. In Figure 15.8, only variables are shown. You can expand some variables, such as `self`. At the top of the Debug pane, controls let you move through the app. From left to right, these controls do the following:

- Close the Debug pane
- Continue
- Step over this line of code (that is, execute one line)
- Step into a function
- Step out of a function to the first line of the calling routine

Checking Out the Split-View Version

As noted previously, this architecture works very well with the iPhone version of the template. That version is based on the navigation bar, and it is very common on iPhone apps. In fact, it is the basic interface paradigm that most iPhone users are used to. This section describes a significant difference that can lead you to reconsider the implementation of your code. The basic architecture is unchanged: At an appropriate place in the code, move data between the interface objects and the managed object that is stored in the persistent store. The issue has to do with where those appropriate places are.

▶ More details about the mechanics of navigation bars are included in Hour 19, "Using `UITableView` on iOS," p. 337.

When you use a navigation bar, the user is presented with a master view controller that presents a list of items usually in a table view. The user selects one item. The table view responds to that selection by creating a new view controller along with its view. That view controller (and its view) is then pushed onto the navigation stack. At that time, the back button is added at the left of the navigation bar. When it is clicked, the previous view controller is popped up the stack and the view on the device changes. All of this is done without you having to write any code because it is part of the template and part of the navigation tools in the framework.

When iPad was developed, the engineers and human interface designers at Apple worked long and hard to find appropriate ways of navigating through data. The navigation-based structure that is appropriate on iPhone is not an optimal experience in many cases when you are working on iPad. The navigation bar structure is efficient at letting people move quickly through ordered data, pushing and popping view controllers and their views.

With the larger iPad screen, those navigation steps are no longer the only way of getting around. The advice from Apple's interface designers to developers working with iPad is to minimize those steps and transitions. The phrase that is used is *flatten your data*. Split-view controllers allow you to place the master view controller with its list of items at the left side of a horizontally held iPad. Instead of swapping views in and out on the navigation stack, the right side of the iPad can contain a detail view controller and its view. As the user taps one object or another in the master view controller at the left, the detail view controller at the right is updated with the new object's data. It is a smoother and simpler transition.

When the iPad is held vertically, a button typically appears at the left of the bar at the top of the screen. That button opens a pop-over that contains the master view controller's list of object. Select an object in the pop-over, and the pop-over disappears. The detail view that has been present behind the pop-over is updated with the new object's data.

This structure is simpler for users and for developers because you are no longer swapping views in and out. And, because you are no longer swapping views in and out, `viewWillAppear` and `viewWillDisappear` no longer can serve as bottlenecks to control the moving of data between interface objects and managed objects.

Instead, you can consider using `setDetailItem` or `configureView` in the templates. Those methods of `DetailViewController` are called when a new detail item is to be set or when its view needs to be updated. Those are the most logical places to insert your data moving code. The disadvantage of this approach is that while these methods or methods like them are very common, they are specific to an individual app, whereas `viewWillAppear` and `viewWillDisappear` are part of Cocoa. This means you might have to implement these methods yourself.

In addition, if several views are needed to display the data, you might want to update only those views that are necessary. Typically, a method like `setDetailItem` does just that. You might want to implement `configureView` in subclasses of your detail view controller so you can call it as needed and perform only the necessary tasks.

If you are using this typical structure in which the master view controller's list is managed by a `UITableView`, you have another option. In `didSelectRowAtIndexPath` (a `UITableView` method in `MasterViewController`), you can do your data moving. More likely, you will call a method in `DetailViewController`, such as `configureView` or another method you create. The advantage of this structure is that `didSelect RowAtIndexPath` is going to be implemented in your master view controller, and that method is going to reference or create the detail view controller. This means both the master and detail view controller are available in that method.

There is one further point to consider in thinking about the iPad version. It is common to combine the navigation interface and the flattened interface. This combination puts the navigation-based stack in the master view controller so users can drill down through an object hierarchy. When they are at the bottom, the data is displayed in the detail view controller in the stack view controller. (This might have been hidden during the navigation.)

Look at Settings on iPhone and iPad to see a number of examples of how these interfaces are implemented.

Adding a Managed Object

In the basic template, `DetailViewController` has an instance variable called `detailItem`. It is set when you select an instance from the master view controller. It is set in `MasterViewController.m` in `didSelectRowAtIndexPath` with these three lines of code:

```
NSManagedObject *selectedObject =
  [[self fetchedResultsController] objectAtIndexPath:indexPath];
self.detailViewController.detailItem = selectedObject;
```

The `detailItem` property is declared in `DetailViewController.h` with this code:

```
@property (strong, nonatomic) id *detailItem;
```

Because it is declared as id, this code is usable in many circumstances. In the case of this app and the template, you know that it is going to be an NSManagedObject, so you can change the property declaration to be:

```
@property (strong, nonatomic) NSManagedObject *detailItem;
```

This will make your code a little clearer because you do not have to coerce it every time you use it as a managed object.

Moving and Saving Data

To save the managed object context, all you need to do is move data between the text field and the managed object and then save it. For this example, the code will go into viewWillAppear.

> **NOTE**
>
> Most of the time when you override a method that includes a call to super, your code either comes after or before that call.

In a method such as viewWillAppear, the call to super comes first because you want the view to do all its initialization before you do your work. In a method such as viewWillDisappear, the call to super comes last. You do your work (such as disposing of objects), and then the view does its own cleaning up. If you reverse this sequence, you might find that objects have not yet been created or have already been disposed of. This pattern is common to almost all the will/did framework methods.

Because key-value coding works on all objects, you can use it to move the data. You have already connected the text field to the name property, so you can refer to it directly. Here is the line of code to add at the end of viewWillAppear. Place it after the call to super, as shown in Listing 15.1.

LISTING 15.1   viewWillAppear

```
- (void)viewWillAppear:(BOOL)animated
{
  [super viewWillAppear:animated];
  self.name.text = [self.detailItem valueForKey:@"name"];
}
```

Moving Data to the Managed Object from the Interface

You use the reverse process to move the data to the managed object from the interface, as shown in Listing 15.2.

LISTING 15.2   viewWillDisappear

```
- (void)viewWillDisappear:(BOOL)animated
{
  [self.detailItem setValue: self.name.text forKey:@"name"];
  [super viewWillDisappear:animated];
}
```

Saving the Managed Object Context

If you experiment with the app now, you will see that it lets you add and remove new customers and that you can change their names. Everything seems to work perfectly, but if you quit the app and restart it, none of your name changes have been saved. The customers you might have added or deleted have been saved because that code has always been in `ManagedObjectController` as part of the template, but the code for the new attributes and the text field does not automatically save itself. You add that code into `viewWillDisappear`.

> **NOTE**
>
> On iOS, you are encouraged by Apple not to ask people to save their work explicitly; instead, you should save it as needed. This architecture has moved into Mac OS X Lion with the autosave feature. In fact, in the world of databases, the concept of saving data has typically not been part of the user interface in many cases. For example, you can search in vain in standard FileMaker projects for a Save button. FileMaker just saves your work as necessary.

For those reasons, you can put the save code into `viewWillDisappear` as an automatic action. The basic code is shown here. You should provide an appropriate error message (see Hour 23, "Interacting with Users," p. 409, for some tips on how to do this):

```
NSError *error;
  if (![self._detailObject.managedObjectContext save:&error]) {
  // Update to handle the error appropriately.
    NSLog(@"Unresolved error %@, %@", error, [error userInfo]);
    exit(-1);  // Fail
}
```

Cleaning Up the Interface

As you test your app (and show your friends!), you might notice some issues you should clean up. You are using the navigation interface in Cocoa Touch, and you have not had to worry at all about how the transitions from one screen to another take place. You can continue to make modifications to the navigation structure without worrying about the architecture (but you will find out more about it in Hour 16 and Hour 17).

For starters, take a look at the app as it might look after you have done some experimentation, as shown in Figure 15.9.

FIGURE 15.9
Experiment with
the app.

One thing you might want to change is to sort the names on the master view. That is a simple task. The sort order is set when you create the fetch request in `fetchedResultsController` in `MasterViewController.m`. If you have followed the steps in converting from the template, you have changed the sort descriptor to sort on the new name attribute instead of the `timeStamp` attribute that was present in the template. The template sorted on the `timeStamp` attribute in reverse order. Here is the code you should have now:

```
NSSortDescriptor *sortDescriptor = [[NSSortDescriptor alloc]
  initWithKey:@"name" ascending:NO];
```

That was appropriate for the timeStamp sorting. Change NO to YES and your list will be alphabetized.

There is one other change you can make to improve the interface. At the moment, the detail view has a title of Detail, as shown in Figure 15.9. You can improve on that by putting the name of the customer into the navigator bar's title.

The Detail title is placed in the navigator bar's title in DetailViewController.m in the initWithNibName method. Here is the code:

```
if (self) {
  self.title = NSLocalizedString(@"Detail", @"Detail");
```

This is fine because the title will always be Detail. However, to make the title change depending on the current data, you need to set it elsewhere after the new detail item has been set.

Begin by removing the code from initWithNibName. Continue in setDetailItem by adding code to set the title to the detail item's data. Listing 15.3 shows the method with this code added.

LISTING 15.3   setDetailItem

```
- (void)setDetailItem:(id)newDetailItem
{
  if (_detailItem != newDetailItem) {
    _detailItem = newDetailItem;

    // Update the view.
    [self configureView];
  }

  // set the controller's title
  self.title = [self.detailItem valueForKey:@"name"];

  if (self.popoverController != nil) {
    [self.popoverController dismissPopoverAnimated:YES];
  }
}
```

Summary

This hour brings together the various components you have seen on their own: managed objects, fetch requests, connections, properties, and interface objects. You have now created an app that lets you create, save, delete, and modify data. This app uses the Master-Detail Application template that includes a master view (and its controller) as well as a detail view (and its controller).

The management of these views is handled by the navigation object, which you do not have to do anything to use from the template. As you will learn, you can build on it in the future with your own features and customizations, but this is the heart of many iPhone and iPad apps.

Q&A

Q. *What are the basic steps you have to implement to save data?*

A. Write a line of code to take data from an interface element such as a text field and place it in the appropriate property of the entity instance.

Q. *How do you save the data?*

A. You save the managed object context, and it saves all its changed data. When you create a managed object, you include its context. So, given a managed object, you can then get its context and ask the context to save itself.

Workshop

Quiz

1. *How do you set the title for a navigation bar?*

2. *How do you move from one view to another?*

Quiz Answers

1. Set the navigation bar's `title` property.

2. You switch view controllers, and they take care of the views. And if you build on the Master-Detail Application template, you do not necessarily know this because it is already done for you. The only time you will need to worry about it is if you need to add another level of detail (such as master – detail 1 – sub-detail a).

Activities

Follow up on Quiz 2 by looking at various apps that use navigation bars. You can tell when you are looking at a master view and when you are looking at a detail view. Master views are table views and have a list of objects or an empty list with faint lines. Detail views do not usually contain table views except for formatting purposes. Look at the Apple apps such as Mail, Calendar, and Address Book on iPhone, iPad, and Mac to see how the same data is presented in different ways.

HOUR 16

Using Split Views on iPad

Moving to the iPad

As much as possible, this book is designed so that you can jump around to the particular information you need at any given moment. For example, if you want to find out how to validate data, you might jump into Hour 18, "Validating Data." This hour is a bit different. It follows directly on Hour 15, "Saving Data with a Navigation Interface." You can download the sample code as it is at the end of Hour 15 as described in the Introduction.

> **NOTE**
>
> Because you are continuing with the project from Hour 15 (or with a copy of it), notice that the file names in the Project navigator still have the Hour_15 prefix.

When you create a universal app, it can be targeted separately for iPhone or iPad. Some of the features are specific to iPhone (such as the navigation controller described in Hour 15), and some are specific to iPad (such as the split view controller used in this hour). In addition, when you work with a universal app, the second device family you use is implemented differently from the first.

This hour shows you some iPad-specific issues, and they are identified for you. Also, in this hour, you learn some code and techniques that are specific to the second device family in a universal app, whether the second one is iPad or iPhone.

When you start to address your second device family, the first step is to take stock of what you have. Change the Xcode scheme to the other simulator and run the app. Figure 16.1 shows the universal app running in the iPad simulator for the first time.

FIGURE 16.1
Run the app for the other device family.

Be sure to select an item and look at its detail view, as shown in Figure 16.2.

As you rotate the simulator, you can see how the split view behaves and how the pop-over can appear when you tap the button in the navigation bar. The master view controller looks pretty much the same whether it is on iPhone or either orientation of iPad. The detail view might be a bit of a surprise.

This is not the detail view you have been working on; this is the original detail view. In a universal app, the basic views have alternative versions for each device. The master view controller is different for the two devices, but the end result is pretty much the same. In Hour 15, you were modifying `DetailViewController_iPhone.xib`; what you are seeing now is the original `DetailViewController_iPad.xib`.

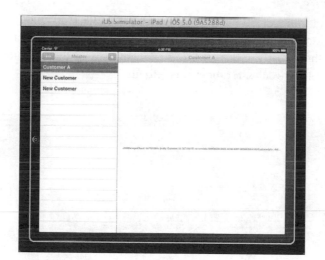

FIGURE 16.2
Check out the
detail view.

Implementing the Second Interface

Whether your second interface is for iPhone or iPad, the implementation task is different from the first task. Hour 15 explained how to add interface elements from the library and how to control-drag to create their properties. That works for the first interface. For the second interface, you can omit the second step because you already have the properties in your header files (and the synthesize directives in your implementation files). For the second interface, you create the interface elements and just connect them to the existing properties.

Try It Yourself ▼

Adding a Field to the Second Interface

Implementing your second interface is simpler than the first one. It is just a matter of adding interface objects and connecting them.

1. Open DetailViewController.h, as shown in Figure 16.3. You will see the properties you added in the first interface (customer and address).

2. The round circle in the gutter indicates that the properties are connected to interface elements. Click on one of them and you will see the object to which it is connected.

3. Click on the round circle and you will go to the connected object in the interface file, as shown in Figure 16.4. Note that this will be in the iPhone nib file if you have followed these steps.

4. Open the other detail nib file (DetailViewController_iPad.xib, in this case). If necessary, delete the label for the detail content. You do not have to delete the property and synthesize statement because that was done when you deleted the label for the iPhone nib file.

FIGURE 16.3
Review proper-
ties and
connections.

FIGURE 16.4
Look at the
connected
object.

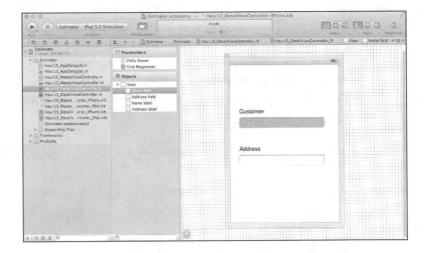

5. Drag a text field from the library, as shown in Figure 16.5. Arrange and size it as you wish. Remember that you are now working on an iPad canvas so you have plenty of room. As part of the creation process, remember to name the field.

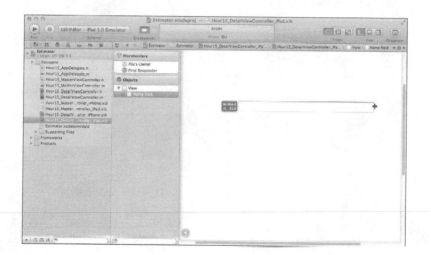

FIGURE 16.5
Add a text field
to the iPad
interface.

6. Control-drag from File's Owner to the new text field and connect the name property, as shown in Figure 16.6.

7. Verify that both connections have been made. Look in DetailViewController.h, as shown in Figure 16.7, to see that both nib files are connected to the controller.

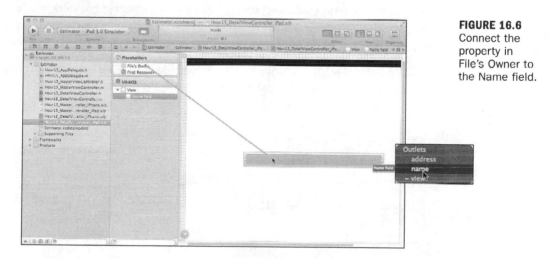

FIGURE 16.6
Connect the
property in
File's Owner to
the Name field.

FIGURE 16.7
Verify the
connections.

Changing the Data Update and Saving Code

As described in Hour 15, using viewWillAppear and viewWillDisappear to move data between the managed object and the interface objects does not work with a split view controller. You can move the code from viewWillAppear to configureView at this point. (You can even argue that the code is more appropriate here in any case.)

Listing 16.1 shows what configureView will look like now. (You can add tests to make certain that the objects exist before using them in this and all cases. That will make your code more robust.)

LISTING 16.1   configureView

```
- (void)configureView
{
  // Update the user interface for the detail item.

  self.name.text = [self.detailItem valueForKey:@"name"];

}
```

As implemented in Hour 15, the data is saved in viewWillDisappear. That is certainly a valid place to put it, but as you start to improve the app and get it ready for future use, you might consider removing methods with dual purposes (particularly if one of the purposes is hidden). The name of the method is not viewWillDisappearAndBeSaved, and you cannot change it because this is an override of a superclass method so you need to preserve the method signature (the name and parameters) so that it will be called by existing code. You may have to do some thinking about what a dual purpose is: Sometimes it is necessary to do several things to accomplish one goal. In this case, saving data and handling the view disappearing are related but different purposes. Putting the saving into its own method is better from an architectural point of view.

Listing 16.2 shows a new save method that contains the code that previously was in viewWillDisappear. Note that a pragma mark has been created for a new section in the source code file. Object lifecycle can be a companion to the existing View lifecycle section. Notice the clarification in the method name.

LISTING 16.2 saveNameData

```
#pragma mark - Object lifecycle

- (void) saveNameData {
  [self.detailItem setValue: self.name.text forKey:@"name"];
  NSError *error;
  if (![self.detailItem.managedObjectContext save:&error]) {
    // Update to handle the error appropriately.
    NSLog(@"Unresolved error %@, %@", error, [error userInfo]);
    exit(-1);  // Fail
  }
}
```

If you remove this code from viewWillDisappear, remember to leave the call to [super viewWillDisappear:animated] in that method. Also, be sure to add the method declaration to the .h file:

```
- (void) saveNameData;
```

Now that you have the saveNameData method, you just have to call it at the appropriate place. Because this app does not ask people to explicitly save their work, you have to anticipate the right place to do so. You already have the context with changes saved automatically when the app quits, but what do you do while the app is running?

With the basic end-of-app save handled for you in the template, all you have to worry about is saving data while the app is running, and the time when you need to do that is when the user navigates to another customer record. Although it might seem a little peculiar, the right place to save data may be when you are loading new data; however, this still leaves a window in which data may not be saved if no new data is loaded because the user has navigated away.

Each app is different. If you can find a method that implies saving unsaved data, you can call your save methods from there. This is a case in which the navigation interface can be very helpful because it makes sense to the user that when the view disappears, the data will be saved. In other cases, you may have Done and Cancel buttons for the user to use. In still other cases, you may want to implement several managed object contexts to handle undo and redo. You can register to receive notifications that editing has ended, which is sent when the keyboard disappears.

Look at the examples on apple.developer.com to get ideas for how to handle the issue of when autosaving occurs. Reviewing the iCloud documentation for iOS and Mac OS may be very helpful because this issue has become a topic of much discussion in the context of autosaving and iCloud.

Check both the iPad and iPhone versions. You should have similar functionality in both. There are still things to do. For example, when you launch the app, no item is selected and users will see an empty detail view.

Part V, "Managing Data and Interfaces," picks up from here and shows you some additional things you can do to enhance the app. For example, you might be wondering what to do about all those other attributes you created (address, email, and so forth). Do you really want to create text fields for each one? Table views will come to the rescue and make your app's interface look very good.

Summary

This hour shows you how to work with the second implementation of a universal app. As you would expect, it is simpler than the first implementation. In addition, you have learned how to optimize the app to run both on iPhone and iPad so the methods are called appropriately on both devices.

Q&A

Q. Why does `viewWillAppear` *not work properly on a split view controller for managing data in the interface the way it does on iPhone?*

A. In navigation-based apps such as the iPhone version, views are moved in and out and that method is called. On iPad, the data is flattened and the views remain in place so you need to update them in a different place.

Q. *When is the right time to save data?*

A. Save data when you know the user is finished with it. That usually means when the user quits the app (you generally do not have to worry about that with the templates).

Workshop

Quiz

1. *Do you need separate connections for every nib file in a universal app?*

2. *Why is saving data inside* `viewWillDisappear` *not necessarily a good idea?*

Quiz Answers

1. This is a trick question (sorry about that). You need separate connections *for every field you use* in a universal app. Some fields might not appear on iPhone, for example, but will appear on iPad.

2. The method name does not indicate that it does anything except work with the view. And you cannot change the method name because it overrides an existing framework method. Furthermore, on iPad split views, views may not disappear in the way that they do in navigation interfaces.

Activities

This is very difficult, but it is something you need to learn how to do. Run your app as if you had never seen it before and look for usability issues.

One way to learn how to do this is to watch someone else use your app. Tell him that you just want to observe, and do not answer any questions he might have unless he gets hopelessly stuck. Keep track of what he does wrong because, ultimately, the error is probably yours in the interface design.

Resist the temptation to point at the interface when someone seems lost. And definitely keep your hands off the device itself. Make certain you explain what you are trying to do because, otherwise, your friend will think you are just rude.

In a class setting, students often pair up for an exercise like this. Many people meet fellow developers in coffee shops or parks where they can show off their apps and experiment with them. You might think about starting a developer group in your own area.

HOUR 17

Structuring Apps for Core Data, Documents, and Shoeboxes

What You'll Learn in This Hour:

▶ Comparing document and non-document templates for Mac OS and iOS
▶ Using the built-in templates and customizing them
▶ Moving data models and data from one project to another

Looking at Apps from the Core Data Point of View: The Role of Documents

In this book, you have seen how the Core Data stack is set up so that, for example, you always have a managed object context and a persistent store. In addition, of course, you have a data model (roughly comparable to a database schema), and with SQLite, a file that contains the persistent store's data.

> **NOTE**
>
> You can customize Core Data to use other data stores than SQLite. However, this topic is beyond the scope of this book.

The Rise and Fall and Rise of Documents for User Data

Against this background, if you have developed Apple software for a while, you have seen the evolution of the major frameworks today—Cocoa for Mac OS and

Cocoa Touch for iOS. They evolved from NeXTSTEP and OpenStep developed by NeXT (purchased by Apple in 1995), as well as from earlier frameworks and development environments built at Apple since 1984. These Apple environments consisted of the early Mac environment, a pioneering object-oriented framework called MacApp (first released in 1985 and used as the basis for many products, including the first versions of Photoshop), and after the NeXT acquisition, a transitional environment called Carbon that was somewhat parallel to Cocoa.

Through this evolution of Apple's various software environments, there was one fairly standard concept. On the desktop, users' data was stored in files that users could move around and rename as they pleased. (This concept was not unique to Apple; it was developed at Xerox PARC and adopted by many graphical user interface-based systems.) Users could send those files to other people and move them to other computers in many cases.

Within Apple and within the developer community, there was some discussion as to whether this was the right model to go forward into the twenty-first century. As personal digital assistants evolved during the 1990s (think of the early Palm devices as well as Apple's Newton and then iPod touch, and, of course, iPhone), users demanded the ability to sync their data across these various devices. They wanted to know where the data was; they wanted to be able to see the files. At various times, these essential data files were hidden in one way or another, and in other cases, users were comforted to be able to see them, move them, and rename them. (There is another side to this story, too. Customer support representatives spent a lot of time helping users find these files after they had been moved and renamed.)

When the first iOS devices were released, one of the criticisms was that users could not see their files. People wanted to see, move, and rename them. With the advent of iOS 4, many data files for apps were visible within iTunes, but a large number of files for many apps were not visible to users in normal use. (There were a variety of work-arounds, such as having apps communicating over the Internet with external data sources.) Perhaps the most important discovery during this period was that the world did not end when users could see, move, and rename their files any more than it did not end when users could not see, move, and rename them. To the extent that people noticed that some of their files were not visible, it did not matter to many people. When pressed, they often provided logical theories of why it made sense for their word processing documents and spreadsheets to be visible to them as files and why their iPhoto and iTunes libraries as well as their calendars and contacts were either invisible or were in some relatively opaque container that was never seen in daily use.

Mac OS X 10.7 Lion and iOS 5 together have presented a more complete and consistent organization of data structure to users. On both Mac OS and iOS, data can be stored in files, and those files can be visible to users in various ways. Often, those files are placed in specific places for each app; the days of organizing your hard disk as you wish are pretty much gone, and with typical hard disks containing millions of files, it is clear to many people that the infinite flexibility of the past might no longer be feasible.

How Core Data Fits Into the Picture

Core Data brings database functionality to apps. Database functionality means that data can be stored and retrieved easily without having to write new code for every app to perform these basic tasks. There is just one question to ask: Where is the database?

Working with Core Data Documents

You can provide a Core Data stack (data model, managed object context, and per-sistent store) for an individual document. This allows you to manage your data on a per-document basis. Sometimes, you have two different views of the same document in two different windows on Mac OS, but it is the same document. A separate document might open in its own window(s), and that document would have its own Core Data stack with a separate data model, managed object context, and persistent store.

The traditional interface functionality for documents is provided in this paradigm: you open a document, make changes, and save it. While the document and its Core Data stack are open, you use Core Data to update the persistent store within the document.

In Lion, the version functionality lets you create multiple versions of a document. Users can continue to use the older way and can make a copy of a document (with its own Core Data) and then work in the copy or the original.

In any of these methods, users can revert to a previous version by simply moving or renaming versions and copies of the document. For document-based apps, each doc-ument has its own Core Data stack.

Working with Library/Shoebox Apps

Library/shoebox apps use a persistent store that is managed by the app itself and not by documents. For example, in iPhoto or iCal, your data is all in a single file that many users do not even notice. It may be hidden in your Library/Application Support folder, which is only accessible by using Option-Go-Library from the Finder menu.

Exploring App Structure for Documents, Mac OS, and iOS

These architectures can be implemented by writing code. Most often, though, you use the built-in Xcode templates to structure your apps. Here are the options as of Xcode 4.2 for Mac OS and iOS, as well as for document-based apps and library/shoebox-based apps. Within these structures, the code to create the Core Data stack is the same.

▶ You might want to review Hour 4, "Getting the Big Core Data Picture," p. 85, to see the code for creating a Core Data stack.

Because the structures are consistent and comparable in both Mac OS and iOS as well as in document-based apps and library/shoebox-based apps, you can move a data model and even a persistent store from one app to another. This means you can run an app on your iPhone and enter some data into it. If you have a companion app on your Mac that uses the same data model, you can move the document from the iPhone app to your Mac and continue editing the data on your Mac. If you have an iPad app that uses the same data model, just move the document from your Mac to your iPad, and you are ready to continue.

Creating a Mac OS Library/Shoebox-Based App

Begin by creating a new Xcode project from the Mac OS Cocoa Application template. As shown in Figure 17.1, provide the usual information about the name, identifier, and App Store category (if you want). Here are the two important settings:

FIGURE 17.1
Create a document-based Mac OS app.

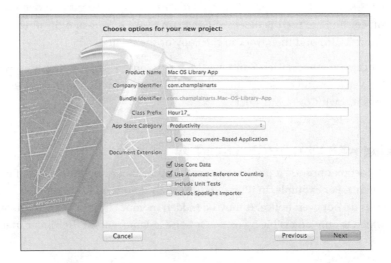

▶ Turn off Create Document-Based Application.

▶ Turn on Use Core Data.

Continue to save the project.

As shown in Figure 17.2, the project will be created. It will contain an app delegate that is properly configured.

FIGURE 17.2
The app dele-
gate is created.

NOTE

As you learned in Hour 3, "Understanding the Basic Code Structure," p. 63, in Objective-C, delegates are often used to extend an object's functionality. In other languages, this is often done with subclasses. Thus, in Objective-C, you typically find that the application class is not subclassed, but a delegate is added to it to perform application-specific functions.

Listing 17.1 shows the code for the app delegate. This consists primarily of the Core Data stack, although the app's main window and a save action are also provided. Both are related to Core Data.

You will need to provide customization based on your data, and that is where the link to Core Data comes in. Just as with the app delegate, you customize windows not by overriding them but by implementing a delegate that adopts the NSWindowDelegate protocol. The _window property and the windowWillReturnUndoManager method in the implementation are used in this way. windowWillReturnUndoManager returns the undo manager for the managed object context. Thus, Core Data manages undo and redo for the window that displays its data.

The saveAction method is a similar link to Core Data. It sends messages to commit editing and to save data to the managed object context.

LISTING 17.1   Setting Up the App Delegate

```
//
//  Mac_OS_Library_AppAppDelegate.h
//  Mac OS Library App
//
//  Created by Jesse Feiler on 8/14/11.
//  Copyright 2011 __MyCompanyName__. All rights reserved.
//

#import <Cocoa/Cocoa.h>

@interface Mac_OS_Library_AppAppDelegate : NSObject <NSApplicationDelegate>


@property (assign) IBOutlet NSWindow *window;

@property (readonly, strong, nonatomic) NSPersistentStoreCoordinator
  *persistentStoreCoordinator;
@property (readonly, strong, nonatomic) NSManagedObjectModel
  *managedObjectModel;
@property (readonly, strong, nonatomic) NSManagedObjectContext
  *managedObjectContext;

- (IBAction)saveAction:(id)sender;

@end
```

Listing 17.2 shows the implementation that has been provided for the app delegate. Note that this is the current (Xcode 4.2) state-of-the-art for creating a Core Data Stack. It differs from some of the sample code that was created for previous versions of Xcode. Going forward, this is the model to use.

TIP

There is nothing you need to change in this code for your own apps if you generate it with the Xcode Cocoa Application template using the no document option. If you copy the code to repurpose it, be sure you replace the name of the app with your own app's name.

You can use the jump bar in Xcode to get an overview of the file, as shown in Figure 17.3.

Most of the code in the implementation listings was shown separately in Hour 3, "Understanding the Basic Code Structure"; Hour 4, "Getting the Big Core Data Picture"; and Hour 5, "Working with Data Models." Here you see it put together.

▶ Note that Hour 23, "Interacting with Users," p. 409, discusses communicating with users. Details of the implementation are shown in Hour 23.

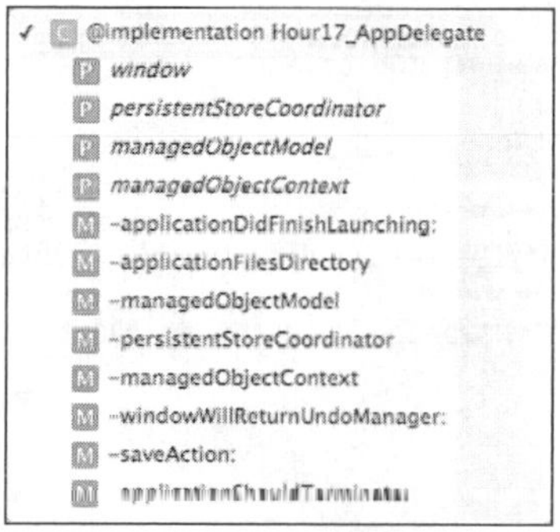

FIGURE 17.3
Use the jump bar in Xcode to see the structure of the implementation file.

LISTING 17.2 Implementing the Mac OS App Delegate

```
//
//  Hour17_AppDelegate.m
//  Mac OS Library App
//
//  Created by Jesse Feiler on 9/22/11.
//  Copyright (c) 2011 another. All rights reserved.
//

#import "Hour17_AppDelegate.h"

@implementation Hour17_AppDelegate

@synthesize window = _window;
@synthesize persistentStoreCoordinator = __persistentStoreCoordinator;
@synthesize managedObjectModel = __managedObjectModel;
@synthesize managedObjectContext = __managedObjectContext;

- (void)applicationDidFinishLaunching:(NSNotification *)aNotification
{
  // Insert code here to initialize your application
}

/**
 Returns the directory the application uses to store the Core Data store file. This
 code usesdirectory named "Mac_OS_Library_App" in the user's Library directory.
 */
- (NSURL *)applicationFilesDirectory {

  NSFileManager *fileManager = [NSFileManager defaultManager];
  NSURL *libraryURL = [[fileManager URLsForDirectory:NSLibraryDirectory
    inDomains:NSUserDomainMask] lastObject];
  return [libraryURL URLByAppendingPathComponent:@"Mac_OS_Library_App"];
}

/**
 Creates if necessary and returns the managed object model for the application.
```

```objc
 */
- (NSManagedObjectModel *)managedObjectModel {
  if (__managedObjectModel) {
    return __managedObjectModel;
  }

  NSURL *modelURL = [[NSBundle mainBundle] URLForResource:@"Mac_OS_Library_App"
    withExtension:@"momd"];
  __managedObjectModel = [[NSManagedObjectModel alloc] initWithContentsOfURL:
    modelURL];
  return __managedObjectModel;
}

/**
  Returns the persistent store coordinator for the application. This
    implementation
    creates and return a coordinator, having added the store for the
      application to it.
    (The directory for the store is created, if necessary.)
 */
- (NSPersistentStoreCoordinator *)persistentStoreCoordinator {
  if (__persistentStoreCoordinator) {
    return __persistentStoreCoordinator;
  }

  NSManagedObjectModel *mom = [self managedObjectModel];
  if (!mom) {
    NSLog(%@ No model to generate a store from", [self class],
      NSStringFromSelector(_cmd));
    return nil;
  }

  NSFileManager *fileManager = [NSFileManager defaultManager];
  NSURL *applicationFilesDirectory = [self applicationFilesDirectory];
  NSError *error = nil;

  NSDictionary *properties = [applicationFilesDirectory
    resourceValuesForKeys:[NSArray
    arrayWithObject:NSURLIsDirectoryKey] error:&error];

  if (!properties) {
    BOOL ok = NO;
    if ([error code] == NSFileReadNoSuchFileError) {
      ok = [fileManager createDirectoryAtPath:[applicationFilesDirectory path]
        withIntermediateDirectories:YES attributes:nil error:&error];
    }
    if (!ok) {
      [[NSApplication sharedApplication] presentError:error];
      return nil;
    }
  }
  else {
    if ([[properties objectForKey:NSURLIsDirectoryKey] boolValue] != YES) {
      // Customize and localize this error.
      NSString *failureDescription = [NSString stringWithFormat:@"Expected a
        folder to
        store application data, found a file (%@).", [applicationFilesDirectory
          path]];
```

```objectivec
      NSMutableDictionary *dict = [NSMutableDictionary dictionary];
      [dict setValue:failureDescription forKey:NSLocalizedDescriptionKey];
      error = [NSError errorWithDomain:@"YOUR_ERROR_DOMAIN" code:101
        userInfo:dict];

      [[NSApplication sharedApplication] presentError:error];
      return nil;
    }
  }

  NSURL *url = [applicationFilesDirectory
    URLByAppendingPathComponent:@"Mac_OS_Library_App.storedata"];
  NSPersistentStoreCoordinator *coordinator = [[NSPersistentStoreCoordinator alloc]
    initWithManagedObjectModel:mom];
  if (![coordinator addPersistentStoreWithType:NSXMLStoreType configuration:nil
    URL:url
    options:nil error:&error]) {
    [[NSApplication sharedApplication] presentError:error];
    return nil;
  }
  __persistentStoreCoordinator = coordinator;

  return __persistentStoreCoordinator;
}

/**
 Returns the managed object context for the application (which is already
 bound to the persistent store coordinator for the application.)
 */
- (NSManagedObjectContext *)managedObjectContext {
  if (__managedObjectContext) {
    return __managedObjectContext;
  }

  NSPersistentStoreCoordinator *coordinator = [self persistentStoreCoordinator];
  if (!coordinator) {
    NSMutableDictionary *dict = [NSMutableDictionary dictionary];
    [dict setValue:@"Failed to initialize the store" forKey:
      NSLocalizedDescriptionKey];
    [dict setValue:@"There was an error building up the data file."
      forKey:NSLocalizedFailureReasonErrorKey];
    NSError *error = [NSError errorWithDomain:@"YOUR_ERROR_DOMAIN" code:9999
      userInfo:dict];
    [[NSApplication sharedApplication] presentError:error];
    return nil;
  }
  __managedObjectContext = [[NSManagedObjectContext alloc] init];
  [__managedObjectContext setPersistentStoreCoordinator:coordinator];

  return __managedObjectContext;
}

/**
  Returns the NSUndoManager for the application. In this case, the manager
    returned is that of the managed object context for the application.
 */
- (NSUndoManager *)windowWillReturnUndoManager:(NSWindow *)window {
```

```
  return [[self managedObjectContext] undoManager];
}

/**
  Performs the save action for the application, which is to send the save:
    message to the
    application's managed object context. Any encountered errors are presented
      to the user.
 */
- (IBAction)saveAction:(id)sender {
  NSError *error = nil;

  if (![[self managedObjectContext] commitEditing]) {
    NSLog(%@ unable to commit editing before saving", [self class],
      NSStringFromSelector(_cmd));
  }

  if (![[self managedObjectContext] save:&error]) {
    [[NSApplication sharedApplication] presentError:error];
  }
}

    - (NSApplicationTerminateReply)applicationShouldTerminate:(NSApplication
      *)sender {
      -
  // Save changes in the application's managed object context before the
    application terminates.

  if (!__managedObjectContext) {
      return NSTerminateNow;
  }

  if (![[self managedObjectContext] commitEditing]) {
    NSLog(%@ unable to commit editing to terminate", [self class],
      NSStringFromSelector(_cmd));
    return NSTerminateCancel;
  }

  if (![[self managedObjectContext] hasChanges]) {
    return NSTerminateNow;
  }

  NSError *error = nil;
  if (![[self managedObjectContext] save:&error]) {

    // Customize this code block to include application-specific recovery steps.
    BOOL result = [sender presentError:error];
    if (result) {
      return NSTerminateCancel;
    }

    NSString *question = NSLocalizedString(@"Could not save changes while
      quitting. Quit anyway?", @"Quit without saves error question message");
    NSString *info = NSLocalizedString(@"Quitting now will lose any changes you
      have made
```

```
        since the last successful save", @"Quit without saves error question info");
    NSString *quitButton = NSLocalizedString(@"Quit anyway", @"Quit anyway button
        title");
    NSString *cancelButton = NSLocalizedString(@"Cancel", @"Cancel button title");
    NSAlert *alert = [[NSAlert alloc] init];
    [alert setMessageText:question];
    [alert setInformativeText:info];
    [alert addButtonWithTitle:quitButton];
    [alert addButtonWithTitle:cancelButton];

    NSInteger answer = [alert runModal];

    if (answer == NSAlertAlternateReturn) {
        return NSTerminateCancel;
    }
}

    return NSTerminateNow;
}

@end
```

Creating an iOS Library/Shoebox-Based App

Create a new Xcode project using Core Data. The templates that allow the Core Data
option are Document-Based, Master-Detail, Utility, and Empty, as shown in Figure 17.4.

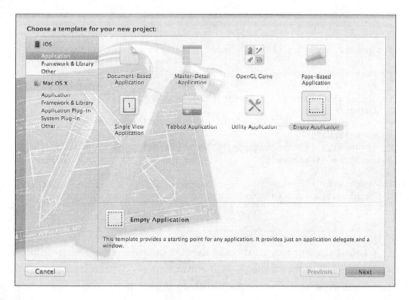

FIGURE 17.4
Choose an iOS
template that
uses Core
Data.

NOTE

All these templates contain a data model and a properly configured app delegate.
They can also contain storyboard files and view controllers. The example shown
here is the Empty template that has none of those so that you can focus on the
Core Data features.

The basic structure is the same as shown previously for Mac OS. The iOS app delegate is a `UIResponder` that adopts the `UIApplicationDelegate` protocol rather than an `NSObject` that adopts the `NSApplicationDelegate` protocol. However, that is mostly a reflection of the different structure of apps on Mac OS and iOS. The code you have to use or write is pretty much the same.

Listing 17.3 shows the header file for the application delegate. The only differences between this code and Listing 17.1 are the `window` property (in Listing 17.1), the accessor `applicationDocumentsDirectory` which is added, and the renaming of `saveAction` to `saveContext`. The functionality of those two methods is basically the same. The differences arise in committing the editing changes to the interface, and that, too, is a reflection of the differences between Mac OS and iOS. Most of the time, you will use the code without modification, so you can just use what you get from the template.

LISTING 17.3   iOS Application Delegate

```
//
//   Hour17_AppDelegate.h
//   Empty
//
//   Created by Jesse Feiler on 9/22/11.
//   Copyright (c) 2011 another. All rights reserved.
//

#import <UIKit/UIKit.h>

@interface Hour17_AppDelegate : UIResponder <UIApplicationDelegate>

@property (strong, nonatomic) UIWindow *window;

@property (readonly, strong, nonatomic) NSManagedObjectContext
  *managedObjectContext;
@property (readonly, strong, nonatomic) NSManagedObjectModel
  *managedObjectModel;
@property (readonly, strong, nonatomic) NSPersistentStoreCoordinator
  *persistentStoreCoordinator;

- (void)saveContext;
- (NSURL *)applicationDocumentsDirectory;

@end
```

Listing 17.4 shows the implementation of the iOS app delegate. The template code contains several shell methods along with comments suggesting how you can use them. They have been removed from this listing. They are:

```
- (void)applicationWillResignActive:(UIApplication *)application
- (void)applicationDidEnterBackground:(UIApplication *)application
- (void)applicationWillEnterForeground:(UIApplication *)application
- (void)applicationDidBecomeActive:(UIApplication *)application
```

Listing 17.4 has been rearranged and modified from the Xcode template. In addition, some titles have been added using pragma mark. Also, some comments about data model migration have been removed. These changes have been made to emphasize the parallel structure between the iOS and Mac OS versions.

▶ See Hour 24, "Migrating Data Models," p. 423, for more information on data model migration.

You might want to compare Figure 17.3 with Figure 17.5 so that you can see the similarities in the rearranged files.

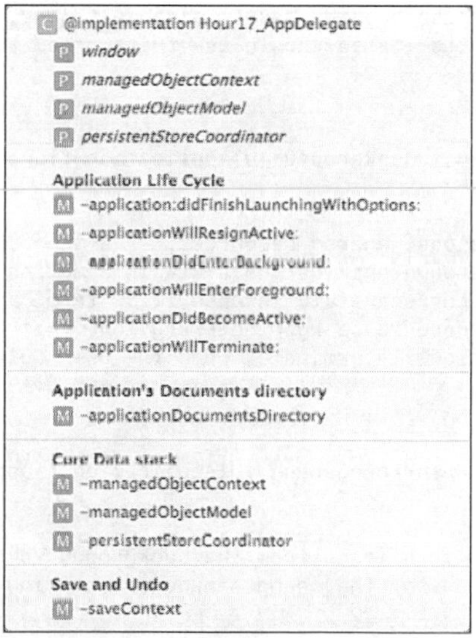

FIGURE 17.5
Use the jump bar to see the structure of the implementation file.

LISTING 17.4   iOS App Delegate Implementation (Rearranged and Titled)

```
//
//  Hour17_AppDelegate.m
//  Empty
//
//  Created by Jesse Feiler on 9/22/11.
//  Copyright (c) 2011 another. All rights reserved.
//

#import "Hour17_AppDelegate.h"

@implementation Hour17_AppDelegate

@synthesize window = _window;
@synthesize managedObjectContext = __managedObjectContext;
@synthesize managedObjectModel = __managedObjectModel;
```

```objc
@synthesize persistentStoreCoordinator = __persistentStoreCoordinator;

#pragma mark - Application Life Cycle
- (BOOL)application:(UIApplication *)application
  didFinishLaunchingWithOptions:(NSDictionary *)launchOptions
{
  self.window = [[UIWindow alloc] initWithFrame:[[UIScreen mainScreen] bounds]];
  // Override point for customization after application launch.
  self.window.backgroundColor = [UIColor whiteColor];
  [self.window makeKeyAndVisible];
  return YES;
}

- (void)applicationWillResignActive:(UIApplication *)application
{
  /*
   Sent when the application is about to move from active to inactive state.
     This can occur for certain types of temporary interruptions (such as an
     incoming phone call or SMS message) or when the user quits the application
     and it begins the transition to the background state.
   Use this method to pause ongoing tasks, disable timers, and throttle down
     OpenGL ES frame rates. Games should use this method to pause the game.
   */
}

- (void)applicationDidEnterBackground:(UIApplication *)application
{
  /*
  Use this method to release shared resources, save user data, invalidate
    timers, and store enough application state information to restore your
    application to its current state in case it is terminated later.
  If your application supports background execution, this method is called
    instead of applicationWillTerminate: when the user quits.
   */
}

- (void)applicationWillEnterForeground:(UIApplication *)application
{
  /*
  Called as part of the transition from the background to the inactive state;
    here you can undo many of the changes made on entering the background.
   */
}

- (void)applicationDidBecomeActive:(UIApplication *)application
{
  /*
  Restart any tasks that were paused (or not yet started) while the application
    was inactive. If the application was previously in the background, optionally
    refresh the user interface.
   */
}
```

```objc
- (void)applicationWillTerminate:(UIApplication *)application
{
  // Saves changes in the application's managed object context before the
    application terminates.
  [self saveContext];
}

#pragma mark - Application's Documents directory

/**
 Returns the URL to the application's Documents directory.
 */
- (NSURL *)applicationDocumentsDirectory
{
  return [[[NSFileManager defaultManager] URLsForDirectory:NSDocumentDirectory
    inDomains:NSUserDomainMask] lastObject];
}


#pragma mark - Core Data stack

/**
 Returns the managed object context for the application.
 If the context doesn't already exist, it is created and bound to the
   persistent store coordinator for the application.
 */
- (NSManagedObjectContext *)managedObjectContext
{
  if (__managedObjectContext != nil)
  {
    return __managedObjectContext;
  }

  NSPersistentStoreCoordinator *coordinator = [self persistentStoreCoordinator];
  if (coordinator != nil)
  {
    __managedObjectContext = [[NSManagedObjectContext alloc] init];
    [__managedObjectContext setPersistentStoreCoordinator:coordinator];
  }
  return __managedObjectContext;
}

/**
 Returns the managed object model for the application.
 If the model doesn't already exist, it is created from the application's model.
 */
- (NSManagedObjectModel *)managedObjectModel
{
  if (__managedObjectModel != nil)
  {
    return __managedObjectModel;
  }
  NSURL *modelURL = [[NSBundle mainBundle] URLForResource:@"Empty"
```

```
      withExtension:@"momd"];
    __managedObjectModel = [[NSManagedObjectModel alloc]
      initWithContentsOfURL:modelURL];
  return __managedObjectModel;
}

/**
 Returns the persistent store coordinator for the application.
 If the coordinator doesn't already exist, it is created and the application's
   store added to it.
 */
- (NSPersistentStoreCoordinator *)persistentStoreCoordinator
{
  if (__persistentStoreCoordinator != nil)
  {
    return __persistentStoreCoordinator;
  }

  NSURL *storeURL = [[self applicationDocumentsDirectory]
URLByAppendingPathComponent:@"Empty.sqlite"];

  NSError *error = nil;
  __persistentStoreCoordinator = [[NSPersistentStoreCoordinator alloc]
    initWithManagedObjectModel:[self managedObjectModel]];
  if (![__persistentStoreCoordinator
    addPersistentStoreWithType:NSSQLiteStoreType
    configuration:nil URL:storeURL options:nil error:&error])
  {
    /*
  Replace this implementation with code to handle the error appropriately.

  abort() causes the application to generate a crash log and terminate. You
     should not use this function in a shipping application, although it may be
     useful during development.

  Typical reasons for an error here include:
  * The persistent store is not accessible;
  * The schema for the persistent store is incompatible with current managed
       object model.
    Check the error message to determine what the actual problem was.


    If the persistent store is not accessible, there is typically something
       wrong with the file path. Often, a file URL is pointing into the
       application's resources directory instead of a writeable directory.

    If you encounter schema incompatibility errors during development, you can
       reduce their frequency by:
    * Simply deleting the existing store:
    [[NSFileManager defaultManager] removeItemAtURL:storeURL error:nil]

    */
```

```
      NSLog(@"Unresolved error %@, %@", error, [error userInfo]);
      abort();
   }

   return __persistentStoreCoordinator;
}

#pragma mark - Save and Undo
- (void)saveContext
{
   NSError *error = nil;
   NSManagedObjectContext *managedObjectContext = self.managedObjectContext;
   if (managedObjectContext !- nil)
   {
      if ([managedObjectContext hasChanges] && ![managedObjectContext save:&error])
      {
         /*
         Replace this implementation with code to handle the error appropriately.

            abort() causes the application to generate a crash log and terminate.
You should not use this function in a shipping application, although it may be
   useful during development.
         */
         NSLog(@"Unresolved error %@, %@", error, [error userInfo]);
         abort();
      }
   }
}
@end
```

Creating a Mac OS Document-Based App

Create a new project in Xcode using the Mac OS Cocoa Application template. As shown in Figure 17.6, use the checkbox to create a document-based application. Provide the name of the document class and the extension to be used on its files.

As shown in Figure 17.7, Xcode will create the project for you. Note that the following files are created for your options of a document-based app and Core Data:

- ▶ Document.h and Document.m are your document class. They are automatically set as descendents of NSPersistentDocument. If you had provided a different name in Figure 17.2, that would be used. It is easier to set a name when you create the project rather than renaming the class with Edit, Refactor, Rename.

- ▶ Document.xcdatamodeld is the empty data model.

- ▶ Document.xib is the nib file.

FIGURE 17.6
Create a docu-
ment-based
Mac OS app.

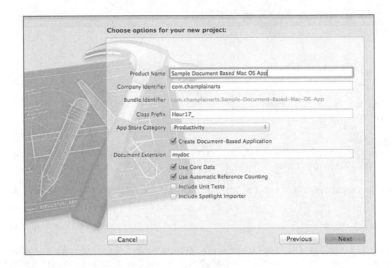

FIGURE 17.7
The project files
are created by
Xcode.

As shown in Figure 17.8, the project is set up appropriately with the name you have
provided. By default, you have three document types on Mac OS: binary, XML, and
SQLite. If you will be using only the SQLite document type, you can delete the other
two, as shown in Figure 17.8.

TIP

Using only SQLite document types can simplify both the user experience and your
own code. For example, users are not presented with a choice of document type
when they save a document.

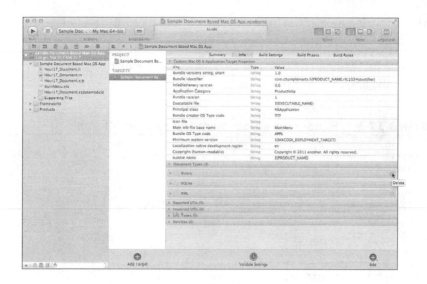

FIGURE 17.8
Delete unnec-
essary docu-
ment types.

Implementing the Core Data Stack

Your document class must implement the Core Data stack. There are several ways of
doing this. One method, which is shown in the Department and Employees sample
code on developer.apple.com, is to make an entity in the document the starting
point. In Department and Employees, each document contains a Department entity
that has its own data such as name and budget. It also has relationships to zero or
more employees. In that sample, each document then becomes a single department's data.

You can extend this concept by, for example, creating a basic company entity that
then can have relationships to departments and they have relationships to their
own employees. This structure with a key entity and subsidiary subentities is common and useful. Without such a key entity in the document, you need to find a
place to store common data for the document, and, although you can do that with
meta data, you might soon find yourself in a situation where you (or your users)
want to add on more data until the construction of a key entity with almost limitless
attributes that can be added is a necessity.

If you do not have common data you want to store in an object, you can forgo that
structure. Instead, you can create a collection object to bring together your top-level
objects.

If you use this structure, this means you will modify the header file for a Mac OS
document-based app to look like Listing 17.5. In this case, the key entity is

customer; each customer can have zero or more jobs that will be estimated using this app.

▶ Note that Listing 17.5 becomes the basis for an example used in Part V, "Managing Data and Interfaces."

LISTING 17.5   Header for a Document-Based Mac OS App

```
//
//  Hour17_Document.h
//  Sample Document Based Mac OS App
//
//  Created by Jesse Feiler on 8/12/11.
//  Copyright 2011 __ChamplainArts__. All rights reserved.
//

#import <Cocoa/Cocoa.h>

@interface MyDocument : NSPersistentDocument {
  NSManagedObject *customer;
}

- (NSManagedObject *)customer;
- (void)setCustomer:(NSManagedObject *)aCustomer;

@end
```

The implementation of the document will contain accessors for the key entity— customer. (That is the code that you add to the basic template; it is shown in italics in Listing 17.6.) As you will learn, the getter contains the core data stack. This means that in your code, you deal with the key entity (customer, company, department, and so forth), and only within that do you work with Core Data.

As you have learned with the previous implementations, Figure 17.9 uses the jump bar to show the structure of the code in Listing 17.6.

FIGURE 17.9
Review the implementation file structure from the jump bar.

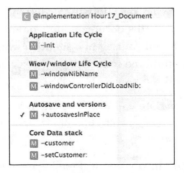

LISTING 17.6   Implementation for a Document-Based Mac OS App

```objc
//
//  Hour17_Document.m
//  Sample Document Based Mac OS App
//
//  Created by Jesse Feiler on 8/12/11.
//  Copyright 2011 __ChamplainArts__. All rights reserved.
//

#import "MyDocument.h"

@implementation MyDocument

#pragma mark - Application life cycle

- (id)init
{
  self = [super init];
  if (self) {
    // Add your subclass-specific initialization here.
    // If an error occurs here, return nil.
  }
  return self;
}

- (id)initWithType:(NSString *)type error:(NSError **)error
{
  self = [super initWithType:type error:error];
  if (self != nil)
    {
      NSManagedObjectContext *managedObjectContext = [self managedObjectContext];
      [self setCustomer:[NSEntityDescription
      insertNewObjectForEntityForName:@"Customer"
        inManagedObjectContext:managedObjectContext]];
      // To avoid undo registration for this insertion, removeAllActions on the
      // undoManager.
      // First call processPendingChanges on the managed object context to force
      // the undo registration
      // for this insertion, then call removeAllActions.
      [managedObjectContext processPendingChanges];
      [[managedObjectContext undoManager] removeAllActions];
      [self updateChangeCount:NSChangeCleared];
    }
    return self;
}

#pragma mark   View/window life cycle

- (NSString *)windowNibName
{
  // Override returning the nib file name of the document
  // If you need to use a subclass of NSWindowController or if your document
    supports
  // multiple NSWindowControllers, you should remove this method and override -
  //    makeWindowControllers instead.
  return @"MyDocument";
}
```

```objc
- (void)windowControllerDidLoadNib:(NSWindowController *)aController
{
  [super windowControllerDidLoadNib:aController];
  // Add any code here that needs to be executed once the windowController has
    loaded
  // the document's window.
}

#pragma mark - Autosave and versions

+ (BOOL)autosavesInPlace
{
  return YES;
}

#pragma mark - Core Data stack

- (NSManagedObject *)customer
  {
    if (customer != nil)
    {
      return customer;
    }

    NSManagedObjectContext *moc = [self managedObjectContext];
    NSFetchRequest *fetchRequest = [[NSFetchRequest alloc] init];
    NSError *fetchError = nil;
    NSArray *fetchResults;

    @try
     {
       NSEntityDescription *entity = [NSEntityDescription entityForName:@"Customer"
         inManagedObjectContext:moc];

       [fetchRequest setEntity:entity];
       fetchResults = [moc executeFetchRequest:fetchRequest error:&fetchError];
    } @finally
    {
      //[fetchRequest release];
    }

    if ((fetchResults != nil) && ([fetchResults count] == 1) && (fetchError == nil))
    {
      [self setCustomer:[fetchResults objectAtIndex:0]];
      return customer;
    }

    if (fetchError != nil)
      {
        [self presentError:fetchError];
      }
    else {
        // should present custom error message...
```

```
    }
    return nil;
}

- (void)setCustomer:(NSManagedObject *)aCustomer
{
  if (customer != aCustomer)
    {
    customer = aCustomer;
    }
}

@end
```

Moving Data Models

Although there are some differences in how the apps are put together, Core Data can fit into any of the basic paradigms for iOS and Mac OS apps. Not only that, a given data model can actually be used in different apps. And, if that data model is used to create and update different persistent stores, they too can move from one app to another.

The apps can use the same data, but they very well might look different—after all, they will run on different operating systems and different devices. Figure 17.10 shows an app running in a split view controller on iPad.

As shown in Figure 17.11, the data from the same persistent store can be edited in an app on Mac OS.

FIGURE 17.10
Use a split view controller on iPad.

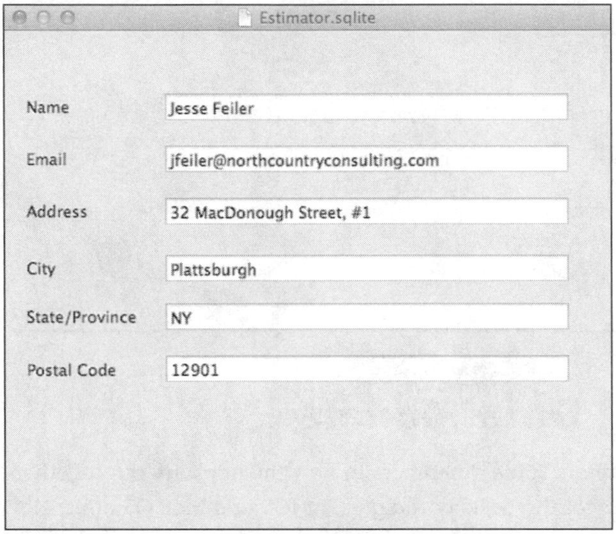

FIGURE 17.11
The same data
can be viewed
and edited on
Mac OS.

NOTE

These figures show the same persistent store being opened from two different apps. Note that this is not shared access: Core Data is not a multiuser environment. What is being shown is the ability to move a persistent store and update it from different devices. This is at the heart of iCloud. For true multiuser data sharing, look at FileMaker and FileMaker Go.

Moving a Data Model from One Project to Another

You can move a persistent store file from one location to another. With a document-based app, you can save it in one place and open it in another. With a library/shoebox-based app, it is a matter of locating the file in the sandbox of the simulator or, with iTunes, in the app's sandbox on the device. On Mac OS, it's a matter of Control-clicking Go in the Finder menu to open the Library/Application Support folder (or wherever you have put the file). All these files have the sqlite extension (if you are using SQLite formats), and in that sense, they are interchangeable providing the projects have the same data model.

Data model files are somewhat more complex. The files in your project are actually file bundles. You can locate one of them in the Finder and, with Command-click, bring up a shortcut menu that lets you open that file bundle. In it you might see several versions of your data model.

The trick in moving data models is not to move pieces of the file bundle. The steps outlined in the next section will help you avoid unintended adventures.

NOTE

Note that the process discussed in the next section relies on working with a new project and a new and unused data model—in other words, working with a new project you have not yet built.

The reason for this is that at build time, the data model (the `xcdatamodeld` files) is compiled into yet another file package with a suffix momd that, in turn, contains references to the versions of the data model. The steps in the next section keep the versions of the `xcdatamodeld` package complete in the file in the Finder and leave the bundle intact.

There are several ways to move a data model from one project to another; the following steps are one method. You can short-circuit it in various ways, but this works:

1. Start by building a Core Data project with a data model. You do not have to make it complete or final; just get the basics working.

2. Create a second Core Data project using an appropriate template. Whether you start from Mac OS or iOS does not matter.

3. Before doing anything else with the new project, find the data model in the Project navigator.

4. Control-click it to bring up the shortcut menu shown in Figure 17.12.

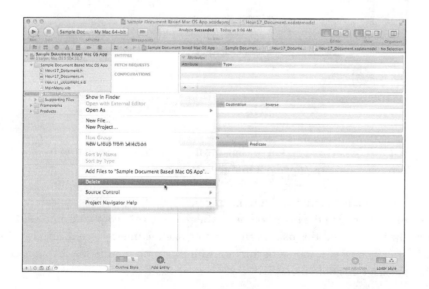

FIGURE 17.12
Delete the existing data model.

5. Delete the existing data model.

6. As shown in Figure 17.13, you have the option to merely remove the reference. This can let you return to the previous data model if you want. If you keep the file, you might want to move it somewhere safe where it is out of the way of your project to avoid confusion.

7. Select the group in which the data model was located and Control-click to bring up the shortcut menu again, as shown in Figure 17.14.

FIGURE 17.13
Removing only the references is safest unless you already have a copy of the file.

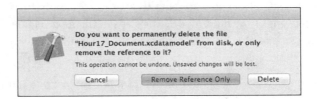

Do you want to permanently delete the file "Hour17_Document.xcdatamodel" from disk, or only remove the reference to it?

This operation cannot be undone. Unsaved changes will be lost.

Cancel   Remove Reference Only   Delete

FIGURE 17.14
Add the other data model file to the project.

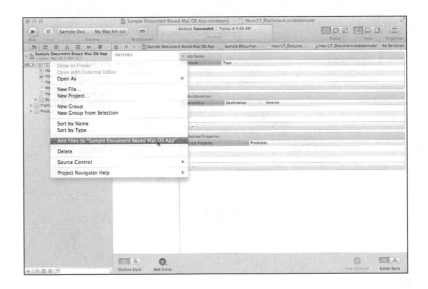

8. Be sure to select the option to copy the file. This should leave it in its old location as well as copying it into the new project.

You should be able to build and run the app now with the new data model. (Remember to change the model name in your code so that your core data stack opens the new file.) At this point, you need to make the interface connections to the model, but by now you should be familiar with that process from the first project you created for this data model.

Summary

This hour shows you how to work with the second implementation of a universal app. It explores the document model of apps on Mac OS and iOS as well as the non-document model (sometimes called the Library/Shoebox model). Both let you store data in any way you want, although Core Data is clearly preferable because of its power and flexibility. The structure of the two types of apps differ, but those differences are confined to the app delegate and document classes—your data model, views, view controllers, and nib files work the same way no matter in which structure they are located.

Q&A

Q. *Where does the Core Data stack go in each of the app structures?*

A. The Core Data stack needs to be always reachable from code that might need it. Thus, it is located in the document class for a document-based app and in the app delegate for a Library/Shoebox app. Each document can have its own Core Data stack—and that is one of the features of the document-based architecture.

Q. *How do you share data models?*

A. Data models are portable from one app to another because they do not contain references to classes or nib files. Classes contain references *to* the data model, and nib files contain connections to outlets in classes and through them to the data model. The data model itself is transportable. Having transported it, you and your users can then use it in several apps to access the same files. But remember that Core Data is not a multiuser environment; you can access the same files but not at the same time. You can look at the iCloud information on developer.apple.com and the author's site at northcountry consulting.com to see how you can take advantage of iCloud.

Workshop

Quiz

1. *How do you create a Core Data app on Mac OS compared to iOS?*

2. *How do you create a document-based app on Mac OS compared to iOS?*

Quiz Answers

1. On iOS, select a template that can use Core Data and then turn on the Core Data checkbox. The templates are Master-Detail, Utility, and Empty. On Mac OS, you use the Cocoa Application template for most development, so the Core Data option is available in all cases.

2. Use the checkbox and document type when you create a Cocoa App. On iOS, start from the Document-Based project template.

Activities

Start looking at each of the apps you use to see whether they are Library/Shoebox apps or document-based apps. Do not limit your research to apps on iOS and Mac devices: Think about apps you use at home, at work, at school, or at a public library. What are the design, interface, and security issues that differ for these two types of apps?

HOUR 18

Validating Data

What You'll Learn in This Hour:

▶ Creating validation rules in the data model
▶ Moving data between interface fields and data model objects
▶ Using formatters
▶ Creating subclasses of NSManaged object

Using Validation Rules in the Data Model

There are two aspects to data validation:

▶ Specifying the validation rules

▶ Implementing them

In this hour, you learn how to set some validation rules for a data model and how they take effect as people enter data. After that, you learn how to modify the default behavior so that you provide your own validation error messages.

The focus in this hour is on the rules. Once you have them in place, some will be managed automatically for you—particularly on Mac OS with its bindings and with document-based apps. Others you need to check on at appropriate times of program execution.

▷ You will find more information about calling validation rules in Hour 22, "Managing Validation."

As you learned in the "Adding Relationships to a Data Model" section of Hour 6, "Working with the Data Model Editor," p. 117, you can specify the behavior to take place when one entity in a relationship is deleted: You do that by selecting the relationship and examining its settings in the Data Model inspector in the utility area. Using the same interface, you can select entities in the data model and set validation rules for them.

The techniques for displaying messages do not differ much whether you are displaying a validation error message or another type of message. You should be aware that modern interface design deemphasizes communications with the user. When it comes to error messages, it has long been the goal to eliminate not only the message, but also the possibility of creating an error condition. You have a variety of interface choices to accomplish this goal:

▶ On Mac OS, disable menu items that do not apply rather than letting someone choose them and then telling them they should not have done so.

▶ On iOS, use the appropriate keyboard so that, for example, alphabetic characters cannot be typed into a numeric field.

In "Setting Up Rules in Your Data Model," you learn how to set up some common data validation rules in your data model. As pointed out in Hour 6, every time you can catch a data error by clicking a checkbox in the data model rather than by writing code, you have saved yourself a lot of time and effort. In addition, for apps that are heavily data intensive, your data validation rules can easily be communicated to users.

With these rules in place, the balance of this hour demonstrates how they can be used with and without modifications.

Relational Integrity, Data Validation, and Data Quality Rules

Rules in the Core Data data model or schema in other data management paradigms enforce data quality. There are three basic types of rules:

▶ Referential integrity
▶ Data validation
▶ Data quality

As you learned in Hour 6, you can specify what happens when an entity on one side of a relationship is deleted. Those rules can help you preserve *referential integrity*. Simply put, this means that if you have a relationship in which one entity points to another, if something happens to cause that second entity to no longer exist, the reference in the first entity must be adjusted. Otherwise, it will point to a related entity that no longer exists. Your choices include preventing such a deletion or automatically setting the reference to a reasonable value. In the absence of referential integrity, you can never be certain that a reference is valid. Referential integrity is usually enforced in the data model or schema, but you can implement it in other ways.

Data validation is the simplest and most common type of data quality control. It also is usually enforced by the data model or schema because this type of edit uses only the information about a given attribute (or field) that is contained in the data model. For example, if you declare an attribute to be an integer, you can edit it so that a user gets an error if he types a noninteger.

You can construct data validation rules that go beyond integers and letters using *regular expressions*. Regular expressions can parse strings of text to find matching sequences of text. For example, you can write a regular expression to check whether a sequence of characters is an email address. The simplest version might check for a single @ in the string that is not in either the first or last position. You can find a wide variety of regular expressions for validating email addresses on the Web using a search engine. In fact, you will probably find a regular expression for just about any edit of this type that you want to perform as long as the edit is limited to syntax or structure. (In other words, checking that an email address is properly formatted can be done with a regular expression, but checking that it is an actual email address requires additional work.)

The final type of data rules are *data quality* edits. (Note that people often refer to data quality as encompassing referential integrity, data validity, and data quality. Those are two separate uses of the phrase.)

When referring to a specific type of data edit, *data quality* generally refers to edits that cannot be performed on the data by itself. You do not need to look at any other data to check to see whether the entered values are an integer or a value greater than zero—typical data validation edits.

A data quality edit often compares entered data with other data. For time series data, a value that differs from the previous period's value by more than a certain amount might trigger a warning. Likewise, in some cases, a value that is too similar to the previous value is a red flag.

For example, checking to see that someone enrolled in a history class is also enrolled in the school could be a quality edit depending on how it is implemented. Quality edits often need to be implemented in code because they might involve retrieving other data to make a comparison. In many environments, quality edits can be overridden, while validity edits cannot be (that integer must be an integer). Referential integrity, like validation edits, often generates error messages that cannot be overridden.

There is one important point to remember about most database rules: They are applied when data is entered or modified. Changing a data rule in most cases has no effect on data that has already been entered. This means that you can only assume that all your integers really are integers for those values that are entered after the rule has been turned on. For the "integers" such as "my bad data" that already exist, the rule will not have any effect.

Setting Up Rules in Your Data Model

This section shows you how to implement data rules in your model. These rules are typical of those that are commonly used. Adding them to your data model does not take much time, and it can dramatically improve the stability and integrity of your data.

▶ This section expands on Hour 6, "Working with the Core Data Model Editor," p. 117.

Working with the Data Model Inspector

In the Core Data data model editor, show the utility area at the right of the workspace and choose the Data Model inspector, as shown in Figure 18.1.

NOTE

In comparing the data model shown in Figure 18.1 with previous data models, you may notice a new field, `customerSince`. This is an example of the complexities of apparently simple database design. For a database that tracks new transactions, this field should logically be a date. However, for a database that is tracking data that may have been converted from older systems and even from paper, a date may not work.

If a firm has been doing business with a client since the 1880s, putting a date into this field might be misleading. (Even the year may be uncertain, but the actual date may be lost in the mists of time.) Using the year (an integer) may bypass the issue. Depending on your needs, you can hone in on the issue, if it is one, by providing a second field, by renaming this one to `customerSinceYear`, or other tactics. Designing databases is dependent on the data they will be using. These choices are for the end-user or client. The database designer's job can be to guide them and to ask questions such as, "How long have the longest-affiliated clients been customers?"

FIGURE 18.1
Use the Data Model inspector.

Select the object you want to edit—typically, this will be an entity or a relationship. You can select multiple objects such as several entities or several attributes within an entity. If you have several entities selected, all their attributes are displayed in the table view, and you can select attributes from several entities at the same time to set properties. (This is particularly useful for setting the Optional property for a whole group of attributes.)

NOTE

Whether you work in the table or graph view of the editor is up to you because Xcode handles them both appropriately. In a graph view, the line representing a relationship actually represents both sides of the relationship (the relationship and its inverse). Good database design includes inverse relationships in all cases, so this can be an issue for you. If it is, simply switch to table view temporarily and then move back to graph view.

The top pane of the inspector displays settings for attributes, entities, or relationships depending on which is selected. You can select multiple attributes or multiple relationships, but you cannot select attributes and relationships at the same time. If you select multiple entities, all their attributes and relationships are shown in the editor view, but the top pane of the inspector displays the entity settings rather than the attribute or relationship settings.

At the bottom of the Data Model inspector are the settings User Info, Versioning, and Relationship Sync; these are beyond the scope of this book. You can find more information about them on developer.apple.com, but rest assured that many developers build many Core Data-based apps and never worry about these.

You are primarily interested in the top section of the Data Model inspector. Depending on your selection, it displays settings for entities, attributes, or relationships. These are discussed in the following sections.

Managing Entity Settings

As shown in Figure 18.1, when the Data Model inspector reflects one or more entities, the top part of the pane lets you configure it. There are five sections of entity settings.

Name

This is the name you have provided in the table or graph view of the editor. Changing it there or here immediately changes it in the other view. As you will learn, the name setting is at the top for entities, relationships, and attributes.

Class

There are two ways of implementing Core Data functionality in your apps. As you have learned so far, you can treat them as `NSManagedObject` instances. You access values using key-value coding (KVC). If you do not type in a class name, the Class field shown in Figure 18.1 contains placeholder text in the typical light gray style that reads `NSManagedObject`. Leave it alone in most cases, unless you have created a class for your entity.

▶ The "Creating Subclasses of `NSManagedObject` for Your Entities" section, p. 331, explains how to create classes for your entities and the circumstances under which you might want to do so. These classes will be subclasses of `NSManagedObject`.

Abstract Entity

Core Data brings object-oriented programming and relational database management together. Abstract entities are common in object-oriented programming, and they are implemented as well in Core Data.

An abstract object (in programming) or entity (in Core Data) is an object or entity that is never instantiated. Instead, its descendants are instantiated.

In a data model, you might create an abstract entity for an inventory object. The abstract object might have attributes such as name and an identifier. The descendant entities would inherit the name and identifier field, but they would also add more specific fields.

You might have one subentity to store items for sale; another subentity would store capital assets. Each of these subentities would have their own attributes with their own rules. For example, within the subentity for capital assets, the identifiers might well be unique, and within items for sale, the identifiers might also be unique. However, across both subentities, the identifiers might not be unique.

> **NOTE**
>
> Using abstract entities can help to organize and clarify your data model. However, you might want to consider the various ways of organizing your data. Instead of subclassing an abstract entity, you might want to create a concrete entity with sufficient attributes so that you can configure a given instance to be either an item for sale or a capital asset. This is a basic data modeling issue, and there often are no clear-cut answers.

Parent Entity

You can specify a parent entity for your entity. The parent can be an abstract entity, but it can also be a concrete one. You can choose only from existing entities.

TIP

If you find yourself needing a parent entity and one does not yet exist, you can create it and come back to continue configuring the descendant.

Indexes

Indexing can improve performance; however, the trade-off of using indexes is that they can degrade performance because they need to be updated when data is updated. Thus, you improve retrieval and degrade updating. In many systems, this is an easy choice to make; in others, it is difficult.

For complex systems, there is only one way to make the choice if you have any doubts: Make a copy of the project including the data store and data model, and try it several ways. Be sure to try it on typical hardware. If you improve performance on Mac OS, you might degrade performance on iPhone (and, theoretically, the reverse might apply but that seems less likely).

The indexes you specify for an entity are *compound indexes* consisting of comma-separated properties of the entity. You can specify indexes for specific attributes, as you will learn in the following section. These are simply the compound indexes for the entity as a whole.

NOTE

Typically, attribute is used in Core Data and data management documentation to refer to what at runtime are properties of objects.

You can specify indexes to be used in retrieving data.

Add compound indexes with + and delete them by selecting one and using –. Type in your comma-separated list of properties. You can have several compound indexes, each with its own set of properties.

▶ See developer.apple.com and the developer discussion groups there for more on this topic. In addition, registered developers can access video sessions from Worldwide Developer Conferences; they often have sessions on Core Data performance.

Managing Attribute Settings

Once you have managed your entity, you can begin to manage the attributes for that entity. Select one or more attributes; the settings are shown in Figure 18.2.

You can see the seven settings in Figure 18.2. Each is described in this section.

▶ **Name**—As is always the case, the first line is the name of the attribute. If multiple attributes are selected, the placeholder text reads Multiple Values.

FIGURE 18.2
Manage attribute settings.

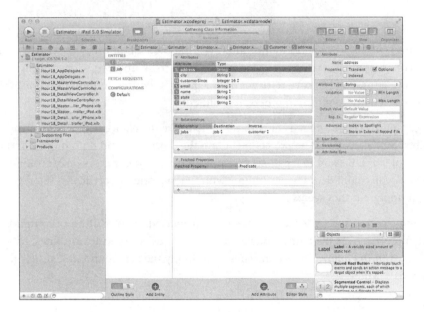

▶ **Properties**—These are the basic settings for any attribute. Many attributes use the default properties (in other words, none of the checkboxes is used). There are three properties:

  ▶ **Transient**—If you are creating a custom class (see "Creating Subclasses of NSManagedObject for Your Entities," p. 331, later in this hour), that class will have a property for your transient attributes. The getter in your entity class will be responsible for returning the value, but it will not be stored in the data store. Typical transient attributes are attributes such as name_last_first, which can be composed at runtime from separate attributes that are stored in the data store as last_name and first_name.

  ▶ **Optional**—Uncheck this box to make the attribute required.

  ▶ **Indexed**—This box causes the attribute to be indexed. Note that this is a single attribute index and not the compound index that you can specify for the entity as a whole.

▶ **Attribute Type**—As shown in Figure 18.3, these are Core Data attribute types that are supported (or not) in particular persistent stores.

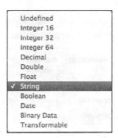

FIGURE 18.3
Select an
attribute type.

▶ **Validation**—These rules depend on the attribute type. For strings, you supply a minimum and maximum length if you want. For numeric types, you specify a minimum and maximum value.

▶ **Default Value**—You can also specify default values,. Default values can be changed; you can use them to speed data entry. (On devices without keyboards, default values can dramatically improve the user experience if they are well-chosen.)

▶ **Regular Expression**—For strings, you can specify a *regular expression* (or *regex*) that is used to validate the string. Search the web for "regular expression" and the type of rule you want to enforce to see examples as in "regular expression email." If you have not used them before, you may want to devote an hour to exploring the tutorials on the web. To the uninitiated, a regular expression can be daunting, but once you learn the rules, you will see how logical and powerful they are. You do not need Core Data-specific regular expressions.

▶ **Advanced**—On Mac OS X, you can index the contents of this attribute in Spotlight for fast searching on the Mac. You also have an option to store the data in an external file. This is most useful for larger data structures such as video that would degrade performance if they were in the persistent store itself. This is a common data management optimization and is not unique to Core Data.

Managing Relationship Settings

In Figure 18.4, the relationship settings are shown for the selected relationship(s). The first three settings are synchronized with the table or graph editor.

FIGURE 18.4
Manage
relationship set-
tings.

▶ **Name**—As always, the first line is the name of the setting. Typically, entity names are singular and capitalized (Job, Customer, and so forth). Relationships are often lowercase and plural for many-to-many relationships. (jobs, customers, and so on). This makes the data model easier to read.

▶ **Destination**—This is the other end of the relationship.

▶ **Inverse**—Most relationships have an inverse in which the destination is the source. This list is only populated when you have created a relationship in a different entity where the relationship in the other entity has this entity as its destination.

▶ **Properties**—These properties have the same meaning for relationships as they do for attributes. Transient relationships exist only at runtime. You can also specify whether a relationship is optional. Note that inverse relationships many times have the reverse optionality. For example, a job-to-customer must have a customer because without one, there is no job. You can, however, have a customer-to-job relationship with no job because the customer has not signed up for a job.

- ▶ **Arranged**—You can now specify that collections are ordered in the data store. You can also provide indexing data such as an order attribute; if you do so, you can reconstitute the order at runtime. It is convenient in many cases to have an ordered relationship maintained by Core Data, but there is a performance penalty. Experiment with your data to see the pros and cons.

- ▶ **Plural/Cardinality**—This is where you can specify whether this is a one-to-one or one-to-many relationship (this is sometimes referred to as *cardinality*). As with the optional property, this often differs for an inverse relationship. One customer can have many jobs, but a job can have only one customer, for example.

- ▶ **Count**—You can provide minimum and maximum counts for each side of the relationship. This is where you implement a one-to-many relationship, but you can also specify other values.

- ▶ **Delete Rule**—The delete rule determines how the relationship behaves when one side of it is deleted (or even if that can happen).

- ▶ **Advanced**—The same advanced settings you have for attributes apply to relationships because, in many ways, they are attributes.

Entering Data into the Interface and Moving It to the Data Model (and Vice Versa)

In the code you have seen so far, it has been simple to enter data and move it into the model. In your interface files, you have created text fields. At the appropriate moments, your detail view controller has moved data from the Core Data managed object to or from the text field. In the examples so far, this has happened in `configureView` (typically called from `viewDidLoad` and other places where necessary) and in `save` or a similar method. Here is the typical code to move data from the view controller (`self`) to a text field in the interface called `name`:

```
self.name.text = [self.detailItem valueForKey:@"name"];
```

This fairly standard code relies on the fact that a text field has a `text` property. It also relies on KVC so that an `NSManagedObject` called `detailItem` has a key called `name` that can be used to set its value.

On the reverse side, this is the code you have used:

```
[self.detailItem setValue: self.name.text forKey:@"name"];
```

Again, it relies on KVC and the existence of a key called name in the managed object called detailItem.

Introducing the Type Conflict Issue

Nothing could be simpler than this pattern. This works very well for all the attributes in the Customer entity shown in Figure 18.5 (it is the same basic data model you have seen previously for the Estimator example in Hour 15, "Saving Data with a Navigation Interface," p. 257).

FIGURE 18.5
Define the Customer entity.

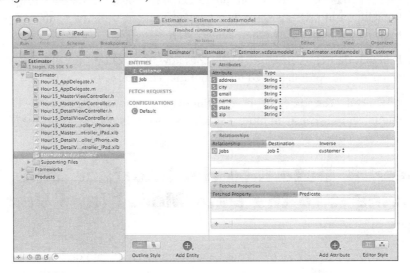

Now consider the Job entity shown in Figure 18.6.

CAUTION

The code snippets shown previously will work well for the job_description and rate attributes, which are strings. For the others, though, you are going to have type conflicts. You cannot set a decimal attribute to text. This is something you might not have worried about in some other languages, but, although Objective-C is forgiving in many ways due to its dynamic nature, type conversions of this sort are not handled automatically for you. (In part, this is because it is not always clear how the conversion should be handled, and as a result, "doing the right thing" might turn into "doing one of the right things.")

Because you know both sides of the issue (that is, that the interface field expects a string and the Core Data attribute expects a decimal), you can convert one to another. There are many conversion methods for objects in the framework, and now you can see the usefulness of having objects.

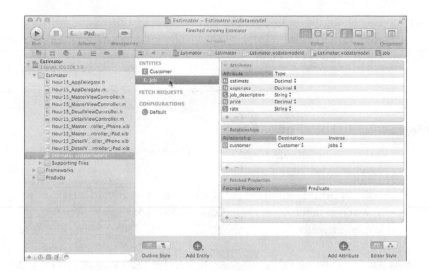

FIGURE 18.6
Define the Job
entity.

Solving the Type Conflict Issue with Formatters

The mechanism you use to do this is a *formatter*. Formatters in Cocoa and Cocoa Touch are used to convert text to and from other types as well as to format the text appropriately.

On Mac OS, you can add formatters from the library to text fields. There are date, number, and custom formatters that you can drag onto a text field. There also is a text field that already contains a number formatter. On either iOS or Mac OS, you can create formatters programmatically.

Not only can a formatter do the actual formatting of text, but it also can serve as a converter to text of a date or number. For example, NSDateFormatter contains dateFromString and stringFromDate methods. The specific conversions depend on the formatter. All formatters are descendants of NSFormatter, and all override stringForObjectValue and getObjectValueForString, which handle the basic conversions.

What you care about is how to add formatters to your text fields and how to use them to convert data. The basic pattern is the same for date and number formatters as well as for any others you might create.

▼ **Try It Yourself**

Using an NSNumberFormatter

The code to create and manage an NSNumberFormatter goes in your view controller (DetailViewController in this example):

1. Inside the DetailViewController.m file, locate the private interface section you added to the example in Hour 15, "Saving Data with a Navigation Interface."

LISTING 18.1   Existing Private Declaration in **DetailViewController.m**

```
#import "Hour18_DetailViewController.h"

@interface Hour18_DetailViewController ()

@property (strong, nonatomic) UIPopoverController *popoverController;

- (void)configureView;

@end
```

2. Add a property for a number formatter. It can go above or below the existing popoverController property. You can rely on the compiler to create the instance variable (numberFormatter):

```
@property (nonatomic, retain, readonly) NSNumberFormatter *numberFormatter;
```

3. Synthesize the new property with the other @synthesize directives. This line can go anywhere, but it is good to keep all the @synthesize directives together:

```
@synthesize numberFormatter;
```

4. Implement the getter for numberFormatter. @synthesize implements one for you, but you can create your own with the same name (that is, the name of the property). You can also use a different name, but the standard name is best in most cases. Listing 18.2 shows the getter. If the property exists, it returns it; otherwise, it creates it.

LISTING 18.2   Getter for **numberFormatter**

```
- (NSNumberFormatter *)numberFormatter
{
  if (numberFormatter == nil)
```

```
{
  numberFormatter = [[NSNumberFormatter alloc] init];
}
  return numberFormatter;
}
```

5. After you have a formatter, you can call its methods. For example, now that you have an `NSNumberFormatter`, you can convert strings to and from numbers with these methods. Notice that in both, you pass in the value to be converted; you are not working off of a value in the formatter itself:

```
- (NSString *)stringFromNumber:(NSNumber *)number
```

and

```
- (NSNumber *)numberFromString:(NSString *)string
```

6. Stored in the number format are the styles and formats to be used in the formatter rather than the value. For more information, see the documentation for `NSNumberFormatter` and `NSDateFormatter`. (Remember that you can search for them in Organizer.)

7. To set the value of a text field from the price attribute of a managed object, convert the decimal to a text with a formatter as follows:

```
self.price.text = [numberFormatter stringFromNumber:

  [NCNumber numberWithInteger:self.detailItem
  valueForKey:@"price"];]]];
```

8. To set the value of a managed object's non-text attribute (the reverse of step 7), use code such as the following. This can be used to set the price attribute of a job that is a decimal value:

```
[self.detailItem setValue: [numberFormatter numberFromString: self.price.text

  forKey:@"price"];
```

When you are going from a string to a class such as `NSDecimalNumber`, you can also use class methods such as `decimalNumberFromString` to handle the conversion. However, the reverse (number to string) is most easily done with a formatter. In view of the fact that you will need a formatter to handle that transformation, it is easier for many people to use the formatter to handle both conversions rather than using a formatter in one direction and a class method in the other direction.

▲

Creating Subclasses of `NSManagedObject` for Your Entities

Creating your own subclass of `NSManagedObject` has its pros and cons. The most noticeable difference between subclasses and `NSManagedObject` is that you have properties with their accessors for your entity attributes. This can mean less code for you to write because you do not have to implement KVC. In addition, KVC can sometimes be slower than accessors in getting to and from the data. In addition, because mistakes in typing accessors are detected as you build the project while mistakes in typing attribute names for KVC are detected at runtime, you have a slight extra margin of security.

Transient properties and relationships must be implemented in subclasses of NSManagedObject, so your decision might be made for you. Many Core Data apps use a combination of subclasses and KVC.

Another important reason for using subclasses of NSManagedObject is that you can implement your own validation rules in them. The validation rules you have seen in this hour are fine for working with individual attributes, but if you want to perform quality edits that compare data values with other fields or attributes or with historical values, you need to implement your own edits.

▶ You will find more about implementing quality edits like these in Part IV, "Building the Core Data Code."

If you want to use subclasses, you can easily create them with Xcode. Select the entity (or entities) that you want to subclass and select Editor, Create NSManaged Object Subclass. You can select several attributes from several entities if you want and then choose the command. If you do that, you will be asked which entities you want to subclass, as shown in Figure 18.7.

FIGURE 18.7
Select your
subclasses.

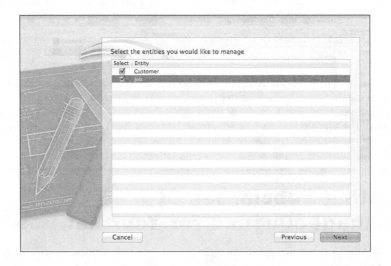

Next, select the group into which the new subclass files (the .h and .m files) will be placed. Of course, you can always move them.

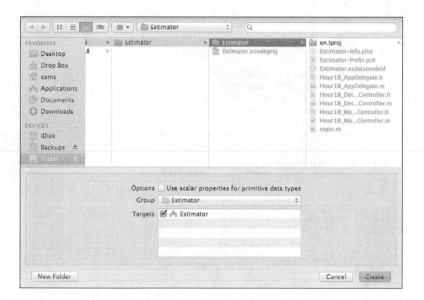

FIGURE 18.8
Set the group
and disk loca-
tion for the
subclass.

In the case of the data model shown in this hour, here are the files that are built for the Customer entity if it is subclassed. Job is very much the same, but Customer is used because it shows how a to-many relationship is implemented in the subclass. In this case, it is customer-to-jobs, and Customer.h contains an NSSet that will be populated at runtime. Note the accessors that let you get and set individual objects within the set of the to-many Jobs relationship. Listing 18.3 shows Customer.h, and Listing 18.4 shows Customer.m.

LISTING 18.3   Customer.h

```
//   Customer.h
//   Test Core Data
//
//   Created by Jesse Feiler on 8/20/11.
//   Copyright (c) 2011 another. All rights reserved.
//

#import <Foundation/Foundation.h>
#import <CoreData/CoreData.h>


@interface Customer : NSManagedObject

@property (nonatomic, retain) NSString * address;
@property (nonatomic, retain) NSString * city;
```

```
@property (nonatomic, retain) NSString * email;
@property (nonatomic, retain) NSString * name;
@property (nonatomic, retain) NSString * state;
@property (nonatomic, retain) NSString * zip;
@property (nonatomic, retain) NSSet *jobs;
@end

@interface Customer (CoreDataGeneratedAccessors)

- (void)addJobsObject:(NSManagedObject *)value;
- (void)removeJobsObject:(NSManagedObject *)value;
- (void)addJobs:(NSSet *)values;
- (void)removeJobs:(NSSet *)values;
@end
```

LISTING 18.4   Customer.m

```
//  Customer.m
//  Test Core Data
//
//  Created by Jesse Feiler on 8/20/11.
//  Copyright (c) 2011 another. All rights reserved.
//

#import "Customer.h"


@implementation Customer

@dynamic address;
@dynamic city;
@dynamic email;
@dynamic name;
@dynamic state;
@dynamic zip;
@dynamic jobs;

@end
```

Summary

In this hour, you have learned how to adjust settings for entities, attributes, and relationships to determine which data values and conditions are legal. The actual management of validation with these rules is described in Hour 22, "Managing Validation."

You have also learned how to use formatters that can be used not only for formatting data, but also for editing it and transforming it to and from strings and object properties. Finally, you learned how to let Xcode and Core Data build subclasses of NSManagedObject based on your data model. You will learn how to use these features through Part V, "Managing Data and Interfaces."

Q&A

Q. Why is NSFormatter **necessary when other languages provide built-in functions for type conversion?**

A. In Objective-C, many simple data types from other languages (integers, for example) are usually objects. As such, they can respond to messages so that instead of building a function to manipulate a basic type, the type itself can respond and convert itself. NSFormatter works in this structure to mediate between objects in the interface (such as UITextField) and objects in the data model (such as NSManagedObject and its subclasses).

Q. What is the difference between validity edits and quality edits?

A. Validity edits typically cannot be overridden, and they have to do with elemental issues—no alphabetic characters in an integer field and no values in a date field greater than today. Quality edits often can be overridden and compare values in one field or attribute with values for the same attribute in another instance with values for a different attribute in the same instance.

Workshop

Quiz

1. *When do you use an inverse relationship?*

2. *What is relationship cardinality or the plural setting?*

Quiz Answers

1. Almost every relationship has its inverse.

2. This setting determines how many objects can be at the destination of the relationship. For example, a one-to-many relationship is actually implemented as a to-many relationship to the destination with an inverse relationship with a to-one destination.

Activities

Learn to think of validation rules in a nonprocedural way. Often, when people think of them or describe them to developers, the discussion is procedural: "Check that X is less than Y, and then check that B is not equal to C unless it is a Thursday." Work with yourself or your users to make the validation rules disjoint—that is, no sequences and no combinations.

Using UITableView on iOS

- ▶ Looking at table views on Mac OS and iOS
- ▶ Understanding the structure of UITableView
- ▶ Setting field labels in UITableView
- ▶ Moving data from Core Data into UITableView

Working with Table Views and iOS, Mac OS, and Core Data

Table views are a powerful way to display data on both Mac OS and iOS. Because Core Data apps often have large quantities of data to manage, these classes in Cocoa and Cocoa Touch are a good way to go about the job. Core Data on Mac OS and iOS is the same technology: As you have learned, you can even use the same data model on Mac OS and iOS apps so the persistent stores on one can be updated on the other.

NOTE

Core Data is not multiuser, so those updates must happen in sequence. You can build your own data store for Core Data, and you can certainly build one that handles concurrency. Enterprise Objects Framework, the precursor of Core Data, worked with databases such as Oracle, Sybase, OpenBase, and Informix.

Comparing Table Views on Mac OS and iOS

Table views on Mac OS and iOS differ in their implementations. On Mac OS, NSTableView relies on bindings in Interface Builder and/or programmatic bindings in your code (usually in the controller for the view containing the table view). On iOS, `UITableView` relies on connections in Interface Builder and programmed bindings in your code (also usually in a controller).

These two approaches differ in their style. Bindings on Mac OS incorporate certain aspects of declarative programming as opposed to procedural programming. In other words, in the binding, you bind core data objects to interface objects, and the framework takes care of implementing those bindings when needed. On iOS, the approach is more procedural so that you implement methods to display a cell, and in doing so, you move data between Core Data objects and interface objects. (With storyboards on iOS, segues in Interface Builder provide a more declarative interface to the task of managing views and their controllers than the older procedural methods.)

On both iOS and Mac OS, table views take advantage of protocols for a data source as well as a delegate, which manages user interaction. The actual implementations of these protocols are different on the two platforms, but the overall objectives are the same.

There is another difference to note, but it, too, is not an enormous practical concern. On iOS, tables have rows and a single column. On Mac OS, they can have multiple columns.

Do not magnify the differences in your own mind. From a design point of view, the similarities outweigh the differences when working with Core Data and table views on either iOS or Mac OS.

Focusing on User Interaction on iOS and Mac OS

There is one significant aspect of `UITableView` on iOS, which is not echoed in `NSTableView` on Mac OS. `UITableView` can be used very comfortably and conveniently to implement an interface that has nothing to do with Core Data, and in fact, it is used for that purpose throughout iOS. `UITableView` can be used to organize data that is not organized in records or rows.

> **NOTE**
>
> Data is referred to as rows and columns in spreadsheet-speak, records and fields in database-speak, and entity instances and attributes in Core-Data-speak.

You can find a good example of this data in the Settings app for iPhone and iPad. It shows `UITableView` in action. It also helps you get a more sophisticated grip on the difference in the user interfaces on iOS and Mac OS. On iOS, you are often dealing with full-screen data and a navigation interface, whereas on Mac OS, you deal with menus and multiple windows. In part because of the size of the Mac OS screen, your windows in that environment might be more complex than on iOS.

NOTE

For a perfect example of the complexity of windows on Mac OS, look no further than Xcode. Moving Xcode to an iOS device would be a fascinating adventure, but it is likely to take more than a few minutes.

As you will find in the "Using UITableView Without Core Data" section later in this hour, p. 344, the methods needed to display data are straightforward, and you can use these methods to display non-database data.

▶ After you have learned how to present simple data, Hour 19, "Using UITableView on iOS," p. 337, and Hour 20, "Using NSTableView on Mac OS," p. 363, will help you complete the picture.

Comparing Interfaces: Settings on iOS and System Preferences on Mac OS

One of the reasons for using UITableView for data entry without Core Data is the ability to easily construct an interface. You will appreciate some of the issues involved when you compare Settings on iOS with System Preferences on Mac OS. Figure 19.1 shows System Preferences on Mac OS.

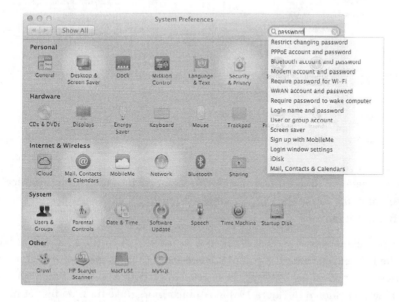

FIGURE 19.1
Use System Preferences on Mac OS.

System Preferences appears in its own window. This window has a toolbar with some specific functionality, such as the Show All button and the search field that lets you highlight relevant settings for your search term.

You can move down into specific settings by clicking on the icons, as shown in Figure 19.2.

FIGURE 19.2
Set specific
settings.

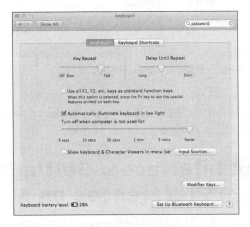

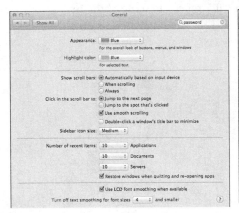 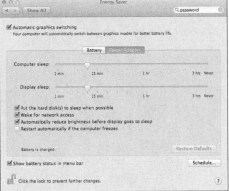

Although there are similarities in the interfaces for each of the settings (particularly the toolbar at the top of the window, which is constant), each view appears basically to be handcrafted.

Things are different on iOS. First of all, look at Settings in Figure 19.3. This is basically the iOS version of both Figures 19.1 and 19.2. There is room at the left of the split view to list all of the settings; the selected one's data appears at the right. The various settings shown in Figure 19.3 look much more alike than do the settings in Figure 19.2. There is a simple explanation for this: They all use UITableView.

Relying on UITableView to format the data has benefits in addition to speeding up development time. As shown in Figure 19.4, the table view is resized and reshaped appropriately for different devices and orientation.

In the Estimator example that has been used in a number of hours, you have encountered some of the issues UITableView solves very easily in Settings on iPad and iPhone. Consider Figure 19.5: This shows the Estimator interface on iPad.

FIGURE 19.3
Use Settings on iOS for iPad.

FIGURE 19.4
Use Settings on
iOS for iPhone.

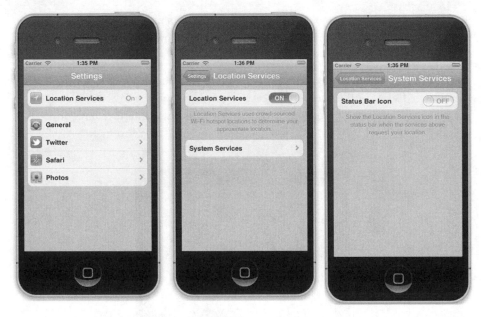

Each field and each label needs to be placed on the interface. Compare Figure 19.5
with Figure 19.3 while paying particular attention to the labels and placement of fields.
Figure 19.3 is neater, and, as you will see, it is easier to construct using UITableView.

FIGURE 19.5
View the
Estimator inter-
face on iPad.

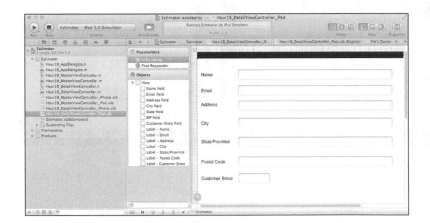

There is also the benefit that comes from being able to reuse the UITableView for both iPhone and iPad. As shown in Figure 19.6, if you have followed the steps so far in this book, your iPad interface is mostly complete, but your iPhone interface still needs most of the fields added.

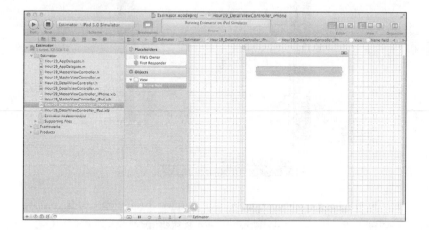

FIGURE 19.6
The iPhone interface is incomplete.

When you use a UITableView, you do not have to worry about the placement of each field and label, especially because you have already worked with a UITableView. Consider the list of customers shown in Figures 19.7 and 19.8 using the Master-Detail Application template.

FIGURE 19.7
View the Master-Detail Application template in landscape on iPad.

FIGURE 19.8
View the
Master-Detail
Application tem-
plate in portrait
on iPad.

If you explore the master view controller nib files (or the storyboard if you are using
a storyboard), you will see that the table view is a single object with dummy data,
as shown in Figure 19.9.

FIGURE 19.9
In Interface
Builder editor,
the UITableView
object has
dummy data.

That data will be replaced at runtime either by data from your Core Data persistent store
or by data that you create programmatically (by hard-coding values, performing calcula-
tions, or accessing external sources including the Internet).

Using UITableView Without Core Data

You can learn the basics of UITableView by supplying hard-coded data in your app.
This lets you focus on UITableView so that you will be ready to move on to adding
Core Data functionality to it. This section provides a bit of terminology followed by
some code you can use to manage your data view and to move from other display
formats to UITableView.

Learning the Table View Language

To start working with table views, you need to know a little terminology. Refer to Figure 19.3 to find the major components.

▶ **Cell**—A UITableView consists of *cells*. In Figure 19.3, there are five cells in the Settings section at the left (Location Services, General, Twitter, Safari, and Photos). Cells can contain data in the form of images and/or text; they also can contain selection controls and accessories such as disclosure indicators and buttons and check marks.

▶ **Sections**—A table view can have *sections*. The table at the left has only one section. At the right, five sections are visible. Three have headers (General, Privacy, and Security). Security also has a footer (Warn when visiting fraudulent websites.) The third group (Clear History and Clear Cookies and Data) has neither a header nor a footer. This particular formatting is accomplished by choosing the *grouped* style for the table.

▶ **Accessory View**—Cells can have an *accessory view*, which is normally located at the right. This might contain a disclosure triangle or a setting as shown in the Safari settings in Figure 19.3. The accessory view can also contain an image or text, as is the case with Location Services at the left.

These are the basics you need to know to talk about UITableView. Other concepts and details will be dealt with as they arise.

Removing the Old Interface of Individual Fields with a Table View

Look back at Figure 19.5. Each of those fields and labels was placed and configured separately. A UITableView can handle a lot of that for you. Figure 19.10 shows what the finished result can be.

FIGURE 19.10
Convert separate fields to a table view.

There are two tasks here. In the first, you need to remove the individual fields from the interface and their references from your code. In the second, you need to add the table view and its supporting code.

NOTE

You can download the files as described in the Introduction. Make certain to download the Hour 19 versions. Note that all of the file names begin with Hour19. For example, references to `DetailViewController.h` will show as `Hour19_DetailView Controller.h` in the downloaded code.

▼   **Try It Yourself**

Remove Separate Interface Fields and Declarations

This task is needed only for a conversion from separate fields. You can skip it entirely if you are starting with a blank interface.

1. Open `DetailViewController_iPad.xib`.

2. Delete all of the fields you added previously—both the text fields and the label fields. Do not delete the View object at the top of the view hierarchy. The View object should be the only Object in the document outline.

3. Open `DetailViewController.h`.

4. Select and delete the properties for the interface fields, as shown in Figure 19.11.

FIGURE 19.11
Delete properties for the interface fields.

5. If you declared local instance variables, delete them, too. If you have followed the steps in this book, you do not have these variables.

6. Open DetailViewController.m.

7. Select the synthesize statements for the properties you deleted in step 2 and delete them, as shown in Figure 19.12. Be careful not to delete any other synthesize statements. (After step 5, you may notice that these lines have errors in then until you delete them.)

FIGURE 19.12
Delete synthesize statements no longer needed.

8. Delete all of the code in configureView. In save, delete all of the code such as this:

```
[self.detailItem setValue: self.name.text forKey:@"name"];
```

Make certain to delete only the lines of code that refer to the fields you deleted.

9. In viewDidUnload, delete all of the code such as this:

```
[self setName:nil];
```

Make certain to delete only the lines of code that refer to the fields you deleted.

▼   **Try It Yourself**

Implement a Table View for Constant Data

Now you are ready to add a table view to your interface. You are beginning with a blank canvas on which to draw your new interface.

1. Open DetailViewController_iPad.xib, as shown in Figure 19.13. The only object in the document should be View, as shown in the figure.

FIGURE 19.13
Start to build the table-based interface.

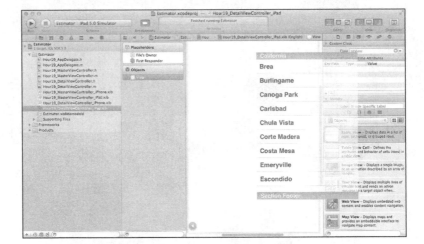

2. Open the utility area and drag a table view onto the canvas as shown.

3. Use the assistant view to open DetailViewController.h next to, above, or below the nib file, as shown in Figure 19.14.

4. As shown in Figure 19.14, control-drag from the view to the interface file.

5. Create an outlet, as shown in Figure 19.15. In the example, it is called estimatorTableView. Xcode will create your property and synthesize commands for you and will configure the connection in Interface Builder.

6. In DetailViewController.h, DetailViewController is declared as a subclass of UIViewController, as shown in the background of Figure 19.14. You will need to change it to a subclass of UITableViewController. In addition, you need to adopt the UITableViewDataSource protocol. Change the declaration to match the code in Listing 19.1.

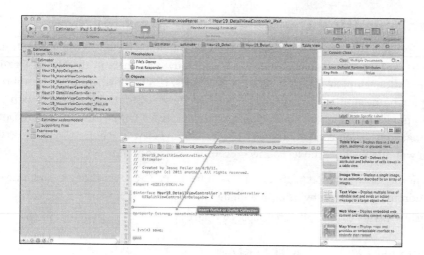

FIGURE 19.14
Use the assistant view to open the interface file.

FIGURE 19.15
Create and attach an outlet for the view.

LISTING 19.1   Interface for DetailViewController with a Table View

```
@interface Hour19_DetailViewController:UITableViewController <UITableViewDataSource,
   UISplitViewControllerDelegate> {
}
```

If you want, you can build and run the app. In the master view controller, you should see any customer entities you have already created. You can delete them or add new ones with the controls at the top of the master view controller in its popover (portrait mode) or at the left of the split view controller (landscape mode).

As for the detail view controller, there is no data to be displayed yet, but you should see the characteristic dim lines indicating that a table view is being displayed. Another set of those lines is visible in the master view controller where there is data to be displayed.

Implementing the Basic Table View Methods

For the table view to begin to function, you need to implement a few methods from the UITableViewDataSource protocol. You already have them in the Master-Detail Application template: They are in the master view controller where they control the display of the entities (customers, in this case). However, that code interacts with the data model. The essential methods can be implemented here without the Core Data connections so you can get an idea of how the table view functions. (Do not worry—you will add the data model connections in the next section.)

All of the following modifications will be in DetailViewController.m. Add a new section to collect them by using the following line:

```
#pragma mark - UITableViewDataSource Protocol
```

Use the jump bar to look at the list of methods and sections in the file so you do not place these in the middle of another section. Consider Figure 19.16, which shows the methods and pragma marks. The Split View section was selected from this menu, and the new code was entered just before that section, so it is not broken up.

FIGURE 19.16
Use the jump bar to help you decide where to put the new section of code.

Most of the methods you will implement have self-explanatory names. Because you are not accessing the data store, you will be using constant data, so it is easy to implement these methods. The comments from the template have been preserved in this code.

There are only two required methods in the protocol: `tableView:cellForRowatAtIndexPath` and `tableView:numberOfRowsInSection`.

> **NOTE**
>
> This is a high-level overview of the process. The following section, "Going Beyond the Basic Table View Methods," gives you more details.

You need to specify the number of rows in each section. Because you are not implementing numberOfSectionsInTableView, the number of sections will default to one, so you will need to specify the number of rows in that section. This method can grow so that it returns different values for different sections (the section is passed in). Count the number of rows in Figure 19.5 and implement the code in Listing 19.2.

LISTING 19.2   numberOfRowsInSection

```
- (NSInteger)tableView:(UITableView *)tableView numberOfRowsInSection:
    (NSInteger)section
{
  return 7;
}
```

For now, you can just hardcode a value to make certain the table view is working. Soon, this method will be enhanced to retrieve data from Core Data. There are three points to note about the code in Listing 19.3:

▶ **A table view can cache a cell, which you then can reuse**—This improves performance and memory usage because you do not have to create the cell for each row. You can use several different configurations of cells—give each one an identifier. Thus, the entire first section of this method (down to Configure the Cell) is usually not modified.

▶ **Each UITableViewCell has a textLabel property**—You can set the text property of the text label, and, in this code, it is hard-coded to be the string @"test".

▶ **An indexPath parameter of type NSPathIndex is passed into the method**—NSPathIndex contains two values—a section and a row. If a variable of type NSPathIndex is called myIndex, access them with myIndex.section and myIndex.row. Because you have the index path passed in, you will be able to set the appropriate value for any row in any section.

LISTING 19.3   cellForRowAtIndexPath

```
// Customize the appearance of table view cells.
- (UITableViewCell *)tableView:(UITableView *)tableView
  cellForRowAtIndexPath:(NSIndexPath *)indexPath
{
  static NSString *CellIdentifier = @"Cell";

  UITableViewCell *cell = [tableView dequeueReusableCellWithIdentifier:
    CellIdentifier];
  if (cell == nil) {
    cell = [[UITableViewCell alloc] initWithStyle:UITableViewCellStyleDefault
      reuseIdentifier:CellIdentifier];
  }

  // Configure the cell.
  cell.textLabel.text = @"test";
  return cell;
}
```

The final step is to connect the table view in Interface Builder to the Data Source property of File's Owner (DetailViewController). Now that you have changed the interface declaration in Listing 19.1, Figure 19.17 shows the connection. Note that the table view (in the background) has been relabeled Estimator Table View in the Identity inspector in the utility area. If you command-click on File's Owner, you will see its connections, including the two to Estimator Table View: It is connected to the data source of File's Owner, as well as to the estimatorTableView property.

FIGURE 19.17
Connect
Estimator Table
View to File's
Owner as data
source and
**estimator
TableView**.

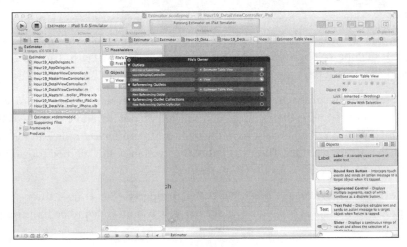

Build and run the app, and you should see the results in Figure 19.18. (Remember that the logic to set a default customer on startup is not yet present. You will have to select or create a customer to see data.)

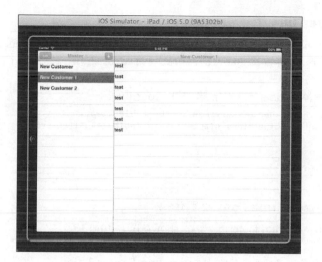

FIGURE 19.18
Test the table
view with
default text.

Going Beyond the Basic Table View Methods

You can build on the basic table view methods to provide more features and functionality. The next section, "Using UITableView with Core Data," goes even further by showing how to replace your hard-coded data with data from the data store.

Figure 19.18 showed you the basic features of using UITableView. Figure 19.19 shows a number of other features before you move on to your Core Data persistent store in the next section.

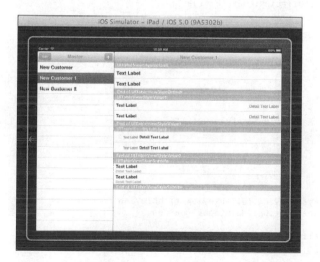

FIGURE 19.19
Use additional
UITableView
features.

Using More Than One Section

If you do nothing, UITableView will assume your table has one section. To use more sections, override numberOfSectionsInTableView, as shown in Listing 19.4.

LISTING 19.4   Use More Than One Section

```
// Customize the number of sections in the table view.
- (NSInteger)numberOfSectionsInTableView:(UITableView *)tableView
{
  return 4;
}
```

Setting Header and Footer Titles

You can set header and footer titles, as shown in Listing 19.5.

LISTING 19.5   Set Section Header and Footer Titles

```
// Customize section titles
- (NSString *)tableView:(UITableView *)tableView
  titleForHeaderInSection:(NSInteger)section
{
  switch (section)
  {
    case 0:
    {
      return @"UITableViewStyleDefault";
    }

    case 1:
    {
      return @"UITableViewStyleValue1";
    }

    case 2:
    {
      return @"UITableViewStyleValue2";
    }

    case 3:
    {
      return @"UITableViewStyleSubtitle";
    }

  }
  return nil;
}

- (NSString *)tableView:(UITableView *)tableView
titleForFooterInSection:(NSInteger)section
{
  switch (section)
  {
    case 0:
    {
      return @"End of UITableViewStyleDefault";
```

```
    }
    case 1:
    {
      return @"End of UITableViewStyleValue1";
    }

    case 2:
    {
      return @"End of UITableViewStyleValue2";
    }

    case 3:
    {
      return @"End of UITableViewStyleSubtitle";
    }
  }
    return nil;
}
```

Creating Styled Cells

You can change the style of cells, as shown in Figure 19.19, by overriding
cellForRowAtIndexPath. More important, this is the method you use to actually set
the data for a cell.

In Listing 19.3, you saw all of this, but now you can see the features in more detail.
The code to let you reuse cells is needed when you use multiple styles, and now you
can see why it is so important. Each UITableViewCell can have a style, but, if you
look in the class reference, you will see the style is not a property. Rather, the style
constants are used in initWithStyle when a cell is created. This means that if you
want to use the same style for several cells (and that makes for a better-looking
table), it is much better to reuse the cells once they are created.

TIP

If style were a property, the matter would be different, because changing a property
from one value to another is a relatively inexpensive process.

In Listing 19.6, you see how cells can be created using each of the defined cell styles.
Each cell's content is displayed in a combination of three properties:

▶ Text is displayed in textLabel and detailTextLabel. Figure 19.19 shows
  the relative style and placement of these properties in the different styles.
  These properties are both UILabel.

▶ Images are displayed in imageView, an instance of UIImageView.

In addition to these views, an accessory view at the right of each cell can contain a disclosure indicator, a detail disclosure indicator, or a checkmark. These are standard images.

▶ You will learn more about using accessory views in Hour 23, "Interacting with Users," p. 409.

LISTING 19.6   Styling Cells

```objc
// Customize the appearance of table view cells.
- (UITableViewCell *)tableView:(UITableView *)tableView
cellForRowAtIndexPath:(NSIndexPath *)indexPath
{

  static NSString *CellIdentifier0 = @"Cell0";
  static NSString *CellIdentifier1 = @"Cell1";
  static NSString *CellIdentifier2 = @"Cell2";
  static NSString *CellIdentifier3 = @"Cell3";

  UITableViewCell *cell;

  switch (indexPath.section)
  {
    case 0:
    {
      cell = [tableView dequeueReusableCellWithIdentifier:CellIdentifier0];
      if (cell == nil) {
        cell = [[UITableViewCell alloc] initWithStyle:UITableViewCellStyleDefault
          reuseIdentifier:CellIdentifier0];
      }
      break;
    }

    case 1:
    {
      cell = [tableView dequeueReusableCellWithIdentifier:CellIdentifier1];
      if (cell == nil) {
        cell = [[UITableViewCell alloc] initWithStyle:UITableViewCellStyleValue1
          reuseIdentifier:CellIdentifier1];
      }
      break;
    }

    case 2:
    {
      cell = [tableView dequeueReusableCellWithIdentifier:CellIdentifier2];
      if (cell == nil) {
      cell = [[UITableViewCell alloc] initWithStyle:UITableViewCellStyleValue2
        reuseIdentifier:CellIdentifier2];
      }
      break;
    }
```

```
    case 3:
    {
      cell = [tableView dequeueReusableCellWithIdentifier:CellIdentifier3];
      if (cell == nil) {
        cell = [[UITableViewCell alloc] initWithStyle:UITableViewCellStyleSubtitle
          reuseIdentifier:CellIdentifier3];
      }
      break;
    }

  } // end switch

  // Configure the cell.
  cell.textLabel.text = @"Text Label";
  cell.detailTextLabel.text = @"Detail Text Label";
  return cell;
}
```

Using **UITableView** with **Core Data**

You can use UITableView to format data from an individual Core Data instance (or record, if you prefer database terminology). This lets you avoid formatting every field and label yourself. To do so, you need to hardcode the field labels and retrieve the data from Core Data. This uses some of the features from the previous section, as well as some new features to access the Core Data. It does not use sections, so if you have experimented with them as described in the previous section, comment out or delete the following:

- ▶ numberOfSectionsInTableView:

- ▶ tableView:titleForHeaderInSection:

- ▶ tableView:titleForFooterInSection:

  ▷ To learn more about using UITableView with multiple instances/records, see Hour 23, "Interacting with Users," p. 409.

As a general rule, using a single style for each row within a section produces the best results. You can use an alternate style for special cases, so that you can draw attention to them. Review the styles from Figure 19.19, and pick one for your data entry.

This example uses UITableViewCellStyleValue2. This means you can use the code from Listing 19.3 to create the cell that will be reused. You will need a new switch statement to set the text for each row because the label and the detail label will change. Listing 19.7 shows the code to create the reusable cell and the switch statement to set the labels.

LISTING 19.7   Create the Cell Labels

```
// Customize the appearance of table view cells.
- (UITableViewCell *)tableView:(UITableView *)tableView
  cellForRowAtIndexPath:(NSIndexPath *)indexPath
{
  static NSString *CellIdentifier = @"CellStyle2";

  UITableViewCell *cell = [tableView dequeueReusableCellWithIdentifier:
    CellIdentifier];
  if (cell == nil) {
    cell = [[UITableViewCell alloc] initWithStyle:UITableViewCellStyleValue2
      reuseIdentifier:CellIdentifier];
  }

  // Configure the cell for each row
  switch (indexPath.row)
  {
    case 0:
    {
      cell.textLabel.text = @"Name";
      break;
    }

    case 1:
    {
      cell.textLabel.text = @"Email";
      break;
    }

    case 2:
    {
      cell.textLabel.text = @"Address";
      break;
    }

    case 3:
    {
      cell.textLabel.text = @"City";
      break;
    }

    case 4:
    {
      cell.textLabel.text = @"State/Province";
      break;
    }

    case 5:
    {
      cell.textLabel.text = @"Postal Code";
      break;
    }

    case 6:
    {
      cell.textLabel.text = @"Customer Since";
      break;
```

```
    }

  } // end switch

  return cell;
}
```

The results are shown in Figure 19.20.

FIGURE 19.20
Check the lay-
out for the cell
labels.

All that remains is to insert the values for the data from the persistent store. In Hour 18, you set the text property of a UITextField with code such as the following:

```
self.name.text = [self.detailItem valueForKey:@"name"];
```

You modify that code and place it in each of the case statements using this syntax that varies simply by the key name:

```
cell.textLabel.text = [self.detailItem valueForKey:@"name"];
```

Because each case of the switch statements has its own cell, you do not need to further identify which cell you are setting. (And, of course, the cells are reused to save memory and improve performance.)

That is all you have to do to display data. Letting users enter and change data is another matter. You will find out how to do that in Hour 23.

TIP

The decimal field has to be handled the way it is handled in Hour 18.

Summary

This hour showed you how to use a UITableView to organize your data display. This avoids the need to manually create fields and labels. And, as you have seen in the last section, it lets you easily move data into the cells of the table view.

Q&A

Q. *Why are cells reused in* UITableView?

A. Cells can have different styles, but styles are set only when initialized. Thus, it is much faster and uses memory more efficiently to initialize one of each type of cell you will use and then reuse it with new data, rather than recreating it each time the data changes.

Q. *How do you customize your iOS table view so it does not look like Settings?*

A. The whole point of table views on iOS is to present users with a consistent interface. Customize your table views only to the extent that is necessary: Users are used to using them as they are.

Workshop

Quiz

1. *How many sections are in a table view?*

2. *How many styles are used within a single section?*

Quiz Answers

1. As many sections as you want. If you do not specify, there is automatically one section.

2. Many designers would use one or two. One should be the common style, and the second one would be for exceptions or some data that is qualitatively different. This is not a hard-and-fast, but it is worth considering.

Activities

Look at System Preferences (Mac OS) and Settings (iOS) to see how they are designed. If you have access to older versions of the operating systems, see how they have changed. Apple and users have learned from experience how to improve them. (If you do not collect old versions of operating systems, check old books in your public library or on your own shelves and search on the Internet. You will often be able to track the refinement and evolution of interfaces.)

HOUR 20

Using NSTableView on Mac OS

What You'll Learn in This Hour:

▶ **Comparing** `UITableView` **with** `NSTableView`
▶ **Building an** `NSTableView` **app**

Exploring the New NSTableView Features

`NSTableView` is more than just a way of displaying data in rows and columns. Its structure and implementation fits in tightly with many of the key features of Objective-C and Cocoa including protocols and delegates as you learned in Hour 19, "Using `UITableView` on iOS," p. 337. For a variety of reasons, `UITableView` is implemented differently from its predecessor, `NSTableView`.

When Steve Jobs presented developers with the first in-depth look at Mac OS X 10.7 (Lion) in autumn of 2010, the presentation was titled "Back to the Mac." The point of the title was to emphasize that in building iOS, some design decisions were made that would have benefits for Mac OS, and, with Lion, some of them would be moving from iOS over to Mac OS. Some of these ideas reflected lessons learned from the mobile devices, but other reflected the opportunities posed by starting over with some key features.

`NSTableView` has benefited from the Back to the Mac experiences. It has been a key component of Mac OS X from the beginning. `UITableView` on iOS represents a different approach to some key aspects of table programming, and now, with Lion, `NSTableView` has received some new features.

▶ The definitive reference on this topic is "Table View Programming Guide," available for download in a PDF as well as interactive viewing from developer.apple.com and through Xcode's organizer. This July 2011 document reflects the current state of the art. If you want a more in-depth approach than this hour permits, this guide would be a good place to continue your reading.

NOTE

Keep the date firmly in mind. Although new documents and sample code will be available on developer.apple.com, remember that table view examples from before July 2011 use features of NSTableView, which still exist. Post-July 2011 examples, however, demonstrate some new features and design patterns. You might want to explore the With and Without Bindings project on developer.apple.com. In addition, TableViewPlayground contains four samples in it with varying uses of table views.

Most important to developers, some of the new features are implemented in UITableView on iOS. If you are building an app that will have both iOS and Mac OS implementations, your work might be easier if you use the same Core Data model in both environments (and you can even use iCloud to share documents) and use the new NSTableView features that parallel UITableView. The code you write will not be automatically portable from one operating system to the other, but your manual port from one to the other can be easier if you use the new NSTableView features.

You will note that on iOS that on iOS, table views are limited to one column. You can use a navigation interface or a master-detail controller design to help people drill down through the data. Typically, the last item is a single row of data that is presented in a column. On Mac OS, that is not necessary. Related to this issue is a structural difference: In NSTableView, there is an NSTableRowView. In the single-column design of UITableView, cells are their own rows. You will see that you can configure the table rows in Interface Builder beginning with Lion.

In addition, there is an NSTableColumn class in NSTableView. When you have only one column in a table, the table itself is the column. Interface elements have identifiers, as shown in Figure 20.1. The identifiers are needed by some methods such as tableView:viewForTableColumn:row, but when you are using automatic identifiers, this is taken care of for you. (You do not enter anything to use automatic identifiers; rather, you make certain that the field is empty, and the default value, Automatic, appears in light gray.)

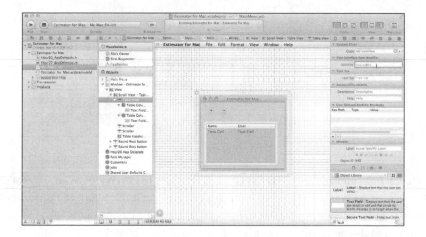

FIGURE 20.1
You can use automatic identifiers.

In addition to providing the data source protocol as an alternative to bindings, NSTableView allows table cells to be based on views rather than being limited to NSCell. A new class, NSTableCellView, provides a good starting point for your own view-based cells. You will notice that you can use it directly from the library without subclassing it in many cases.

When you explore early iPhone apps, you will see that displaying views in table views (particularly in navigation interfaces) was essential. That part of UITableView has evolved particularly in versions 3 and 4 to what is now iOS 5. You could not have easily written some of the early iPhone apps using NSTableView on Mac OS.

This is one of the rare cases in which the history of the development of operating systems is important for your understanding of the current state of the art as well as where the technologies are likely to move in the future. With this in mind, it is time to look at NSTableView as it is today on Mac OS.

Building an NSTableView App

NSTableView can take advantage of Core Data and bindings so that you may not need to write very much if any code. In this hour, you will see how to build the app shown in Figure 20.2.

FIGURE 20.2
Build a Mac OS app with Core Data and bindings.

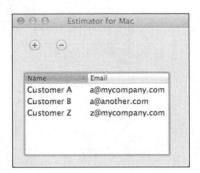
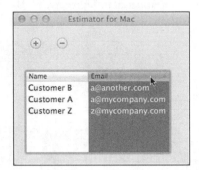

In Figure 20.1, you see an NSTableView with buttons to add a row or to remove a selected row. As you see at the left, you can click in a column header to select it and set a sort order of ascending or descending. Clicking in a header sorts the column according to the order you have selected, as you see at the right.

▼ **Try It Yourself**

Build an NSTableView Based on Core Data and Bindings

Here are the steps to build the bare-bones example shown previously in Figure 20.2. You can enhance it with your own data to build your own app. As you work through these steps, keep a running total of the lines of code you write.

▶ When completing these steps, you may want to refer back to Hour 1, "Introducing Xcode 4," p. 7 and Hour 6, "Working with the Data Model Editor," p. 117, as well as the "Integrating Views and Data on Mac OS" section in Hour 8, "Controllers: Integrating the Data Model with Your Code," p. 143.

1. Create a new Mac OS project using the Cocoa Application template.

2. Use the Core Data option for your project. The automatic reference counting option is recommended for new projects, but it is not essential to this one. Choose a class prefix if you want.

   Your project should look like Figure 20.3.

FIGURE 20.3
Create the project.

3. Create your Core Data model, as shown in Figure 20.4. This is the same model that is used in many hours.

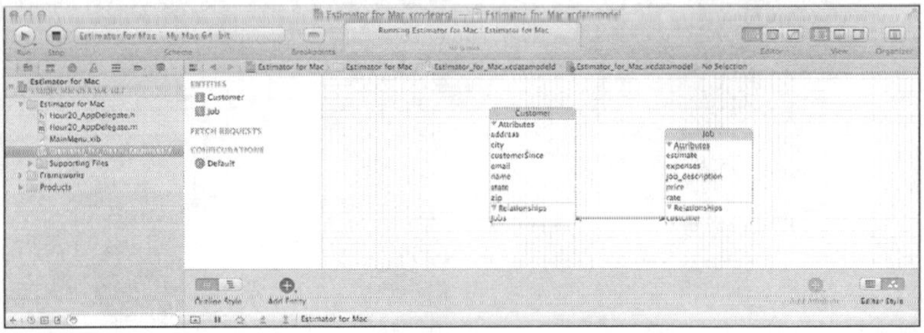

FIGURE 20.4
Create your data model.

4. Using Interface Builder editor add an array controller from the library to your document outline, as shown in Figure 20.5. This will control your top-level objects—customers in this example.

5. Set the Xcode-specific label in the Identity section of the Identity inspector to Customers. When you click out of the text field, the name of the array controller in the document outline should be changed

FIGURE 20.5
Add an array
controller.

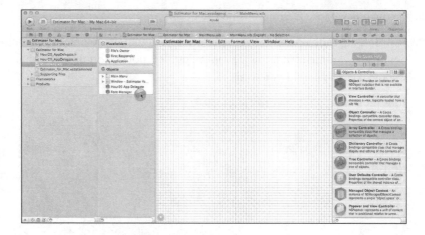

6. As shown in Figure 20.6, switch to the Attributes inspector and choose Entity
Name for the mode and type in Customer for the Entity Name. Make sure
Prepares Content and editable are checked. If you have another entity, you can
add an array controller for it, too.

FIGURE 20.6
Set the entity
name in the
Attributes
inspector.

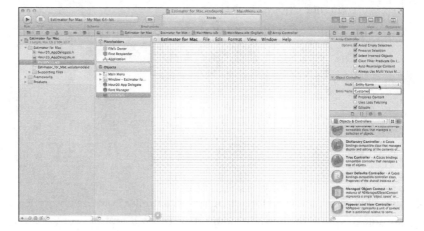

TIP

The name in Step 6 must be the name of the entity in your Core Data model.

7. With the array controller still selected, switch to the Bindings inspector and in
the Parameters section (at the bottom), bind the array controller to the app delegate, as shown in Figure 20.7. For the model key path, start typing, and you
will see that Xcode will auto-complete your typing with the properties from the
interface of the app delegate.

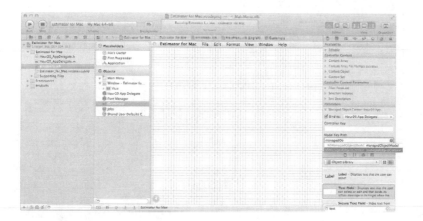

FIGURE 20.7
Bind the con-
troller to the
app delegate

8. In model-view-controller terms, you now have the data model and your array
   controller. So, now you just need the view. Add a table view to the canvas, as
   shown in Figure 20.8.

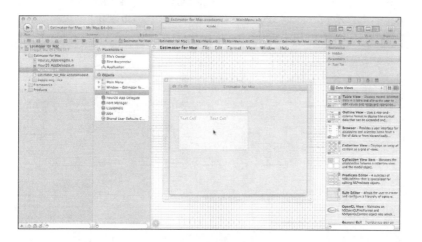

FIGURE 20.8
Add a table
view.

9. Connect a table column to an attribute in your data model. In this case, the
   first table column of the two in the template will be connected to the name
   attribute. Begin by selecting the column.

   Either select it in the document outline or shift-right click on the table view, as
   shown in Figure 20.9, and select the column in the shortcut window. Make certain you click in the appropriate column of the table view: It will be highlighted after the click. With Lion and a trackpad, use shift-two finger tap.

FIGURE 20.9
Select the table
column to
connect to the
array controller.

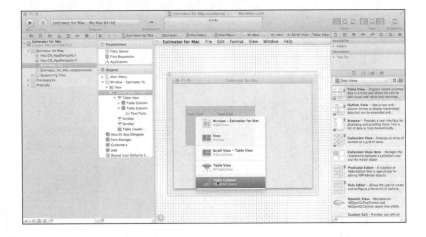

10. With the column selected, open the Bindings inspector, as shown in Figure
20.10. In the value section at the top of the inspector, bind the column to Customers with a controller key of `arrangedObjects` (you always use this value
here) and with a model key path that matches the attribute of your data model
to be displayed in the column (`name` in this case).

FIGURE 20.10
Bind the
column value
to the array
controller.

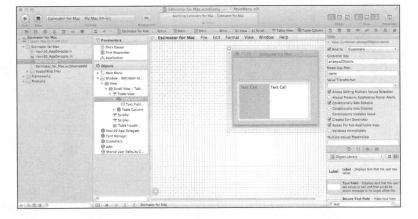

11. Repeat Steps 9 and 10 for the second column and another attribute such as
email in this example.

12. Create the Add button for the table view. Add a rounded rect button from the
library to the view, as shown in Figure 20.11.

13. With the button still selected, use the Attributes inspector to set the image to
NSAddTemplate (about halfway down the Attributes inspector). Delete the title
and, with the button (not its interior cell) still selected, choose Editor, Size to Fit
Content.

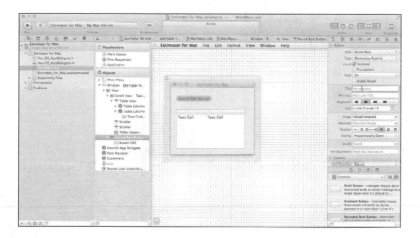

FIGURE 20.11
Insert an Add button.

14. Repeat Step 11 with another rounded rect button; use the NSRemoveTemplate image. You should see the results, as shown in Figure 20.12.

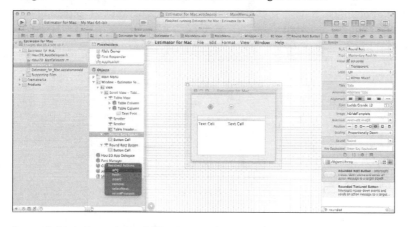

FIGURE 20.12
Connect the Add button.

15. Control-drag from the Add button to the Customers array controller in the document outline. Connect the button to the Add action, as shown in Figure 20.12.

16. Similarly, connect the Remove button to the array controller's Remove action by command-dragging from the button to the controller in the document outline.

17. Type titles in the table's header row.

18. Run the app. As you see in Figure 20.13, you can use the Add and Remove buttons. Click in a row to select it (you will see a highlight). Click in a cell to begin editing it. Quit the app and then rerun it. Experiment with sorting the columns and changing the column widths. Quit and restart. You'll see that your changes have automatically been saved by Core Data based on the bindings to the array controller.

You're done.

Running total of lines of code written: 0.

FIGURE 20.13
Run the app.

When typing in text to Interface Builder editor, make certain you complete the edit by clicking out of each field. If you receive runtime errors that an attribute is null or cannot be found, check that you have completed the edit.

Summary

This hour has shown how you can put together the features you saw in Hour 8 to a no-code basic app. The example in this hour is a tried-and-true Core Data standby. What is important for many people is that with this basic app, you can get into the world of Core Data with very little coding. For people who are not comfortable with databases, Core Data and NSTableView can be a good introduction.

Q&A

Q. *Why would you choose to use bindings over programmatic connections between data and a table view?*

A. In one case, you really have no choice. If you have an existing app that needs a relatively minor modification, you do not rewrite it from scratch, so you should stick with bindings. For new apps, the choice can also be easy. If you are sharing an app and even a Core Data model between an iOS app and a Mac app, the closer you can make the two sets of code, the easier your development and maintenance work will be.

Q. *What is the most important structural difference between* NSTableView *and* UITableView?

A. The biggest difference is that NSTableView can have multiple columns. This means all of the routines have to work in a multi-column environment even if you only need one column.

Workshop

Quiz

1. *What is the best way to create identifiers for user interface elements?*

2. *What are the two required methods for the data source?*

Quiz Answers

1. Use the Automatic setting (which is the default) in the Identity inspector for the interface element.

2. `numberOfRowsInTableView` and `tableView:objectValueForTableColumn:row`.

Activities

Search for example code on developer.apple.com using the keywords CoreData and table view. Look for example code that has been modified in or after July 2011 to see the new features described in this hour.

> **TIP**
> When completing this activity and searching developer.apple.com, use CoreData—no space—rather than Core Data.

Rearranging Table Rows on iOS

NOTE

This hour applies only to Cocoa Touch and its touch interface.

Handling the Ordering of Table Rows

When you use table views with Core Data, you have a powerful way of displaying sets of records. As you have learned in Hour 19, "Using UITableView on iOS," p. 337, and Hour 20, "Using NSTableView on Mac OS," p. 363, you also can use table views to display single records in an easily formatted manner. In the case of using a table to display fields from a single record, your nib or storyboard file together with the view controller code you write determines the sequence of the data, as you see in the detail view at the right in Figure 21.1. The master view at the left of Figure 21.1 displays data dynamically based on a sort order (in this case, it is the name).

Handling Display Order

One of the classic problems in designing databases is specifying the sort order for data to be displayed. The most common solution—sorting on a specific field—breaks down in a number of cases. Perhaps the most common case in which it breaks down is when number data is presented as text. For example, if the following values are sorted numerically, they appear in this sequence:

1

10

15

100

250

FIGURE 21.1
You can use
table views to
sort records
and code to
order specific
fields within a
record.

If those values are sorted as text, they appear as follows:

1

10

100

15

250

The reason is that each character is sorted by its alphanumeric value. 0 sorts before 5; therefore, 100 sorts before 15. You can get around this issue by storing the data as numbers and displaying it as text.

▶ The conversion is often done in an NSFormatter, as shown in "Using an NSNumberFormatter" in Hour 18, "Validating Data," p. 317.

As long as you can store or generate values that can be automatically sorted, you can let your database or interface do the work. In fact, in Cocoa Touch, NSFetched-ResultsController is responsible not only for the fetching, but also for the sorting. You create a sort descriptor and store it in the fetch request. This means everything you get from the fetch request is already sorted and you do not have to worry.

Listing 21.1 shows the getter for a fetch request from a typical Xcode project template (Master-Detail Application, in fact). The code is heavily annotated with indications of where you can extend it. The sort descriptor is definitely one such place: The sort key will vary depending on your data model.

LISTING 21.1   Setting Up the Fetch Request

```
- (NSFetchedResultsController *)fetchedResultsController
{
  if (__fetchedResultsController != nil)
  {
    return __fetchedResultsController;
  }

  /*
   Set up the fetched results controller.
  */
  // Create the fetch request for the entity.
  NSFetchRequest *fetchRequest = [[NSFetchRequest alloc] init];
  // Edit the entity name as appropriate.
  NSEntityDescription *entity = [NSEntityDescription entityForName:@"Customer"
    inManagedObjectContext:self.managedObjectContext];
  [fetchRequest setEntity:entity];

  // Set the batch size to a suitable number.
  [fetchRequest setFetchBatchSize:20];

  // Edit the sort key as appropriate.
  NSSortDescriptor *sortDescriptor = [[NSSortDescriptor alloc]
    initWithKey:@"name"
    ascending:YES];
  NSArray *sortDescriptors = [[NSArray alloc] initWithObjects:sortDescriptor,
    nil];
  [fetchRequest setSortDescriptors:sortDescriptors];


  // Edit the section name key path and cache name if appropriate.
  // nil for section name key path means "no sections".
  NSFetchedResultsController *aFetchedResultsController =
    [[NSFetchedResultsController
    alloc] initWithFetchRequest:fetchRequest
    managedObjectContext:self.managedObjectContext
    sectionNameKeyPath:nil cacheName:@"Master"];
  aFetchedResultsController.delegate = self;
  self.fetchedResultsController = aFetchedResultsController;

  NSError *error = nil;
  if (![self.fetchedResultsController performFetch:&error])
    {
      /*
      Replace this implementation with code to handle the error appropriately.

      abort() causes the application to generate a crash log and terminate.
        You should
      not use this function in a shipping application, although it may be
        useful during
```

```
       development. If it is not possible to recover from the error, display an
         alert
       panel that instructs the user to quit the application by pressing the Home
         button.
       */
       NSLog(@"Unresolved error %@, %@", error, [error userInfo]);
       abort();
   }

   return __fetchedResultsController;
}
```

Handling Ad Hoc Display Order

The simplest way of ordering data is by using a data value such as a name, the date created, customer since, and so forth. With the exception of the numeric/text issue described in the previous section and the intricacies of ordering names (last-name-first, first-name-last, and various combinations), letting the data itself provide its order is simple and intuitive.

You also can argue that in some ways, it breaks the model-view-controller design pattern. If the display order is based on the data itself (the model), then that is the first and last word on the topic. However, if you want to allow the display to be variable, the display order needs to be managed dynamically by the view and might need to be stored somewhere which generally means it is considered as part of the model. Unfortunately, this is one of a handful of cases in which the simplicity of model-view-controller becomes a bit over-simplistic.

> **NOTE**
>
> Another such case is related to the concept of documents particularly with regard to undo and redo. The intermediate states of the document in the various iterations of undo and redo are logically part of the controller or even view. However, in some cases, they might need to be stored, which seems to put them in the model. Fortunately, most people are worried about getting their code to work and making it maintainable. There are excellent examples of managing undo and redo on developer.apple.com.

The way in which this is often handled is by creating a new attribute called *displayOrder* in some of the sample code on developer.apple.com. This attribute provides the display sequence for the data. You can set up your fetched results controller with a sort based on this attribute, and all will be well.

Of course, you have to provide a way of setting the display order. The next two sections explain the two ways of doing this. One works only on iOS; the other works on both iOS and Mac OS.

Setting displayOrder Manually (Mac OS or IOS)

After you have created a displayOrder attribute in your data model, you can allow people to set it.

TIP

Alternatively, you can dynamically set the displayOrder attribute to be the count of the number of items in the set plus one when you create a new item. This means the items start out in creation sequence order but can be reordered later on if the displayOrder attribute is changed.

If this field is editable, people can rearrange items by changing the value. It is important in these cases that displayOrder is not limited to integers. If you have three records with displayOrder set to

1

2

3

a user can change the 3 to 1.5. Then, sorting by displayOrder will give you

1

1.5 (formerly 3)

2

Now the records are in order. All you need is a Reorder command or button that takes the new sequence and renumbers displayOrder as 1, 2, 3. Users quickly get used to this. You can even refine the process by limiting the reordering function to power users in which other users never see displayOrder or the Reorder command or button.

Setting `displayOrder` by Touch

One of the wonderful features of a touch interface is that the shenanigans involved in setting display order can disappear—users can just rearrange rows in a table by dragging them. A simple way of handling this is to create an `NSMutableArray` for the sorted items. They are loaded into the mutable array at runtime based on a `displayOrder` attribute. As the rows are rearranged in the touch interface, those numbers are regenerated. At the end, the entire array is written out to the persistent store.

This is necessitated because in Core Data, relationships are normally represented by sets, which are unordered (`NSSet`). This provides for very fast performance at the expense of a slight complication for ordered relationships. With the advent of iOS 5 and the latest versions of Core Data, ordered relationships are now implemented. They use `NSOrderedSet`, which is not a descendant of `NSSet`; it is a different object entirely, and its performance is somewhat slower.

> **NOTE**
>
> Of course, *slower* is a relative term. If your app manages a recipe with a dozen or so ingredients, the performance impact is less than if it manages data for every city or town in the United States—all 194,502 of them.

▶ An excellent example of using manual rearrangement of rows is the iPhone Core Data Recipes example on developer.apple.com. The code in this hour is modified from the example found there. Look at the ordering of ingredients in a recipe to see the exact code.

Allowing a Table Row to Be Moved

Figure 21.1 showed you the basic Master-Detail Application template with a table view used for the various rows at the left and another table viewed to show data from a single record at the right. Clicking Edit at the top of the master view controller at the left sends a message to the table view so that it can be edited. Figure 21.2 shows the result with the default settings.

To make rows movable, you need to do two things: explicity make a row movable and create a method to handle the move. The method does not need to do anything, but it has to be there.

FIGURE 21.2
Default settings
for table view
editing.

Try It Yourself ▼

Making a Row Movable

You can make the settings for each row different, but in most cases you make all of the rows movable. You also can control whether rows can be moved between sections.

1. Change the default value of tableView:canMoveRowAtIndexPath to YES from NO as it appears in the default template code shown here. You can use IF or SWITCH statements to set different values for different rows or sections of the index path:

```
- (BOOL)tableView:(UITableView *)tableView canMoveRowAtIndexPath:
  (NSIndexPath *)indexPath
{
  // The table view should not be re-orderable.
  return NO;
}
```

2. Implement tableView:moveRowAtIndexPath. As shown here, you do not need to provide any more than the shell:

```
- (void)tableView:(UITableView *)tableView moveRowAtIndexPath:
    (NSIndexPath *)fromIndexPath
    toIndexPath:(NSIndexPath *)toIndexPath {
}
```

With these two changes, clicking Edit gives you the reordering controls shown in Figure 21.3.

FIGURE 21.3
You can now
reorder rows.

Doing the Move

There are four aspects to the move in this type of structure:

▶ Create a subclass of NSManagedObject for the entity that will own the list of items that can be rearrranged. (This is a one-time process you do when you are creating the data model and your code.) Many people automatically make an entity that will have a list of related objects in a relationship into its own subclass of NSManagedObject.

▶ Retrieve a set of related objects from the persistent store and put the objects into a mutable array.

▶ As the user moves the objects around, update the displayOrder values.

▶ When saving, take the mutable array objects and store them in the persistent store.

This code goes into the master (formerly root) view controller in the Master-Detail Application or a similar project. For example, if you are using the Core Data Recipes example, this code is in RecipeDetailViewController, which lists the title of the recipe as well as the list of ingredients. A separate controller, IngredientDetailViewController lets users view and edit a specific ingredient. It is the higher-level controller that controls the list of ingredients or other items in an app. Similarly,

RecipeListTableViewController provides the list of recipes each of which is then managed by RecipeDetailViewController.

Creating the Subclass of NSManagedObject

When you subclass NSManagedObject, you get a custom class that will automatically load data from your persistent store. You can access the class properties directly without worrying about key-value coding. You need to create such subclasses to handle transformable attributes. In addition, handling relationships is simpler with subclasses because the code to manage the relationship is built for you. Here's how you create a subclass of NSManagedObject.

1. Open your data model in Xcode, as shown in Figure 21.4.

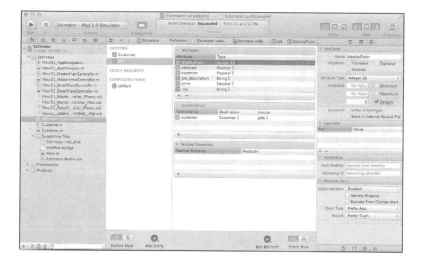

FIGURE 21.4
Start from your data model.

2. Select the entity that will be ordered in the data model and add a displayOrder attribute with type Integer 16 to it. In this example, jobs can be ordered within a customer. You don't have to worry about the non-integer order values in the previous ordering scenario.

3. Select Editor, Create NSManagedObject Subclass.

4. The sheet shown in Figure 21.5 lets you choose the location on disk for the class files as well as the group in your project into which to put them.

FIGURE 21.5
Choose the set-
tings and loca-
tion for your
new class.

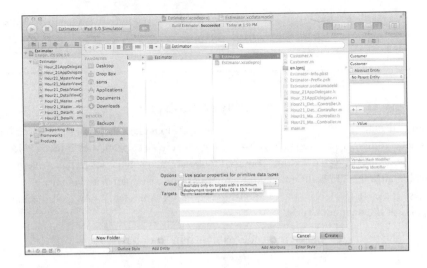

Beginning with Lion, you have the ability to choose scalar properties for primi-
tive data types. In the case of the data model shown in Figure 21.4, this means
the two Integer 16 properties will be created as int16_t. In other words, with
scalar properties, you get

```
@property (nonatomic) int16_t displayOrder;
```

instead of

```
@property (nonatomic, retain) NSNumber * displayOrder;
```

This is often a matter of personal preference. For many people, as they get used
to using the Cocoa types with all of their built-in functionality instead of the
older style of scalar properties.

TIP

As always, for projects in which very high performance goals are set, you should
test and compare the two strategies. The data store is going to be the same; the
classes are run-time artifacts and can be changed against the same data store for
comparison.

5. Listing 21.2 shows the header file that is built. You do not need to do anything
with it unless you want to add additional method declarations.

LISTING 21.2   Header for a Custom NSManagedObject Class

```
#import <Foundation/Foundation.h>
#import <CoreData/CoreData.h>
```

```
@interface Customer : NSManagedObject

@property (nonatomic, retain) NSString * address;
@property (nonatomic, retain) NSString * city;
@property (nonatomic, retain) NSNumber * customerSince;
@property (nonatomic, retain) NSNumber * displayOrder;
@property (nonatomic, retain) NSString * email;
@property (nonatomic, retain) NSString * name;
@property (nonatomic, retain) NSString * state;
@property (nonatomic, retain) NSString * zip;
@property (nonatomic, retain) NSSet *jobs;
@end

@interface Customer (CoreDataGeneratedAccessors)

- (void)addJobsObject:(NSManagedObject *)value;
- (void)removeJobsObject:(NSManagedObject *)value;
- (void)addJobs:(NSSet *)values;
- (void)removeJobs:(NSSet *)values;

@end
```

6. Listing 21.3 shows the implementation file for the custom class.

LISTING 21.3   Implementation for a Custom NSManagedObject Class

```
@implementation Customer

@dynamic address;
@dynamic city;
@dynamic customerSince;
@dynamic displayOrder;
@dynamic email;
@dynamic name;
@dynamic state;
@dynamic zip;
@dynamic jobs;

@end
```

TIP

You do not need to make any changes to the code in Listing 21.3 unless you are implementing additional methods.

The compiler directive @dynamic replaces @synthesize for Core Data properties. You can see from the absence of implementations of the add and remove methods that just as @synthesize automatically creates the accessors (getters and setters),

@dynamic automatically creates methods such as addJobs and removeJobs, which are declared in the header file.

In addition, the two pairs of methods add and remove single objects from the relationship (addJobsObject and removeJobsObject) or the entire relationship (addJobs and removeJobs), which works with NSSet instead of NSManagedObject.

Once you move into the world of subclasses of NSManagedObject, it is often easiest to use custom classses for everything except the smallest classes.

Loading the Mutable Array

If you have created a subclass of NSManagedObject as shown in the previous section, you can use it to access its properties, including displayOrder, which is the property that you will use to manage moving rows in the table. Your subclass objects may be at the top level of your data structure, as is the case with Customer. They also could be in a relationship (as is the case with Jobs); a relationship is represented at runtime as an NSSet containing the related entities for the relationship.

TIP

Keep in mind that this is not an issue if you are sorting the data by an existing data attribute such as name or customerSince.

▼   Try It Yourself

Move the Relationship Entities into an NSMutableArray

The standard way of handling rearrangeable rows is to create an NSMutableArray, which can be reordered. You will use your subclasses of NSManagedObject (Job or Customer or your own subclass), so be certain to import the appropriate .h file at the top of the .m file in which you place your code.

1. In your view controller file for the view that will contain the list, create a property for the mutable array:

   ```
   @property (nonatomic, retain) NSMutableArray *customers;
   ```

2. Add a @synthesize directive in the implementation file of the view controller:

   ```
   @synthesize customers:
   ```

3. Move the objects you have retrieved from your Core Data persistent store into a mutable array. This code typically goes in `viewDidLoad` of the controller for the list view. The process is similar but slightly different for objects that are at the top level of your data structure (such as Customers) than for objects that are part of a relationships (such as Jobs).

  a. For top level data (such as Customers), Listing 21.4 shows you how to fill the mutable array in `viewDidLoad` in your master view controller. The mutable array is loaded from the fetched objects in the fetched results controller. In this listing, the code is placed at the end of the method. The only changes you need to make are the name of the sorting property (`displayOrder` here) and the name of the mutable array you declared in step 1; it is used in the next to last line (`self.customers`).

LISTING 21.4   Moving the Top-Level Objects into a Mutable Array.

```
- (void)viewDidLoad
{
  [super viewDidLoad];
  // Do any additional setup after loading the view, typically from a nib.
  // Set up the edit and add buttons.
  self.navigationItem.leftBarButtonItem = self.editButtonItem;

  UIBarButtonItem *addButton = [[UIBarButtonItem alloc]
    initWithBarButtonSystemItem:UIBarButtonSystemItemAdd target:self
    action:@selector(insertNewObject)];
  self.navigationItem.rightBarButtonItem = addButton;

  // THIS IS THE CODE TO LOAD THE MUTABLE ARRAY
  NSMutableArray *sortedElements = [[NSMutableArray alloc]
    initWithArray:self.fetchedResultsController.fetchedObjects];
  NSSortDescriptor *sortDescriptor = [[NSSortDescriptor alloc]
    initWithKey:@"displayOrder" ascending:YES];
  NSArray *sortDescriptors = [[NSArray alloc]
    initWithObjects:sortDescriptor, nil];
  [sortedElements sortUsingDescriptors:sortDescriptors];
  self.customers = sortedElements;

  [self.tableView reloadData];
}
```

  b. For related data (such as Jobs), move the Core Data relationship entities (in the `NSSet` of your `NSManagedObject` subclass) to the mutable array. (Compare this with moving the objects from the fetched results controller for top level entities shown in a.) This code typically goes in `viewDidLoad` of the controller for the list view, which in the case of a relationship would be located in `DetailViewController`. The code in Listing 21.5 assumes a `displayOrder` attribute stored in the data store. If you are basing your code on the Master-Detail template as shown in this hour, the specific entity for which the relationship is being displayed is `self.detailItem` in `DetailViewController`.

LISTING 21.5   Moving Related Objects into a Mutable Array

```
- (
void)viewDidLoad
{
  [super viewDidLoad];

  // Do any additional setup after loading the view, typically from a nib.

  NSSortDescriptor *sortDescriptor = [[NSSortDescriptor alloc]

  initWithKey:@"displayOrder" ascending:YES];

  NSArray *sortDescriptors = [[NSArray alloc] initWithObjects:&sort
    Descriptor count:1];

  Customer* myCustomer = (Customer*)self.detailItem;

  NSMutableArray *sortedElements = [[NSMutableArray alloc]

  initWithArray:[myCustomer.jobs allObjects]];
    [sortedElements sortUsingDescriptors:sortDescriptors];

  self.jobs = sortedJobs;

  [self configureView];
}
```

NOTE

For some people, it is easiest to use the same name for the `NSMutableArray`, which is a property of the view controller and for the property of the override to `NSManagedObject` (in this case, `listElements`). Other people prefer different names such as `jobs` and `sortedJobs`. Just document what you are doing.

Moving the List Elements (Relationship Entities)

As you have seen, enabling the ability to rearrange rows requires at least the shell of tableView:moveRowAtIndexPath. Listing 21.6 shows the standard code for handling the move. It updates the displayOrder property of the objects in the range of movement as specified by fromIndexPath and toIndexPath. Because the objects are updated when the move occurs, whenever their context is saved, the new order will be saved. This is the code for moving customers in the master view controller; substitute jobs for customers in the detail view controller to handle rearranging jobs for a customer.

LISTING 21.6   Handling the Move

```
- (void)tableView:(UITableView *)tableView moveRowAtIndexPath:(NSIndexPath *)
  fromIndexPath toIndexPath:(NSIndexPath *)toIndexPath {

  Customer *customer = [self.customers objectAtIndex:fromIndexPath.row];
  [customers removeObjectAtIndex:fromIndexPath.row];
  [customers insertObject:customer atIndex:toIndexPath.row];

  NSInteger start = fromIndexPath.row;
  if (toIndexPath.row < start) {
    start = toIndexPath.row;
  }

  NSInteger end = toIndexPath.row;
  if (fromIndexPath.row > end) {
    end = fromIndexPath.row;
  }

  for (NSInteger i = start; i <= end; i++) {
    customer = [self.customers objectAtIndex:i];
    customer.displayOrder = [NSNumber numberWithInteger: i];
  }

}
```

Saving the Moved Data

If you test the code, you will notice that all seems to work well, but the next time you run it, the rearrangement is lost. So, the last step is to save the new values for displayOrder, as shown in Listing 21.7. This is a bare bones override of setEditing, which is called as part of the processing of the edit-done button by UIViewController. All you need to do is just save your managed object context. No customization is required in this code.

LISTING 21.7   Saving the Data

```
- (void)setEditing:(BOOL)editing animated:(BOOL)animated {

  [super setEditing:editing animated:animated];

  [self.tableView beginUpdates];

  [self.tableView endUpdates];

  /*
  If editing is finished, save the managed object context.
  */
  if (!editing) {
    NSManagedObjectContext *context = self.managedObjectContext;
    NSError *error = nil;
    if (![context save:&error]) {
      /*
      Replace this implementation with code to handle the error appropriately.
      */
      NSLog(@"Unresolved error %@, %@", error, [error userInfo]);
      abort();
    }
  }
}
```

Summary

This hour introduced you to the issues involved in displaying sorted data in a table. You have seen how Cocoa Touch implements direct manipulation for rearranging table rows and what you have to do to use it in your apps.

Q&A

Q. When do you need to implement an instance variable such as displayOrder?

A. Whenever you want data to be sorted based on ad hoc or user-supplied criteria instead of intrinsic data values (names, dates, and so forth), you need to store the sort order. It does no harm to routinely add a sort order attribute to data that will be sorted so that adding a user-specified sort in the future is easier.

Q. Why do ordered relationships (in iOS 5 or Lion and later) impose a performance penalty?

A. This is exactly the same issue as the slight performance penalty in databases that is caused by indexes. In the case of ordered relationships and indexes, an update to the data itself requires additional updating of the index or sort order. Despite the fact that these performance penalties are real, in practice, they often are not worth worrying about except in very high-performance systems.

Workshop

Quiz

1. *Why do you copy relationships into a mutable array to reorder them?*
2. *How do you display the reordering icon in a table view?*

Quiz Answers

1. Relationships in Core Data are returned to you in an NSSet, which is unordered. In fact, as shown from the data model (and almost any data diagram), relationships in relational databases are usually not ordered. They can accidentally be ordered by the sequence in which related items are added, but that is usually not guaranteed by the specification of the database.

2. Make sure you have an Edit button on your table view. Change (or implement) canMoveRowAtIndexPath to return YES and implement tableView:moveRowAtIndexPath. tableView:moveRowAtIndexPath does not need to do anything.

Activities

Explore the iPhone Core Data Recipes example from developer.apple.com. Experiment as a user with rearrranging recipe ingredients, and then follow the code that implements the feature. Pay particular attention to how only the ingredients section is reorderable. How would you change the interface to make other items reorderable?

HOUR 22

Managing Validation

What You'll Learn in This Hour:

▶ Exploring the validation interface you do not have to write

▶ Performing validations

Validation for Free

Hour 18, "Validating Data," p. 317, shows you how to set up validation rules in your Core Data model. This is a good start, but you need to apply them to keep your data valid. The whole point of implementing validation rules in the database is to avoid or at least minimize the code you have to write to keep your data clean. Not only does this save time, but it also helps to reduce the possibility of validation code being written incorrectly or of loopholes occurring so that under some circumstances, the validation tests are not even performed.

There are two basic approaches to getting validation for free—that is, with as little effort as possible. One of these approaches is widely known. The second approach might come as a surprise to you, but when you think about it, you will see how it works.

You get validation easily by using existing code that is built into frameworks and sample apps. As you will see in "Validation on Mac OS" later in this hour, there are cases in which you have to do nothing beyond clicking checkboxes in the Core Data model editor. Before writing a single line of validation code, always check to see if the validation can be done elsewhere and with code that is already written. There is no absolute guarantee the code in a sample app from developer.apple.com will be superior to the code you write, but chances are good that the more people who use a section of code, the more stable and reliable it will be.

TIP

Templates that rely on the document model make it easy to implement and test validation rules because each document is validated automatically when it is saved. (You can also use Interface Builder to specify validation to occur when the user exits a data entry field.) In a library/shoebox app, you may have to quit the app to force validation.

The second approach to getting validation with very little effort is the one that is not always obvious: Make your validation rules reasonable. If you get too complicated in your validation rules, you can create circumstances in which people have to disable them in one way or another to finish their work.

NOTE

Of course, one way to have it both ways when it comes to validation is to allow users (sometimes only privileged users) the ability to override errors. Every time you allow an override, you open a backdoor to potential data corruption. Before you know it, the rare occurrence of a validation error override becomes part of the standard operating procedures, and all you have done is slowed down and complicated what people are trying to do with your app.

This subject is a matter of system design regardless of whether it is implemented in Core Data or not. In fact, the ability to approve the entry of invalid data is a management issue that applies if people are using parchment and quill pens.

Validation on Mac OS

You can see how Mac OS validation comes for free by creating a new Cocoa Application in Xcode. Make certain you use the options for Core Data as well as a document-based app as you set up the project, as shown in Figure 22.1.

You can use the same data model you have used in other hours either by retyping it or by deleting the existing data model in the project and then adding and renaming a data model you have worked on elsewhere. If you give it the same name as the default data model, you will not have to make other adjustments beyond cleaning the old files out of the project. Figure 22.2 shows the project and the data model.

NOTE

The Estimator data model that is used elsewhere in this book is used again in this hour. Download examples as described in the Introduction. Be particularly careful with the examples for this hour. They use the same basic data model as used in other hours, but the data model for the two examples in this hour have been modified to focus on validation. Building on an example from another hour might give you different results than you expect. Also, remember that in the downloadable files as well as the screenshots, class names are prefixed with Hour22. In the text, the prefixes are omitted so that, for example, Hour22_Document.h is referred to simply as Document.h.

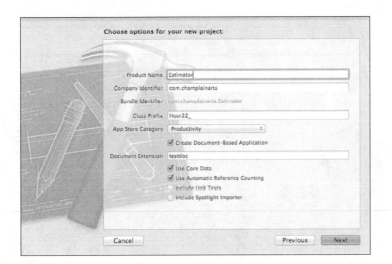

FIGURE 22.1
Create a new
project.

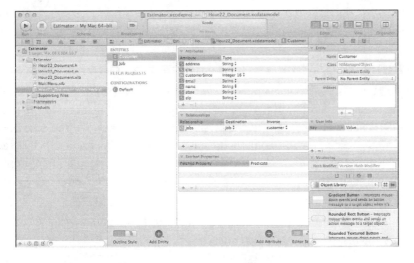

FIGURE 22.2
Create the Core
Data model.

Set up a validation rule in the data model. The simplest rule to set up is to make certain that one or more attributes is not optional, as you see in Figure 22.3. If an attribute is not optional *and* if it does not have a default value, users will need to enter some data. If they do not, a validation error occurs.

▶ You may want to refer to Hour 18, "Validating Data," p. 317 to review how to set up validation rules. In this hour, you will see how to do work with validation rules up to the point of interacting with the user with a dialog, sheet, or popover. That topic is covered in Hour 23, "Interacting with Users," p. 409.

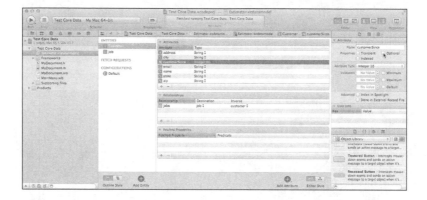

In addition to your data model, you will need a nib file to display the data and allow it to be edited. You also need to build the Core Data glue into your project. Fortunately, as you have seen in other hours, these processes are not complicated once you have done them a few times. The next section can serve as a review and reinforcement of the techniques you have seen before.

Building the Core Data Glue in `Document.h`

Listing 22.1 shows what `Document.h` should look like. To the basic code that is generated from the template, you need to add an instance variable for an entity that will automatically be created in a new persistent store (`Customer` in the data model used here). Instead of a declared property, an instance variable and explicit accessors are used in this example. Although it is a best practice to use declared properties, existing code including many examples still use explicit declarations so you need to be comfortable with both styles.

As Listing 22.2 demonstrates, this allows the managed object context to be created if necessary the first time the getter is called.

LISTING 22.1   `MyDocument.h`

```
#import <Cocoa/Cocoa.h>

@interface MyDocument : NSPersistentDocument {
  NSManagedObject *customer;
}

- (NSManagedObject *)customer;
- (void)setCustomer:(NSManagedObject *)aCustomer;

@end
```

Building the Core Data Glue in MyDocument.m

Here is the code for the implementation of Document. This is standard Core Data glue code; the only thing not standard is the name of the default entity. Remember that it must match your Core Data model—Customer in this case.

LISTING 22.2   MyDocument.m

```
#import "Document.h"

@implementation Document

- (id)init
{
  self = [super init];
  if (self) {
  }
  return self;
}

- (id)initWithType:(NSString *)type error:(NSError **)error
{
  self = [super initWithType:type error:error];
  if (self != nil) {
    NSManagedObjectContext *managedObjectContext = [self
      managedObjectContext];
    [self setCustomer:[NSEntityDescription
      insertNewObjectForEntity-ForName:@"Customer"
      inManagedObjectContext:managedObjectContext]];
  }
  return self;
}

- (NSString *)windowNibName
{
  return @"Document";
}

- (void)windowControllerDidLoadNib:(NSWindowController *)aController
{
  [super windowControllerDidLoadNib:aController];
}

+ (BOOL)autosavesInPlace
{
  return NO; // see comment about testing
}

#pragma mark - Core Data stack

- (NSManagedObject *)customer
{
```

```
if (customer != nil)
{
  return customer;
}
NSManagedObjectContext *moc = [self managedObjectContext];
NSFetchRequest *fetchRequest = [[NSFetchRequest alloc] init];
NSError *fetchError = nil;
NSArray *fetchResults;

@try
  {
  NSEntityDescription *entity = [NSEntityDescription
    entityForName:@"Customer"
    inManagedObjectContext:moc];
  [fetchRequest setEntity:entity];
  fetchResults = [moc executeFetchRequest:fetchRequest
    error:&fetchError];
  } @finally
  {
    // for non-ARC projects, this would be [fetchRequest release];
  }
if ((fetchResults != nil) && ([fetchResults count] == 1) && (fetchError
  == nil))
  {
  [self setCustomer:[fetchResults objectAtIndex:0]];
  return customer;
  }

if (fetchError != nil){
    [self presentError:fetchError];
  }
  else {
   // your own error message
  }
return nil;
}

- (void)setCustomer:(NSManagedObject *)aCustomer
{
  if (customer != aCustomer)
    {
      customer = aCustomer;
    }
}

@end
```

NOTE

Note that `autosavesInPlace` returns NO in this code. For most purposes in new code, it should return YES, but in this example, being able to control when the document is saved (that is, when validation is run) is important.

Building the Core Data Glue in a Nib File

In the document window nib file, add text fields and labels for data entry. Next, you will need to connect and bind them to the data model.

Figure 22.4 shows you how the nib file is set up. (Refer to Hour 8 if necessary.) Note that the object controller has been added from the library and been labeled Customer. Also, note that as the fields have been added, their Xcode Specific Labels have been set in the Identity section of the Identity inspector so you do not have a series of Text Field objects in the document outline with no clue as to which is which.

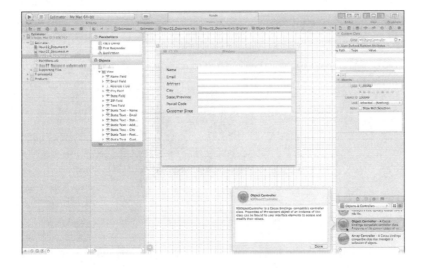

FIGURE 22.4
Add an object controller and label it Customer.

Bind the Customer controller to `managedObjectContext` in File's Owner, as shown in Figure 22.5.

Finally, connect the bindings from the Customer controller to the data fields, as shown in Figure 22.6. The process is the same for each field once you have created your Customer object controller:

1. Show the Bindings inspector in the utility area.

FIGURE 22.5
Bind the Customer object controller to `managed Object Context` in File's Owner.

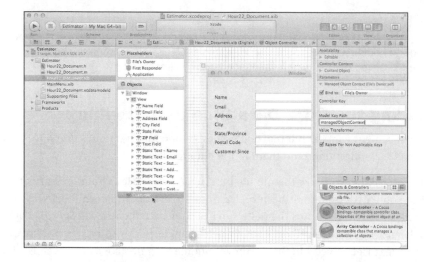

FIGURE 22.6
Finish the bindings between the managed object context and the text fields.

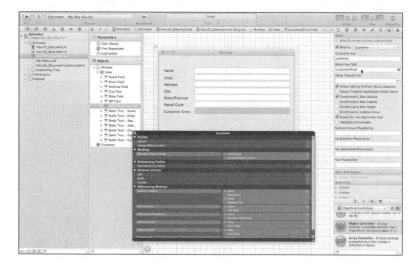

2. Select a field.

3. In the Value section, bind the field to the Customer controller (in the pop-up menu) and also check the box next to the menu.

4. Controller Key should be filled in with `selection`.

5. For Model Key Path, type in the name of the attribute in your data model.

When you are done, control-click on Customer in the document outline to review the referencing bindings, as you see in Figure 22.6.

Testing the Free Validation

You should now be able to build and run the app. Be careful not to enter data for the required field and try saving the data. (This is why you made certain that autosaving is turned off.) You get a standard save dialog, asking you to name the document and select its location.

As soon as you agree to the save, you should see the sheet shown in Figure 22.7. It presents the validation error without any further work on your part.

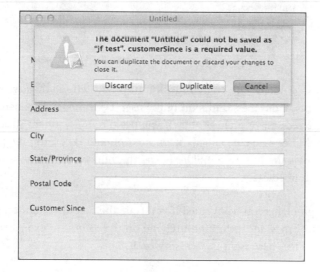

FIGURE 22.7
Core Data catches the error.

Quit and go back to your data model. Make another field required. Now repeat the process: The result is shown in Figure 22.8.

Summarizing Free Validation on Mac OS

By specifying validation rules like these and using documents, you can implement validation without much effort on Mac OS. There are two limitations you should be aware of:

▶ **Only one error is identified by name in the default implementation**—If there is more than one error, the report is simply "multiple errors."

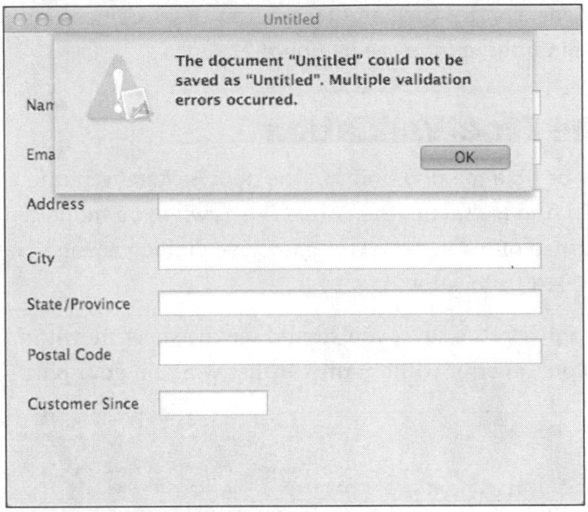

FIGURE 22.8
Core Data can
catch multiple
errors.

▶ **If you use a document, the validation happens when you save each document**—From the standpoint of the user, even the fairly general multiple errors message is often usable. If you use a non-document structure, the user might have no clue exactly what area of data is causing the problem. You can also use Interface Builder to specify that controls such as text fields validate immediately.

Both of these problems can be avoided if you code the actual validation so that you produce the error message rather than relying on the default message. You need to know how to do this because it is necessary on iOS.

Programming Validation for iOS or Mac OS

The reason validation can work on Mac OS without effort on your part is because Cocoa knows how to present error messages. In the multi-window environment and with sheets available, the mechanics of presenting information to the user is simple.

On Cocoa Touch, however, things are a bit more complicated. The error message can be shown in a popover or in a modal view. In some cases, the message is shown in a constrasting color such as red in real time as the mistake is made. (This model has gained a lot of popularity with the rise of JavaScript on web pages.)

▶ Presenting the error can use any of the techniques described in Hour 23, "Interacting with Users," p. 409.

There are three concepts that combine to implement validation on Cocoa: key-value validation, NSError, and support for quality editing. If you do not need to use quality editing, you do not need to bother with that one, but you should be familiar with the other two. One important word of warning: when it comes to key-value validation, it is important to understand the basic structure, but be certain to read to the end of that brief section because what you need to implement is not part of that structure. What you will need to implement will *use* the structure.

Key-Value Validation

The NSKeyValueCoding protocol is used extensively throughout Cocoa and Cocoa Touch. You have seen how you can use it to set and access values for keys on managed objects. The heart of the protocol is the methods that let you get and set values using key:

- (id)valueForKey:(NSString *)key
- (void)setValue:(id)value forKey:(NSString *)key

Key-value validation is an API built on the same concepts that allows you to validate properties. The heart of this API is the method that performs validation on a value given the key to which it might be set:

- (BOOL)validateValue:(id *)ioValue forKey:(NSString *)key
  error:(NSError **)outError

The result of this method is YES if the value passsed is valid for the key; NO otherwise. Note that the value is passed in as a pointer to an object reference (id). Most of the time, you simply use an object reference by itself (id), but the indirection provided by the pointer (id *) allows you to replace the value that is passed in by changing the pointer to point to another object. (If you changed the object reference itself, there might be unintended consequences.)

The reasoning behind this is that if the method can perform an operation that makes invalid data valid (perhaps coercing its type or making some other adjustment), then you can avoid an error message to the user and fix up whatever needs fixing. In these cases, the method returns YES because the modified data is, indeed, valid, and the user never knows there was ever a problem.

CAUTION

Before making changes to the value that is passed in, read Apple's "Core Data Programming Guide" on developer.apple.com or in the Organizer in Xcode. Look for the "Managed Object Validation" chapter (use search tools because page numbers change in documentation). Read the warnings and cautions about problems such as infinite loops that can occur. If you understand the issues and believe your implementation does not fall into an area that might be dangerous, read the documentation one last time and then go ahead.

Problems in validation code are notoriously difficult to track down because they are entirely data-dependent. Your testing suite must include the various conditions that might cause the validation code conditions to fire, and, because it only fires when there is something wrong with the data, it is entirely possible a large and complex system can run literally for years without ever encountering the combination of events that triggers the validation code to fire—and then, the first time it does fire, it can bring down the system. Experienced developers will be glad to regale you with horror stories of this nature.

You never should override `validateValue: forKey: error`. It is implemented in `NSManagedObject` so it is available there and in subclasses you might create. The default implementation processes all of the relevant validation rules you have implemented in your data model. It then checks to see if you have implemented any specific validations. It does this by checking for methods with standard names.

If you are calling (not overriding) `validateValue` for a key such as `price` (or any attribute of an entity you have declared), it will look for a validation method for that key. The name of the key is not passed in as a parameter; rather, it is part of the method name. In this case, what you would implement would be the following:

```
- (BOOL)validatePrice:(id *)ioValue error:(NSError **)outError
```

You implement it, but you do not call it. Instead, `validateValue: forKey`—when called with a key of `price`—will call it if it exists. Violating this rule can lead to infinite loops. In your implementation, you do whatever error checking you want to do and then you return YES or NO. You also return an `NSError` object as described in the following section.

▶ You will see an example of a validation error presented to a user in Hour 23, "Interacting with Users," p. 409.

NSError

`NSError` is a direct descendant of `NSObject`. It contains three primary pieces of information in its properties:

▶ **code**—An `NSInteger` that identifies the error. Integer error codes often pinpoint the exact error for developers and technical support.

▶ **domain**—An `NSString` identifying the general area from which the exception was raised. The four most basic domains defined in Cocoa are as follows:

  ▶ `NSMachErrorDomain`

- NSPOSIXErrorDomain

- NSOSStatusErrorDomain

- NSCocoaErrorDomain

You can define your own domains such as com.yourorganization.yourapp
.ErrorDomain. Domains can provide information both to users and to support
staff.

- **userInfo**—An NSDictionary that provides text (often localized) that identifies the problem in detail. The dictionary entries are localized strings for
any of the following supported keys:

  - NSLocalizedDescriptionKey

  - NSErrorFailingURLStringKey

  - NSFilePathErrorKey

  - NSStringEncodingErrorKey

  - NSUnderlyingErrorKey

  - NSURLErrorKey

  - NSLocalizedFailureReasonErrorKey

  - NSLocalizedRecoverySuggestionErrorKey

  - NSLocalizedRecoveryOptionsErrorKey

  - NSRecoveryAttempterErrorKey

  - NSHelpAnchorErrorKey

  - NSURLErrorFailingURLErrorKey

  - NSURLErrorFailingURLStringErrorKey

  - NSURLErrorFailingURLPeerTrustErrorKey

If you do not see an error key you like, try NSUnderlyingErrorKey.

Quality Edit Support ("Inter-Property Validation")

Many people make a distinction between quality and validity edits. Typically, validity edits cannot be overridden. You can rely on the fact that all data in the database

conforms to those edits (with the exception of data entered before the edits and constraints were implemented).

Quality edits can often be overridden. In addition, validity edits typically can be performed based solely on the rules for a specific field (or key). They do not require any other data.

Quality edits often involve comparisons with additional data values, and can often be overridden by users. For example, an edit of this type could check for a combination of driver's license number and age. Each of those fields can have its own validation rules, but to check that you do not have driver's license numbers for people under age 16, you need to use data from two fields. This is an *inter-property* validation in Apple's documentation. The phrase *quality edit* is used for any edit that requires two data values even if it comes from two instances of the same field.

A common edit of this type is an edit that fails if the difference between two values of the same field exceed a certain tolerance. For example, if a customer's bank balance varies from one day to another by more than $10 million, this issue might be flagged for manual review in a bank.

Because quality edits need to be performed when any of the values change, the structure used for validity edits does not work. For this reason, NSManagedObject provides three methods that you can override:

- (BOOL)validateForInsert:(NSError **)error
- (BOOL)validateForDelete:(NSError **)error
- (BOOL)validateForUpdate:(NSError **)error

You handle these just as the validation routines, returning YES or NO along with an NSError object.

Just as validateValue does its own checking before calling a validatePrice method if you have implemented it (or whatever key is involved), these validation routines must also be called after the built-in validations, which are defined in your data model. Because you are overriding these methods rather than calling a different method such as validateValue or validateConsistency, you have to be careful to call the superclass method as the first line of code in your own method. Here is a sample:

```
- (BOOL)validateForUpdate:(NSError **)error {
  [super validateForUpdate: error];
  // your quality edit
}
```

Summary

This hour shows you how to implement validation rules for your data entry interface. You have also reviewed the process for binding data entry fields to an object controller (Customer) on Mac OS.

Q&A

Q. What does NSError contain?

A. It contains an integer error code, a string representing a domain (which can be your own app identification), and a dictionary with the actual localized error message. The error message can contain variable data (such as the record ID that caused a problem).

Q. Why is it hard to catch errors in editing code?

A. This code only executes in rare circumstances (error conditions), so it is not tested with heavy use. That is one reason why special unit tests that can be devised to test unusual conditions are often used.

Workshop

Quiz

1. *When do you override* `validateValue:forKey:error?`

2. *Why does Cocoa provide error messages to users on Mac OS and not on iOS?*

Quiz Answers

1. Never. Create a new method for the key (such as price). It will be of the form:

```
- (BOOL)validatePrice:(id *)ioValue error:(NSError **)outError
```

2. On Mac OS, sheets are available so the form of the user interaction is well defined for Cocoa to use it. On iOS, there are more options for interaction, so you have to implement your own messages.

Activities

Experiment with implementing your own error messages and validation routines. To create the NSError dictionary, refer to "Using Dictionaries for Key-Value Pairs in Cocoa" in Hour 10, "Working with Predicates and Sorting," p. 171.

HOUR 23

Interacting with Users

What You'll Learn in This Hour:

- ▶ Using an editing interface
- ▶ Putting up sheets and alerts on Mac OS
- ▶ Putting up popovers on iOS

Choosing an Editing Interface

There are two primary ways of allowing users to edit data, and both of them apply to Core Data:

- ▶ **Editing-in-place**—Lets you directly manipulate the data using the same interface you use to display it.

- ▶ **Editing interfaces**—Replace the interface that people use to view data.

Neither is better than the other, and many apps on both iOS and Mac OS use both techniques in various places. In fact, the Estimator example that you have seen in this book is based on the Master-Detail Application template for iOS and uses both of the techniques. One of the most important interface issues to consider is letting the user know when he is able to edit data. This can be done with both editing-in-place and separate editing interfaces.

In the Master-Detail Application template, editing in place is used to edit the table layout itself—that is, deleting or moving rows. A separate editing interface is used to edit the data in the table itself.

A separate editing interface is created with a modal sheet or window or on Mac OS or with a popover or other view on iOS. Those processes are summarized later in this hour, but the details of implementation are beyond the scope of this book.

▶ You can find information about building user interfaces on developer.apple
.com. Look particularly for the Human Interface Guidelines documents and
the sample code. The focus in this hour is on user interactions as they
pertain to Core Data, so you will find references to specific sample code
projects on developer.apple.com that you can download and explore to see
how the entire app fits together beyond the Core Data details.

NOTE

In this section, the Master-Detail Application template is used with the options set
for a universal project for both iPad and iPhone as well as storyboards and automatic reference counting.

In the master view controller (also called the root view controller), you tap Edit to
enter edit mode, as shown in Figure 23.1.

FIGURE 23.1
Tap Edit to
begin editing.

NOTE

The terminology of the controllers, beginning with Xcode 4.2, is a little different than it
has been in the past. For example, `rootViewController` is a property of `UIWindow`; it
is the controller that provides the window's content view. (Remember that the Mac OS
counterpart of `UIWindow` is `NSWindow`; it does not have a `rootViewController` property.) In the `Split View-Controller` Application template from Xcode
versions before 4.2, what is now called the `masterViewController` was called
the `rootViewController`. With the renaming, `rootViewController` has a

more general meaning (the controller for the window's content view), and the specific use of that term for the master view of a master-detail architecture is no longer used.

As shown in Figure 23.2, edit mode on iPad (and iPhone) features editing-in-place. This is the same basic layout as the display of data, but some new features are added when you tap the Edit button. Note how the same view appears in a popover or a split view depending on the iPad's orientation.

FIGURE 23.2
Edit-in-place builds on your basic interface.

Tapping the delete icon at the left of each row then brings up the delete button at the right, as shown in Figure 23.3.

FIGURE 23.3
You need to tap Delete to actually delete the row.

TIP

On iOS with its touch interface, these repeated taps often replace dialogs and alerts on the non-touch interface of Mac OS in which you are warned to confirm that you really want to do something irreparable such as deleting data. In place of that familiar confirmation dialog, you cannot delete data on an iOS device that uses this interface without three separate taps:

1. Tap Edit to enter edit mode.
2. Tap the delete icon at the left of the row you want to delete. Alternatively, swipe across the row.
3. Tap the Delete button at the right of the row.

This is a good example of how the same process that is important to a good interface (confirmation of a potentially dangerous action such as deleting data) can be implemented differently on touch devices and desktop-based devices. It is not the alert or sheet on the Mac that is important, and it is not even the confirmation that the alert or sheet can provide that matters. Rather, what is important is that the act of deleting data is protected as much as possible from accidental use.

NOTE

Of course, notwithstanding all these precautions, you—along with just about every other computer user—have probably confirmed repeatedly that you really do want to delete data which, in retrospect, you realized you did not want to delete. This is the logic behind widespread use of the undo command: Users should be able to recover from deliberate but incorrect actions. How far back you want to go depends on the app and its data. At a certain point, the history normally needs to be frozen without the possibility of undo.

The editing interface shown in Figures 23.1, 23.2, and 23.3 is part of the standard iOS interface. The functionality is provided by a table view that handles all the updating and displays. As is often the case with iOS, this requires several very small sections of code to be written rather than one lengthy method. As you implement edit buttons for table views, you will become familiar with the process. If you are working from a template or sample code, you might already have the view and its controller configured.

TIP

Although you can certainly use an edit button with your own views, using them with table views brings you so much automatic functionality that it is worthwhile to explore the features you get for free.

Communicating with Users

You need to communicate with users in two general situations:

▶ **Error messages.** You need to alert users to errors such as validation errors, as described previously in Hour 18, "Validating Data," p. 317 and Hour 22, "Managing Validation," p. 393.

▶ **Changed views.** In response to user requests, you may need to display a new view, which is done by swapping in a new view controller.

▶ You will find extensive documentation on these two processes on developer.apple.com.

The next section provides a summary or refresher of methods you can use to communicate with users.

Swapping Views on iOS

You often need to swap views when a user taps a disclosure triangle in a table view cell. You may also need to swap views in response to a tap in a toolbar or navigation bar item. You have seen how this is set up for you in the Master-Detail Application template. However, this section shows you how to do it yourself.

The example used is the common one of a detail disclosure button in a table view cell. This can let your users drill down on data. In the Estimator example shown in this book, that could be the case after someone has selected a customer in the master view controller. The master view controller can then show all the jobs for that customer; your user can tap one job and display its details in the detail view. (A navigation interface is great for this.)

Alternatively, you can handle the navigation from customer to individual job in the detail view controller. On iPad, the best practice is to flatten the structure the user sees as much as possible so there is very little navigation: Everything should just be there. However, on iPhone and in some cases on iPad, you do need an intermediate level of detail.

In this scenario, you need a detail view controller and view for the customer (with name and address), as well as a detail view controller for the job (with description and price). On iPad, the list of jobs can be placed on the customer detail view, but you still are going to need to navigate down to the job detail view.

TIP

One way to decide whether to place the navigation in the master or detail view controller is to think of what the user is likely to want to see. Will the user want to switch from one customer to another? If so, keep the master view controller for customers and drill down to the list of jobs in the detail view controller. If the user is likely to want to switch from job to job within a single customer, it may be worth doing the navigation in the master view controller.

In addition to navigation, you may need to swap a view to swap in an editable view. In either case, the process is the same.

▼   **Try It Yourself**

Drilling Down from a Table View to Details or Swapping in an Editable View

No matter which of method you choose, you need to swap views, and then you need to display a table view in one controller or the other that starts the swapping process. This is pseudo-code to walk you through the basic steps. However, the details vary from app to app.

1. When you display the table view from which you want to navigate, add a detail disclosure button to each row in `tableView:cellForRowAtIndexPath`, as shown in Listing 23.1. This is accomplished by setting the accessory type of the cell.

    This code is placed in whichever controller is displaying the list of jobs for a customer, so its main item is the customer. In the Master-Detail template, this is typically `detailItem`. So, in this example, `self` in the following listing is a customer.

LISTING 23.1   Add a Detail Disclosure Accessory to the Row

```
- (UITableViewCell *)tableView:(UITableView *)tableView
  cellForRowAtIndexPath:(NSIndexPath *)indexPath {

  static NSString *CellIdentifier = @"AgendaCell";

  UITableViewCell *cell = [tableView
    dequeueReusableCellWithIdentifier:CellIdentifier];
  if (cell == nil) {
    cell = [[[UITableViewCell alloc]
      initWithStyle:UITableViewCellStyleSubtitle
      reuseIdentifier:CellIdentifier] autorelease];
    cell.editingAccessoryType = UITableViewCellAccessoryNone;
    cell.accessoryType = UITableViewCellAccessoryDetailDisclosureButton;
  }
```

```
  // Configure the cell.
  if (indexPath.row < [self.jobs count]) {
    Job *myJob = [self.jobs objectAtIndex:indexPath.row];
    cell.textLabel.text = myJob.job_description;
    cell.detailTextLabel.text = myJob.rate;
    // you might want to add an image to the cell with cell.imageView.image
    // = something.
  }
  return cell;
}
```

2. Next, handle the tap on the detail disclosure button. Do this in `tableView:did SelectRowAtIndexPath:`, as shown in Listing 23.2. This code will vary with your particular implementation. The key point is that somewhere in this method, you need to create a new view controller and set it to the item in the row that has just been tapped.

3. Then, in the case of a split view controller, set the detail view for the root view controller to be the new view controller you just created. Alternatively, reset the master view controller to be the new view controlled. You may call a method in your master view controller to do this (you will create that method in the next step).

LISTING 23.2   Handle the Tap in the Selected Row

```
- (void)tableView:(UITableView *)tableView didSelectRowAtIndexPath:
(NSIndexPath *)indexPath {
  Job *myItem = [self.jobs objectAtIndex:indexPath.row];
  nextViewController = [[JobDetailController alloc]
  initWithNibName:@"JobView"bundle:nil];
  nextViewController.detailItem = myItem;
  self.rootViewController setDetailView: nextViewController;
}
```

4. Finally, implement the method to set the new detail view, as shown in Listing 23.3. This code is based on the Substitutable View Controller sample code on developer.apple.com. In the scenario described here, this would be in the master view controller that controls the controller for the detail view, which is one of its properties.

LISTING 23.3   Set the New View Controller

```
(void)setDetailView: newDetailView {

detailViewController = (DetailViewController*)nextViewController;

// Update the split view controller's view controllers array.
```

```
NSArray *viewControllers = [[NSArray alloc]
initWithObjects:self.navigationController,
  nextViewController, nil];
splitViewController.viewControllers = viewControllers;
[viewControllers release];

// Dismiss the popover if it's present.
if (popoverController != nil) {
  [popoverController dismissPopoverAnimated:YES];
}

// Configure the new view controller's popover button (after the view
// has been
// displayed and its toolbar/navigation bar has been created).
if (rootPopoverButtonItem != nil) {
  [nextViewController
showRootPopoverButtonItem:self.rootPopoverButtonItem];
  }
}
```

Using Popovers on iOS

Popovers are actually quite similar to swapping views. You create a new view and then, instead of placing it inside a split view controller or pushing it onto a navigation interface, you place it inside a pop-over.

▶ There is an excellent pop-overs example on developer.apple.com. Some of its code is shown here.

Figure 23.4 shows the popovers example in action.

FIGURE 23.4
Experiment with the pop-overs example.

The example in the following Task implements a subclass of UIViewController called UIPopoverContentViewController.

Using a Popover

In this task, you will see how the UIPopoverContentViewController and its view are used by the popover. If you look in the code, you will see that, rather than using a nib file, viewDidLoad adds a UILabel to the view and sets its text, font, and so forth. All of this is standard interface development.

There are two pieces of code you need to write:

1. Create the view controller you want to display in the popover. This typically means declaring a new view controller such as UIPopoverContentView-Controller and setting it up just as you would set up any view controller.

2. Instantiate that view controller at the appropriate place. In the case of display-ing errors, the appropriate place might be when validation is performed. In the popovers example, it is created in DetailViewController.viewDidLoad with the code shown in Listing 23.4.

LISTING 23.4   Creating a Popover View Controller

```
- (void)viewDidLoad {
[super viewDidLoad];

PopoverContentViewController *content = [[PopoverContentViewController
  alloc] init];

// Setup the popover for use in the detail view.
detailViewPopover = [[UIPopoverController alloc]
  initWithContentViewController:content];
detailViewPopover.popoverContentSize = CGSizeMake(320., 320.);
detailViewPopover.delegate = self;

// Setup the popover for use from the navigation bar.
barButtonItemPopover = [[UIPopoverController alloc]
  initWithContentViewController:content];
barButtonItemPopover.popoverContentSize = CGSizeMake(320., 320.);
barButtonItemPopover.delegate = self;

[content release];
}
```

As you can see, two popover content views are created, and they are stored in instance variables for the detail view controller. You might want to create a single popover content view and keep it around for use with error messages. Alternatively, you can create such a view totally as needed.

3. When you are ready to display the view, call this code. (You might also be performing step 2 at this time depending on your app's structure.) Display the popover you created in step 2 with this line of code for a tap in a rect on the main view:

```
[detailViewPopover presentPopoverFromRect:tappedButton.frame
  inView:self.view
  permittedArrowDirections:UIPopoverArrowDirectionAny animated:YES];
```

Display a popover controller from a toolbar item with the following code. Note that the human interface guidelines state that if a popover is shown from a toolbar item, tapping the toolbar item again will dismiss the popover:

```
if (barButtonItemPopover.popoverVisible == NO) {
  [barButtonItemPopover presentPopoverFromBarButtonItem:tappedButton
    permittedArrowDirections:UIPopoverArrowDirectionAny animated:YES];
}
else {
  [barButtonItemPopover dismissPopoverAnimated:YES];
}

[barButtonItemPopover presentPopoverFromBarButtonItem:tappedButton
  permittedArrowDirections:UIPopoverArrowDirectionAny animated:YES];
```

There is additional code in the the example to handle popovers with split view controllers because the guidelines state that only one popover can be visible at a time.

▲

The valid arrow direction values for pop-overs used in Step 3 are:

```
UIPop-overArrowDirectionUp
UIPop-overArrowDirectionDown
UIPop-overArrowDirectionLeft
UIPop-overArrowDirectionRight
UIPop-overArrowDirectionAny
UIPop-overArrowDirectionUnknown
```

If you choose UIPopoverArrowDirectionAny, iOS will choose the most appropriate direction. This is not only the easiest, but also generally the best-looking, of the choices. As is usually the case on iOS, setting animated to YES also typically produces the best results.

Using Sheets and Modal Windows on Mac OS

Not everything on Mac OS happens in a window. Messages can appear in alerts, dialog boxes, and sheets that interrupt the user's actions. Mac OS X brought about the concept of *sheets*, which appear to roll down from a window's title bar. A sheet stops user interaction with the window until the sheet is dismissed (usually with an OK or Cancel button). The advantage that sheets have over tools such as alerts and dialog boxes is that they freeze a specific window while letting users continue to work in other windows and the menubar. Among other things, this means that the user might be able to use commands or another window to handle the issue the sheet identifies. In addition, because sheets are attached to windows, you cannot lose them. Free-floating dialogs—particularly if they are in another space on a Mac—can immobilize the computer.

However, sheets do not work in all circumstances. If no window is open in an app, there is nowhere for a sheet to be displayed. In addition, sometimes an app encounters a situation that needs to be brought to the user's attention immediately but that does not relate to a specific window. Sometimes these are system-wide messages such as the ever-popular "The disk was not ejected properly," which is displayed if you unplug a disk without the benefit of a Finder command. For a given app, app-wide alerts can indicate that a resource is no longer available inside the app or that it is time to back up data, and so forth.

From your point of view, there is very little to think about when you create an alert or a sheet on Mac OS X. Your job is to create a view controller and a nib file just as you would for any window. What is different is how the view controller presents the sheet or alert.

NOTE

You can use other interface elements to stop the action and get the user's attention, but sheets and alerts are the most common.

Try It Yourself ▼

Creating and Dismissing a Sheet

As with any other view, you need a view controller and a nib file to display These are the steps that are specific to working with a sheet. The process typically starts with the user selecting a menu command or clicking a button. Here is what you do from there:

1. Create the window and any views within it using Interface Builder. Make certain to uncheck the checkbox Visible at Launch: You do not want it to appear until you show it.

2. Load the sheet from a bundle. Often the sheet is reused as the app runs; a reference to it is stored in a local variable, such as mySheet in the following code. As always, check that the load operation has succeeded.

   This code typically goes in the sheet controller:

```
if (mySheet == nil)
  {
  NSBundle *myBundle = [NSBundle bundleForClass:[self class]];
  NSNib *nib = [[NSNib alloc] initWithNibNamed:@"MySheet"
    bundle:myBundle];
  BOOL success = [nib instantiateNibWithOwner:self
    topLevelObjects:nil];
  [nib release];

  if (success != YES)
    {
      // handle error
      return;
    }
  }
```

3. Use beginSheet to start the modal session. Typically, you pass in the window from which the button was clicked or the key window in the case of a menu command; the modal delegate is the sheet controller that is managing the sheet (self in the following code). You pass in a selector to be called when the sheet is dismissed. mySheetDidEnd in the following code is custom code for your app:

```
[NSApplication *app = [NSApplication sharedApplication];
[app beginSheet:mySheet
  modalForWindow:documentWindow
  modalDelegate:self
  didEndSelector:returnCode:contextInfo:)
  contextInfo:NULL];
```

4. After the user has finished with the window, remove it from the screen. The return code will be returned to the selector you specified (mySheetDidEnd in this example).

5. In your custom code (mySheetDidEnd), perform any necessary processing. The key line of code in that method is:

```
if (returnCode ==
NSOKButton)
```

6. Attach the button that dismisses the sheet to an action you create. The key line of that action is usually one of these two lines of code. The action frequently has only one line. This calls the code referred to in step 3:

```
[NSApp endSheet:mySheet returnCode:NSOKButton];
[NSApp endSheet:mySheet returnCode:NSCancelButton];
```

Those are the steps involved in posting a sheet.

Creating and Dismissing a Modal Window

If you need an app-wide modal window or a modal window when no document is open, you can use runModalForWindow. Create the window as usual with a nib file and controller. Make it modal with the following method:

```
- (NSInteger)runModalForWindow:(NSWindow *)aWindow
```

▶ You can find more information on modal windows on developer.apple.com in Window Programming Guide; there is a section called "How Modal Windows Work."

Summary

This hour has presented a brief overview of the interaction tools that are available to you in Mac OS and iOS. You have seen that the pattern of views and view controllers applies to popovers, sheets, and modal windows just as it does in other cases.

Q&A

Q. *Why do you use popovers on iOS?*

A. Because you cannot have multiple windows on an iOS device, the popover is the only tool that allows users to see to views at the same time. Multiple views within a single container view allow you to see several views at the same time, but the popover multiple views are transient.

Q. *How do you create a new nib file or a new storyboard file?*

A. For a nib file, select File, New, New File, iOS, Cocoa Touch, UIViewController subclass. This gives you the option to create the view controller files (.h and .m) as well as the nib file. For a storyboard file, select File, New, New File, iOS, User Interface, Storyboard.

Workshop

Quiz

1. *What is the difference between a sheet and a modal window?*

2. *What is the best way to position popover arrows?*

Quiz Answers

1. A sheet is attached to a window and immobilizes that window until it is dismissed. A modal window immobilizes the entire app.

2. The best way is to use UIPopoverArrowDirectionAny. It is easiest and also looks best in most cases.

Activities

Use yourself as a test subject. Observe modal windows, sheets, and pop-overs as you use your computers. Look for patterns of which ones are helpful and which are annoying.

Migrating Data Models

What You'll Learn in This Hour:

▶ Exploring the data migration continuum for Core Data

▶ Working with data model versions

▶ No-effort data migration: undestanding the changes that do not matter

▶ Using automatic lightweight migration

▶ Understanding basic mapping migration

▶ Moving beyond basic mapping migration

Introducing the Core Data Migration Continuum

There really is no single Core Data migration process. As you learn in this hour, data migration (a necessary part of all databases in the real world as described in "Managing Data Migration" following this section), is a continuum of tools and approaches. At its most simple, Core Data provides functionality that lets you modify a data model and continue to use it with your existing code in many cases. That is because when evaluating a data model that has been used to create a persistent store and checking to see whether it is compatible with the model used in an app, Core Data focuses only on the persistent store values. Certain changes you make in your app development just do not make the data model incompatible with existing stores. In other words, there are plenty of things you can do to your app or data model without breaking existing persistent stores.

Moving along the continuum, you will find *lightweight migration* (generally used automatically and referred to as *automatic lightweight migration*). A number of changes that you make to your data model will automatically work the way you expect them to if you set the appropriate options at the time you open a persistent store.

NOTE

In some cases, you have to be careful about the specific types of changes you make to the model. Understanding the different types of migration, you may want to limit your changes to those that will be compatible with a migration strategy that you have implemented. Remember that during development, your migrations may be different and more frequent than during production. One of the actions to take at the end of a phase of the development process may be to turn off automatic migration so that Core Data is stricter about matching the persistent store to the data model.

More complex are migrations that involve *mapping*. In these migrations, you build a *mapping model* that tells Core Data which data maps from which fields to which new fields. You can add code to your mapping model so that you can even examine the data. For example, if you have a single address field in your database, you might be able to parse it into street address, city, state/province, and ZIP/postal code. Depending on the quality of your data and the complexity of the code you write, you might need to preserve the raw data as-is and move the parsed data to new fields that can be manually reviewed and updated as necesssary.

This hour shows you the incompatibilities you do not have to worry about, automatic lightweight migration, and the basics of the mapping models.

Managing Data Model Migration

You have only to look to the story of the Rosetta Stone to start to appreciate how the ways in which data is stored affect its usability over time. From time to time, you might find unreadable floppy disks at the bottom of a catch-all desk drawer, and many a yard sale is replete with collections of music and video on now-unused formats. When a computer program accesses data, both the physical medium and the format of the data need to be consistent. Mainframe programs written in Cobol during the 1950s no longer run on most computers, and even the most carefully archived data is useless to many people.

Databases make life simpler for developers and users, but they add complexity in that you need not only a program to read the database, but also the database manager that may be yet another program (such as MySQL, Oracle, or DB2) or an embedded library such as SQLite. And the data itself might be located on a different computer that might run an operating system that is not even under your control.

On top of all this, the design of the database (its *schema* in technical parlance) must match the design that the application program implements. In other words, if the schema defines a column (or field) for a telephone number and, if over years of careless maintenance, the name of that field has become salary, the software needs to retrieve the telephone number from the salary field. (Experienced database administrators will nod their heads; this is far from uncommon or even a worst-case scenario.)

The need for consistency between the database that stores the data and the software that accesses the data is essential to the use of databases. However, over time, circumstances change and the data might need to change (a few extra digits for a salary field, for example). On the software side, changes might also take place (tax rates can change, for example).

There are many ways to handle consistency as changes are made to both the software and the database. Here are three of the most common methods to handle consistency as changes are made on either side (or both) of the database/software connection.

▶ **Modify the data store and the software at the same time**—Although this might require some complex logistical planning (particularly in multiuser environments), it is the simplest approach in the long run. In many cases, however, it is not feasible. As part of the change-over, the data from the database might be unloaded to a standard format, the database itself can be modified, and the data can be reloaded. Add this interruption in service to the list of reasons this approach may not be feasible.

▶ **Leave the data store unchanged and modify the software**—This works when the change is not part of the data (in other words, giving all employees a specified percent increase or recognizing that a telephone number with a certain area code now must be dealt with as if it had a different area code).

▶ **Attach versioning information to the database as a whole or to individual records within it**—Records can be read in a format that matches their stored versions. For this approach to work, a version must be attached to the database itself or to individual records at the beginning of the process; otherwise, the first change to the database will need to be the addition of a version field, and that change cannot be managed without difficulty.

Core Data uses built-in versioning to give you control over migration. The first two choices can be implemented with any database including Core Data because they are operational in nature.

Core Data can start with the version identification of the data model your app uses and the version identification of the persistent store you open. If they do not match, you get the error that the data model in the project and the data model in the persistent store do not match. The app will usually stop running with an error unless you intercept the error message and programmatically take whatever action is appropriate. You can extend the default behavior in many ways. Certain changes to your database schema can be managed automatically if you provide Core Data with some guidelines and rules. That is what this hour addresses.

> **NOTE**
>
> If you never change your database schema after you complete your app, you can skip over this hour. Do not laugh: That is a common situation, particularly for simple apps. There are even some very complex database schemas that have remained unchanged for decades. And now with the increasing use of Core Data in document-based apps, you may find that your data model is unchanged for years at a time, even though the data stored in your documents changes.

▶ The definitive reference on Core Data migration is "Core Data Model Versioning and Data Migration Programming Guide" on developer.apple .com. You can find it in both the iOS and Mac OS developer libraries under Guides; search on Core Data migration to find it and other references. At the time of this writing, the same document applies to both Mac OS and iOS.

Working with Data Model Versions

You can create multiple versions of your data model in your project. Assuming you have started with a template that gives you Core Data functionality, you already have a data model.

Creating a New Data Model

If you have not started in that way, select File, New, New File and choose a data model, as shown in Figure 24.1. Both iOS and Mac OS have the same functionality and interface for this sheet.

It is almost always better to start from a template that includes Core Data (and to use the checkbox to add that functionality). The reason is that these templates contain the code that implements Core Data functionality for your app. Creating a new data model file does just that: It creates a new data model file. You are on your own for implementing Its use.

Creating a New Data Model Version

Most of the time when you think about creating a new data model for your project, you are better off creating a new version of your existing data model. This allows you to take advantage of data model migration features in Xcode and Cocoa. If you have used pre-4.2 versions of Xcode, you will notice that these steps are fewer and simpler than the steps you are used to in creating a new version of your data model. The result is the same at runtime.

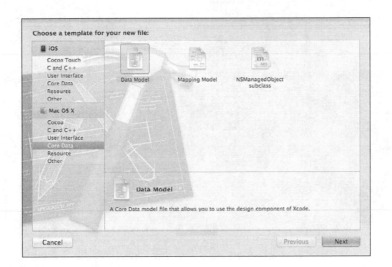

FIGURE 24.1
Create a data
model.

The versioning mechanism relies on the Mac OS package concept—what appears to be a single file is actually a folder. If you command-click on a data model in the Finder, you will see a shortcut menu that includes the Show Package Contents command. That will open the contents of the selected file (the data model in this case), and you will see the individual files.

Try It Yourself

Create a New Version of a Core Data Model

The various versions of your data model are contained within the package. Each has a unique name. (This is a change from previous versions of Xcode.) Do the following:

1. Select your data model from the project navigator, as shown in Figure 24.2.

2. Select Editor/Add Model Version to begin the process (this is also shown in Figure 24.2).

3. As shown in Figure 24.3, name the new version and select the version on which it is based. By default, the new version will have a 2 following the name of the data model (and then 3, and so forth), but you can change the name to be more meaningful, as you see in Figure 24.3.

FIGURE 24.2
Start to create the new version.

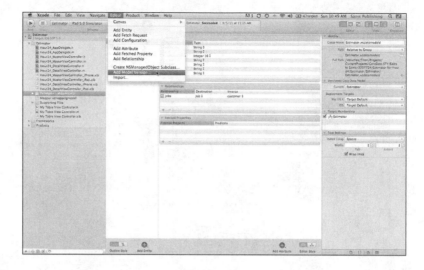

FIGURE 24.3
Name the new version.

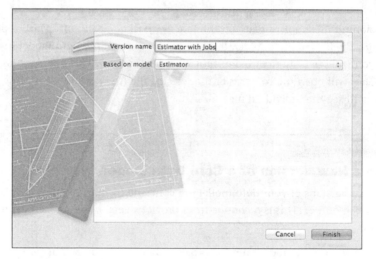

Providing a meaningful name is helpful. Note that part of the synchronization of database, data model, and code is being able to identify versions, so you might want to use terminology that will withstand the test of time.

TIP

A data model called Friday Test will not do you much good when you are trying to change something a year from now. You can always identify the current version, but checking back on previous versions is more helpful with fuller names.

4. As shown in Figure 24.4, the new version is shown in an expandable display for the data model.

FIGURE 24.4
The new version is added to the project.

5. As shown at the right of Figure 24.4, you select the current version in the File inspector. A small green dot is placed on the name of the current version in the project navigator.

TIP

Once you have more than one version of your data model, changing to another version is just a matter of changing the Versioned Core Data Model pop-up in the Data Model inspector.

6. You can also set an identifier in the File inspector, as shown in Figure 24.5.

A data model with only one version is represented by a single file icon in the project navigator. That changes as soon as you add a second version so you can expand it and view the various versions. The identifier shown in Figure 24.5 can be set for a specific version. In the case of a one-version data model, the File inspector looks like Figure 24.5. In other words, you can't select which version is the current version because there is only one.

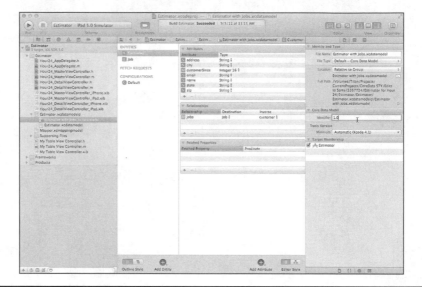

Determining Version Compatibility

There are a lot of moving pieces in the version mechanism of Core Data, but each
one has its own role to play. First of all, your data model has a name. You set this
when you create it (it is picked up automatically in a template from the name you
assign to the project). You can change it by selecting the data model in the project
navigator and using the File inspector.

In the File inspector for a version of a data model, you can set a free-format identifier, as shown previously in Figure 24.5.

You also can set the name for a version when you create it (as shown previously in
Figure 24.3).

At runtime, the framework needs to make certain that the current data model version is compatible with the data model version used to create the persistent store.
And to do this, it uses exactly none of the various identifiers just described (the data
model filename, the version filenames, and the version identifiers).

Core Data uses a fast and efficient way of summarizing data models so it can quickly
compare the data model from the app with the data model that was used to create
the persistent store. It constructs a 32-bit hash code from the data elements in each

entity of the data model that it cares about. This provides a 32-bit summary of the entities in the data model in the persistent store and the data model in the app.

NOTE

This method is commonly used for comparing data such as passwords. It allows a test for matching without providing the underlying data.

This means you can make changes to aspects of your data model that are not included in the hashing process without worrying about version incompatibility. Figure 24.6 shows the project's Core Data inspector where you can see some of the attributes that go into the hashing process:

▶ Name (Customer in Figure 24.6)

▶ Parent (changing the parent or even from a parent to none or vice versa is an incompatibility)

▶ Abstract Entity

▶ Properties (shown in the main part of the editor)

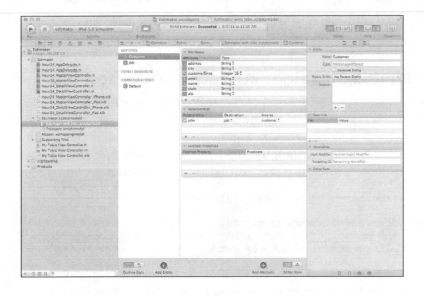

FIGURE 24.6
Here are the entity attributes that are hashed and that, therefore, will cause incompatibilities if you change them.

NOTE

Note that Class (NSManagedObject in Figure 24.6 but a custom class if you want) is not part of the hash, nor are the key/value pairs of User Info. These are not parts of the persisistent store itself; they are parts of the linkage between the persistent store and the code that accesses it.

Forcing Incompatibility

In the versioning section of Figure 24.6, you see a hash modifier, and you can use it to override the default hashing behavior for an entity or attribute. There are cases in which Core Data will treat two data models as compatible, and you do not want that to happen.

The most frequently cited example of this is an attribute that is binary data—a BLOB. If you change the internal format of the binary data, you want the data model to appear different, even though neither the name nor the type has changed.

To do this, set a hash modifier. This value will be used in constructing the hash for the entity or attribute. It is normally blank, but if you change it to anything at all, that will cause the new version of the model to no longer compare cleanly to an old version. If you change the BLOB structure again, just change the hash modifier and, once again, without modifying the name or data type, you will force Core Data to see the models as incompatible.

Using Automatic Lightweight Migration

The version mechanisms let you manage changes to the model and in your code. You can have Core Data do some of the migration work automatically for you.

Making Lightweight Migration Work for You

You can take advantage of Core Data's *lightweight migration* feature. If the data model in the persistent store is incompatible with the one in your app, lightweight migration will make the necessary adjustments so you can run with the incompatible versions. This is particularly useful during development. As a rule, you should clean up the data model so it does exactly match before you move into production.

Here are the changes lightweight migration handles:

▶ Adding a new attribute to an entity.

▶ Making a required attribute optional.

▶ Making an optional attribute required. (In this case, you must also provide a default value; otherwise, you leave open a validation trap for users.)

Renaming Attributes and Entities

You can also rename entities and attributes using the renaming ID in the Versioning section of the Data Model inspector shown previously in Figure 24.6. In your data model, just rename the entity or attribute to the new name you want to use. In the Renaming ID field, enter the previous name for the entity or attribute. When lightweight migration is run, Core Data will handle the conversion for you. This is a convenient way of handling a misspelling in a name.

It also handles the all-too-frequent case in which the user or client decides that from now on, all customers will be "patrons" (or "clients" or "guests"). This can be important for operational reasons, particularly in the customer service area, and the fact that you can adjust quickly might earn you some extra points for getting along well with your own customers, clients, guests, patrons, and so forth (until the next name change).

Turning On Automatic Lightweight Migration

If you have made changes to your data model that can be handled by automatic lightweight migration, you turn it on by setting options for addPersistentStore-WithType. You can search for it in your project; it usually appears only once in the template projects. It typically is located in the getter for the persistent store coordinator. That code is shown in Listing 24.1.

LISTING 24.1 Opening a Persistent Store

```
/**
  Returns the persistent store coordinator for the application.
  If the coordinator doesn't already exist, it is created and the
  application's store added to it.
 */
- (NSPersistentStoreCoordinator *)persistentStoreCoordinator
{
  if (__persistentStoreCoordinator != nil)
  {
    return __persistentStoreCoordinator;
  }

  NSURL *storeURL = [[self applicationDocumentsDirectory]
    URLByAppendingPathComponent:@"Estimator.sqlite"];

  NSError *error = nil;
  persistentStoreCoordinator = [[NSPersistentStoreCoordinator alloc]
    initWithManagedObjectModel:[self managedObjectModel]];
  if (![__persistentStoreCoordinator
    addPersistentStoreWithType:NSSQLiteStoreType
      configuration:nil URL:storeURL options:nil error:&error])
    {
....code continues....
```

options is set to nil in the standard code. It is a dictionary—the structure used throughout Cocoa for sending a collection of named values to as a single object. You create the dictionary to launch automatic lightweight migration and then pass it in with the code in Listing 24.2. (Variable names may differ in your project.)

LISTING 24.2   Creating the Dictionary for Lightweight Migration

```
NSDictionary *options = [NSDictionary dictionaryWithObjectsAndKeys:
  [NSNumber numberWithBool:YES], NSMigratePersistentStoresAutomaticallyOption,
  [NSNumber numberWithBool:YES], NSInferMappingModelAutomaticallyOption, nil];

if (![__persistentStoreCoordinator addPersistentStoreWithType: NSSQLiteStoreType
  configuration: nil URL:storeURL
  options:options error:&error]) {
  // Handle the error.
```

It is a good idea to test auto migration in a copy of the app environment (including a copy of the persistent store). Check to see what has happened. You can also do this programmatically using the NSMappingModel class method shown here

```
+ (NSMappingModel *)inferredMappingModelForSourceModel:
    (NSManagedObjectModel *)source
    destinationModel:(NSManagedObjectModel *)destination
    error:(NSError **)error
```

You pass in the existing model, and it will return nil or new model that is the result of mapping.

Looking at a Mapping Model Overview

Automatic lightweight conversion handles many of the issues that arise during development of a great many Core Data projects. However, sometimes you do need the ability to make substantial changes to a data model. Core Data can accommodate you.

▶ For more details, see "Core Data Model Versioning and Data Migration Programming Guide" on developer.apple.com.

Using a Basic Mapping Model

A basic mapping model is really only slightly more complex than automatic lightweight migration. The primary difference is that you must provide the map, showing which old field goes into which new field and how this should happen. Before you begin, you need two data models: the source model and the destination model. They can be versions of a single data model, or they can be separate data models.

NOTE

Most frequently, these are two versions of your model. However, sometimes you need to jettison old versions to clean up your code. They do not take much space on disk, but focusing on live code can make project maintenance easier.

The first step is to create a new mapping model. Do that (as shown previously in Figure 24.1) using File, New, New File and selecting Mapping Model. As shown in Figure 24.7, you will be prompted to select the source data model (the "before" version).

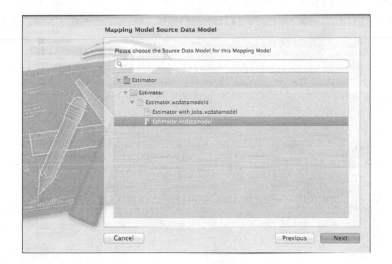

FIGURE 24.7
Select the source data model.

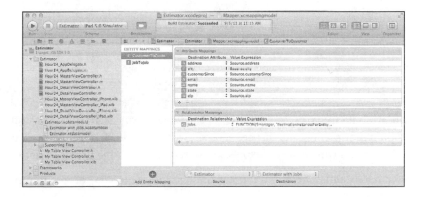

FIGURE 24.8
The mapping model is created automatically.

Next, you will choose the destination data model and then name the file for the mapping model. The mapping model opens, as shown in Figure 24.8. In the center of the window where you normally find the Data Model editor, you now find the mappings. You have new entities created here that map a source entity to a destination entity. For the attributes of the destination entity, by default fields from the source entity are mapped as shown.

At the bottom of the mapping window are pop-ups for the source and destination. Each contains a Choose option that lets you navigate outside your project to a data model in another project or even outside a project. This is how you use an external data model.

TIP

Normally, you use an external data model only for the source, but nothing prevents you from using it as the destination. Keep in mind that this works only if you are going to move the mapping model elsewhere to actually use it.

As shown in Figure 24.9, select an entity mapping and examine it in the Data Model inspector in utilities at the right of the window. Here is where you can change the entities if you do not have a direct one-to-one mapping.

FIGURE 24.9
Customize entity mappings.

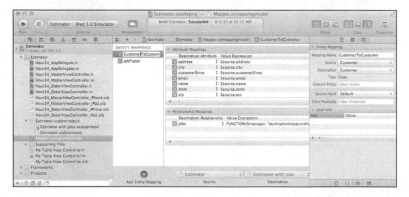

Select an attribute mapping in the center of the window, and you will see the attribute mapping in the Core Data inspector, as shown in Figure 24.10. You can change the fields, and you can create an expression to modify the value that is migrated.

As shown, additional options and settings are available that you can use to further customize the process.

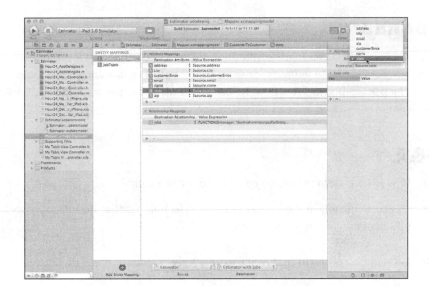

FIGURE 24.10
Change attribute mappings.

Summary

This hour introduced you to the continuum of Core Data migration techniques and tools. The data model in your app must be compatible with the data model used to create the persistent store. This hour helped you understand the ways in which database schema changes do and do not create incompatibilities.

Q&A

Q. *Why is Core Data migration considered a continuum?*

A. It is customizable and consists of tools and techniques that handle incompatibilities of different types and scales.

Q. *Is there one problem that many people have with data migration?*

A. Whether you are talking about Core Data or other technologies, many developers are nervous about data migration. You see signs of this in many databases in which fields have been repurposed and Postal Code becomes something like Preferred Shipper without having its field name changed. The takeaway from Core Data's continuum of migration is not to be afraid: There are many simple ways to migrate your data model and make it easy for people to use and maintain.

Workshop

Quiz

1. *How does Core Data test for compatibility between data models in the app and in a persistent store?*

2. *Do you have to write code to use a mapping model?*

3. *Is it a good idea to back up your database before running migration?*

Quiz Answers

1. Core Data generates a hash of the attributes for each entity in the data model in the persistent store and the app. It then compares those hashes.

2. No. You can, but the default code that is generated in many cases will do the work for you.

3. Absolutely. More than one person has been so eager to try the Core Data migration tools that this step is sometimes omitted. And, because life is the way it is, migration fails and corrupts your database only if you have forgotten to back up the database before migration.

Activities

Hands-on experience with Core Data migration really helps you to understand the processes. Take an existing data model and database and experiment with the continuum, making changes to the data model at each step of the way.

Remember that this is basic familiarization. Data migration is something that happens fairly rarely, so your objective should be to understand the basic process. When you actually need to work with data migration, skim over this chapter again to remind yourself of the steps involved. Very few people commit the entire data migration process to memory.

What's Old in Core Data, Cocoa, Xcode, and Objective-C

Core Data, Xcode, and the Cocoa frameworks are evolving along with the hardware they run on. Mobile devices in particular have changed dramatically in the last few years as millions of people around the world have discovered new ways of using them and communicating with their friends. Hardware, software, and the ways in which people use them do not move in lockstep. One of the big challenges is keeping everything working together even as these changes occur.

This book focuses on Xcode 4, iOS 5, and Mac OS 10.7 (Lion). All of them have a number of new features. But when you are actually working with existing code, you may be looking at code written some time ago for a different environment. This appendix points out some of the features of Core Data, Cocoa, Xcode, and Objective-C that either are deprecated or are no longer best practices.

Declared Properties

Beginning with Objective-C 2.0, declared properties were introduced. If you use the @property directive, you no longer need to declare instance variables inside objects most of the time (the exception is @private instances). You also no longer have to write your own accessors because you can use the @synthesize directive to create them.

Most people use named properties for new code. This can mean living with both styles of programming for a while unless you want to renovate existing code.

> See "Using Declared Properties" in Chapter 3, "Understanding the Basic Code Structure," p. 68.

Required and Optional Methods in Protocols

In Objective-C 2.0, you can mark protocol methods as @required or @optional, and it is a good idea to do so for legibility and ease of maintenance in the future. If the directive is omitted or if this is pre-Objective-C code, @required is assumed.

▶ See the "Using Protocols and Delegates" section in Chapter 3 for more information.

Storyboards in Interface Builder

Xcode 4 implements storyboards to combine your various interface elements within a storyboard file. Nib files are displayed in the same editor you are used to, but when you create new storyboard files, you add views to them so that in fact your new nib files are part of the single storyboard file on which you are working. Whenever you are working with an older project's interface, remember to leave a little extra time to become familiar with the new arrangement.

▶ There is more on this in Chapter 11, "Finding Your Way Around Interface Builder: The Graphics Story."

Ordered Relationships

New features in the development environment often make existing code superfluous. In fact, that is one of the reasons they often are implemented: Many developers ask for the feature because they are tired of implementing and reimplementing it in their software.

Ordered relationships, new in Lion, are one such structure. Many apps never had the need for them, but in some cases, large chunks of existing code can be removed. Make certain to read Apple's documentation to see the pros and cons of using ordered relationships. The actual class is NSOrderedSet, and that is where you will find the documentation.

Index

code listings

M

FREE Online Edition

Your purchase of **Sams Teach Yourself Core Data for Mac and iOS in 24 Hours** includes access to a free online edition for 45 days through the Safari Books Online subscription service. Nearly every Sams book is available online through Safari Books Online, along with more than 5,000 other technical books and videos from publishers such as Addison-Wesley Professional, Cisco Press, Exam Cram, IBM Press, O'Reilly, Prentice Hall, and Que.

SAFARI BOOKS ONLINE allows you to search for a specific answer, cut and paste code, download chapters, and stay current with emerging technologies.

Activate your FREE Online Edition at www.informit.com/safarifree

> **STEP 1:** Enter the coupon code: DJGMNVH.

> **STEP 2:** New Safari users, complete the brief registration form.
> Safari subscribers, just log in.

If you have difficulty registering on Safari or accessing the online edition, please e-mail customer-service@safaribooksonline.com